Community Governance and Citizen-Driven Initiatives in Climate Change Mitigation

One of the most heartening dev   .igation in
recent years has been the increasin̦ .... паіɑ to the principle of 'thinking
globally and acting locally'. The failure of the international community to reach
significant global agreements on the reduction of greenhouse gas emissions has
led local governments, environmental organisations and citizens themselves to
focus increasingly on the local possibilities for action on climate change.

This book analyses the strengths and weaknesses of the co-production of
climate policies that take place where citizen engagement and local initiatives
converge with public agencies. Case studies from Northern Europe,
Australia/New Zealand and the USA reveal that traditional individualist
approaches to promoting environmental behaviour epitomised by information
campaigns and economic incentives cannot trigger the deep behavioural changes
required to materially improve our response to climate change. Only by
marshalling the forces of thousands, and eventually millions of citizens, can we
manage to reach environmental sceptics, reinforce political action and create the
new social norms that are sorely needed in our local, and global, response to
climate change.

This book will be of great relevance to scholars and policy makers with an
interest in climate change politics and governance, community engagement and
sustainable development.

Jens Hoff is Professor in National and International Governance and Public
Policy at the Department of Political Science, University of Copenhagen.

Quentin Gausset is a Lecturer at the Institute of Anthropology, University of
Copenhagen.

Routledge Advances in Climate Change Research

'Full of new insights into the potential of citizens and their communities, this book provides a fresh perspective on how we can move beyond the promise of technological fixes or individual behaviour change to address new forms of governing climate change that place forms of active citizenship and collaboration at their heart. The book makes a convincing case for the need for policy makers to engage with new approaches to engaging citizens in responding to climate change across multiple scales.'

Harriet Bulkeley, Durham University, UK

'A paradox of climate change is that this most global of problems is simultaneously profoundly local in its causes, impacts, and solutions. Hoff and Gausset have assembled a wonderful collection that explores the multiple and diverse ways that local communities from around the world are grappling with climate change and the transformations needed to respond to it. This book is not only cutting edge scholarship, it is also provides a crucial window into the practices, challenges, and practical politics of local responses necessary for solving this global problem.'

Matthew Hoffmann, Department of Political Science, University of Toronto

Community Governance and Citizen-Driven Initiatives in Climate Change Mitigation

Edited by Jens Hoff and Quentin Gausset

LONDON AND NEW YORK

First published 2016
by Routledge
2 Park Square, Milton Park, Abingdon, Oxon OX14 4RN

and by Routledge
711 Third Avenue, New York, NY 10017

First issued in paperback 2017

Routledge is an imprint of the Taylor & Francis Group, an informa business

British Library Cataloguing-in-Publication Data
A catalogue record for this book is available from the British Library

Library of Congress Cataloging-in-Publication Data
Community governance and citizen driven initiatives in climate change mitigation / edited by Jens Hoff and Quentin Gausset.
pages cm. — (Routledge advances in climate change research)
1. Local government and environmental policy. 2. Climate change mitigation—Government policy. 3. Climate change mitigation—Citizen participation. 4. Environmental policy—Decision making—Citizen participation. I. Hoff, Jens. II. Gausset, Quentin.
GE170.C64135 2016
363.738'746—dc23
2015007624

ISBN 13: 978-1-138-09134-4 (pbk)
ISBN 13: 978-1-138-90109-4 (hbk)

Typeset in Goudy
by FiSH Books Ltd, Enfield

Contents

Figures

Tables

Contributors

Stefanie Baasch works as a freelance project consultant and coach in advanced training. She holds a doctoral degree in geography (University of Hamburg), a master's degree in environmental psychology (University of Hagen) and a diploma in public administration economy (University for Applied Public Administration Hamburg). For more than ten years, she worked in several international and German scientific projects on sustainable development, adaptation to climate change and climate protection, energy transition and participation.

Anders Christian Erichsen holds a MSc. degree in Environmental Engineering. He has more than 15 years of experience at DHI, a not-for-profit company dedicated to solving challenges related to water environments worldwide. He has been involved in different research projects related to the environmental impacts of climate change and climate change adaptation, and has contributed to several publications related to these topics.

Quentin Gausset received his PhD in anthropology from the Free University of Brussels in 1997 and is Associate Professor in the Department of Anthropology, University of Copenhagen. He has more than 15 years of experience with interdisciplinary research on natural resource management and environmental conflicts, including fieldwork in African and Asian countries. He has published extensively in scientific journals and anthologies on the socio-cultural aspects of natural resource management, and has edited a book titled *Beyond Territory and Scarcity: Exploring Conflicts over Natural Resource Management* published by the Nordic Africa Institute in Uppsala in 2005. He is currently writing a textbook on environmental anthropology.

Jens Hoff is a Professor in the Department of Political Science, University of Copenhagen. He received his PhD from the same department in 1990. He teaches and conducts research in the areas of governance, citizen participation, climate change, and information and communication technology. He has directed a number of major national and international research projects, sits on the editorial board of several journals and has worked as reviewer for Norwegian, UK and US research councils. From 2010–14 he directed the interdisciplinary research project CIDEA (Citizen Driven Environmental Action). Among his publications in English are *Digital Governance://Networked Societies. Creating Authority, Community and Identity in a Globalized World*, Nordicom 2006 (ed); *Democracy and Citizenship in Scandinavia*, Palgrave 2001; and *Democratic Governance and New Technology*, Routledge, 2000 (ed).

Kasper Hornbæk is a Professor of Computer Science at University of Copenhagen. He received his PhD and MSc from University of Copenhagen and has worked there since. His core research interest is human-computer interaction, including usability research, shape-changing interfaces, large displays and information visualization.

Ebba Lisberg Jensen is an Associate Professor of human ecology at Malmö University, Sweden. Her research interests focus on the relationship between humanity and nature, originally from an anthropological standpoint. Her dissertation was about the aesthetics and ideology of biological diversity, and how it has been deployed when environmentalists fight to preserve old-growth forests. She has also conducted research on local opinions about nuclear waste depositories, outdoor recreation, ecological literacy and urban nature.

Michael Søgaard Jørgensen is Associate Professor in sustainable innovation and transition at the Centre for Design, Innovation and Sustainable Transitions at Aalborg University's campus in Copenhagen. He holds an MSc in Chemical Engineering (1981) and a PhD in Technology Assessment (1988) from the Technical University of Denmark. He has conducted research about the impact of community-based research, technology foresight, environmental innovation in companies, sustainable transition and the role of quality and values in different professions. He is deputy chair of the Society of Green Technology in the Danish Society of Engineers, and one of the coordinators of a network for local environmental ambassador programmes.

Emilie Møllenbach is an Assistant Professor at the IT University of Copenhagen in Interaction Design. She has an MSc degree from the IT University of Copenhagen and a PhD in Computer Science from Loughborough University in the UK. She was subsequently a post-doctoral student at DTU (Denmark's Technical University) followed by another post-doctoral position at the Department of Computer Science at Copenhagen University. Her research concerns human-computer interaction, interaction design methodologies, innovation, sustainability and learning.

Emilie Nørregaard is an MSc student in the Department of Political Science, University of Copenhagen. She specialises in the field of quantitative methods and has worked extensively with data analysis. As an extension of her chapter in this book, she is writing a master's thesis concerning environmental behaviour and examining 'nudging' as a possible method to promote sustainable behaviour among citizens in municipalities.

Irina Papazu is a PhD candidate at the Department of Political Science, University of Copenhagen, and visiting researcher at the Centre for the Study of Invention and Social Process at Goldsmiths, University of London. Her PhD project focuses on Denmark's renewable energy island Samsø and the socio-technical changes the island has been through, making it a world-famous political laboratory that showcases a successful energy transition.

Stine Rahbek Pedersen is coordinator of the environment and climate ambassador programme in Furesø Municipality. She holds an MA degree (cand.techn.soc., 2005) from Roskilde University and has experience with action research, local public participation involving parents and children and has been a director of a local environmental centre in Copenhagen. She is member of the board of the Society of Green Technology within the Danish Society of Engineers and was a member of the Centre for Democracy and Nature Management 2003–2005 at Roskilde University. She is one of the coordinators of a network for local environmental ambassador programmes.

Christian Elling Scheele holds a post-doctoral position at the Department of Public Health at the University of Copenhagen. His contribution to this book constitutes part of his PhD dissertation at the Department of Political Science, University of Copenhagen. Christian also has more than ten years work experience with Danish local governments.

Bjarne W. Strobel defended his PhD in environmental chemistry at The Royal Veterinary and Agricultural University in Copenhagen in 2000 and is an Associate Professor in the Department of Plant and Environmental Sciences, University of Copenhagen. He is experienced in applied research with environmental chemistry in ecosystems, which focuses in large part on the distribution and fate of chemicals in the environment. He has a long record of scientific articles and teaching materials for national and international bachelor, master and PhD courses, including a concept for student-produced video assignments at the university. He now heads a European double degree master's program called 'Environmental Sciences – Soil, Water and Biodiversity (EnvEuro)' that is geared to the international education of the next generation.

Lise Tjørring is a cultural anthropologist and industrial PhD candidate at SE (Danish Energy Company) and the Department of Food and Resource Economics, University of Copenhagen. Her PhD project is about practices and decision-making processes concerning energy consumption in private households in southern Denmark.

Mette Wichmand is a doctoral student at Roskilde University, Denmark in the Department of Communication, Business and Information Technologies. She holds a master's degree in Communication and Educational Planning. Before becoming a doctoral student, she was a lecturer in communication and creative management at Fonty's University of Applied Science in Eindhoven,

The Netherlands. In addition to her teaching position, she has researched and produced documentaries and children's programs about human rights that have been broadcast internationally. Her research interest includes empowerment, social change and civic media. She is currently researching how social network games can empower players to become post-game social innovators.

Acknowledgements

With this note we would like to express our gratitude to the many people and organisations involved in funding, carrying out, discussing and reporting the research that provides the foundation for this book.

First and foremost, our thanks to Innovation Fund Denmark (formerly the Danish Council for Strategic Research), which funded the cross-disciplinary Citizen Driven Environmental Action (CIDEA) research project from 2010–2014. To convert the data gathered in the project into interesting and insightful analyses takes skilful researchers, and we would therefore like to thank all the researchers, including PhD and MA students, for the enthusiasm, willingness to discuss and endurance they displayed during the project.

The unsung heroines and heroes of any publishing project are the research assistants. Special thanks go to Anders Ellesgaard, Andreas Larsen, Emilie Nørregaard, Leni Shapira, Lone Sørensen Hoff and Mikkel Kjer and project secretary Anne Thomsen, who were indispensable in the process of organising the project and related events, collecting, organising and analysing data and preparing this manuscript for publication. In relation to the CIDEA project, the organisation's steering group – Professors Lars Bo Kaspersen, Finn Kensing and Bo Jellesmark Thorsen – provided invaluable support and guidance throughout the whole project.

The CIDEA project involved close collaboration with seven Danish municipalities around a number of climate change mitigation projects and also involved local governments in Australia and New Zealand. Here, we would like to thank the climate change managers or civil servants who constituted our link to the 'real world': Ane Kollerup and Esther Juel Jepsen in Køge, Casper Marott, Berit Haahr Hansen and Lene Bjerg Christensen in Copenhagen, Connie Juul Clausen in Odense, Morten Westergaard in Middelfart, Merete Valbak, Annica Myrén and Torsten Zink Sørensen in Kolding, Susanne Skaarup and Bente Hornbæk in Skanderborg, Line Thastum in Herning, Kerry Prendergast, former mayor of Wellington and Wayne Wescott, former director of ICLEI Oceania.

We would also like to recognise and thank the more than 50 mayors, politicians and civil servants in the seven Danish municipalities as well as in Australia and New Zealand, who volunteered to be interviewed for this project.

In order to discuss our research findings in a broader academic environment and to solicit articles for this book, we organised a workshop at the 2013 Nordic Environmental Social Science (NESS) Conference in Copenhagen. We would like to thank the organisers of this conference, especially Associate Professor Tove Boon, for giving us this opportunity.

Finally, we are grateful for our contacts at Routledge: Associate Editor Annabelle Harris and Editorial Assistant Margaret Farrelly, and before them Louisa Earls and Bethany Wright, for all their encouragement and help in getting this book to the final stage of publication. And last but not least, a special thanks to Susan Michael, who did a thorough linguistic revision and the copy editing of all chapters in the book.

Copenhagen, January 2015
Jens Hoff
Quentin Gausset

1 Community governance and citizen-driven initiatives in climate change mitigation

An introduction

Jens Hoff and Quentin Gausset

Introduction

Global warming is one of the greatest challenges faced by humanity today. The international community is still hoping to limit global warming to no more than 2°C as compared to pre-industrial levels, and the scenario proposed in 2014 by the Intergovernmental Panel on Climate Change (IPCC, established under the auspices of the United Nations) requires reducing global carbon dioxide (CO_2) emissions by 41 to 72 per cent by 2050 as compared to 2010 (IPCC 2014, 23). This objective requires no less than a drastic transformation of the way we produce energy and goods.

The traditional emphasis in the field of climate change mitigation has been on the technical and infrastructural aspects of such a transformation. Thus, mitigation policies have been concerned with the transformation of energy systems towards renewable energy, improving energy efficiency and trading CO_2 quotas. Yet, even though benefits from this transformation are now becoming visible, CO_2 emissions continue to grow at a rate that is higher than ever (IPCC 2014). Because the changes in energy systems do not seem to be enough to keep global warming under the stated goal of 2°C, attention is now increasingly directed towards effecting changes in individual behaviour to reduce people's carbon footprints.

This emphasis upon individual behaviour poses an enormous political and social challenge. Curbing consumption goes against many values we take for granted, such as the idea that our well-being depends on an ever-increasing consumption of goods, as if there were no limits to growth. Curbing consumption also faces widespread scepticism about its effect on individual consumption, coupled with a 'tragedy of the commons', in which no individual feels personally responsible for securing the sound management of collective goods, and in which individuals do not want to be the first to change behaviour.

In addition, this stress on individual behaviour also poses serious ethical and political challenges regarding the environmental legitimacy of political action and the best strategies to encourage sounder environmental behaviour. Overall, the problem we face today is not due to a lack of adequate technology to mitigate climate change; it is a general reluctance to apply these technologies, and in so doing, to bear the social, political as well as financial costs. The challenge of climate change mitigation is therefore, first of all, a problem of governance.

The basic tenet of this book is that citizens, as individuals or as parts of smaller or bigger communities, can and must play an important part in the efforts to mitigate climate changes. Indeed, 'we, the people', as victims of climate change, are also the ones who can act on this immanent threat. This role of citizens as *active agents* in climate change mitigation was brought to the foreground of climate change mitigation efforts following the failure of the international community to reach significant global agreements on the reduction of greenhouse gas emissions. This inability of global institutions to grapple with the issue collectively has left the challenge on our doorstep. This book is about how this challenge has been embraced by both citizens and local communities.

We argue that the disillusionment about the failure to reach global environmental agreements, especially after the 2009 United Nations Conference of the Parties 15 (COP 15) summit in Copenhagen, led local governments, policy makers, environmental organisations and 'green' movements as well as citizens themselves to focus on local possibilities for action on climate change. This 'reorientation towards the local' is the framework within which this book is written.

This book takes different case studies as points of departure in order to answer the following questions: How and why do citizens become engaged in climate change mitigation? What motivates citizens to take action, and what are the factors that hold them back or discourage them? What are the effects of this engagement on local communities and their organisational framework, on the broader political/democratic system and on citizens themselves?

The different chapters of this book approach these research questions from different theoretical and methodological perspectives, most of which come from the social sciences – sociology, anthropology and political science. Whilst we do not attempt to apply a unified theoretical perspective, we have been guided by a common, overall frame of reference. We focus on citizen initiatives, engagement and participation in climate change mitigation, but only insofar as these activities are embedded in a relationship between public agencies and citizens as individuals or as members of different types of communities, and only insofar as they attempt to influence people's behaviour. What we are interested in here is what some have called 'collaborative arrangements' (Healey 1997/2006), and others have called 'co-creation' (Joiner and Josephs 2007), in which citizens and public authorities can play bigger or smaller roles. Because such collaborative arrangements can be seen as governance technologies (Bang 2003), what we discuss in this book is therefore citizen engagement in climate change mitigation *as a governance technology* (Chapters 2 to 11). In some of these governance arrangements, artifacts such as websites or computer games play an important role in mediating the relationship between public agency and citizens, thereby becoming social software (see Chapters 12 and 13).

This way of approaching the subject has important implications for both how we define citizen participation in climate change mitigation (see Chapter 3), and for the roles that citizen initiatives and green movements play in this book. Thus, in the specific cases we analyse here, we only deal with organisations insofar as they engage in some form of collaboration/co-creation with local public agencies.

We use Figure 1.1 as a heuristic device to present the field of possible collaborative arrangements between local public agencies and citizens. The figure combines a vertical axis representing the initiation of climate change mitigation interventions with a horizontal axis representing the focus of these interventions. The vertical axis is presented as a continuum and shows that interventions can be initiated either by government agents or by citizens, but most often in a collaboration in which one of the two poles weighs more than the other. As noted above, there is always an element of involvement of local authority and local citizen participation in our case studies, however minor the contribution of either party might be.

The horizontal axis of the figure, also presented as a continuum, shows that interventions can target either individual change (consumption patterns, transport habits) or collective changes (creation of a low-energy housing cooperative, a sustainable village, building of new collective infrastructures). Since collective change requires the participation of a large number of individuals, and since individuals are influenced by collective behaviour, most interventions mix both aspects, to various degrees.

The figure contains four squares (1–4); we deliberately sought out cases that illustrate each of the squares. Our underlying idea is to investigate whether projects and initiatives belonging to one of these squares might be consistently better than those belonging to other squares in engaging citizens and having measurable effects on the reduction of CO_2 emissions.

Square 1 of the figure denotes arrangements/projects that are clearly initiated by a public agency, and are focused primarily on influencing individual behaviour. These arrangements rely most often on policies influenced by rational

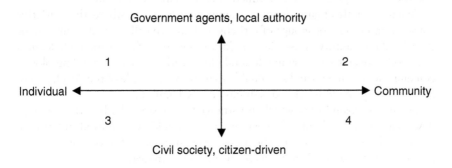

Figure 1.1 The field of possible collaborative arrangements concerning climate change mitigation. Vertical axis represents the initiation of intervention and horizontal axis represents the focus of intervention

choice theory, which posits that individuals will always choose the most rational options that maximise their advantages. The type of policies that this approach entails focuses on providing the right information to actors and influencing behaviour mainly through economic (dis)incentives. Information campaigns, taxes or subsidies are therefore the most common social technologies found among these arrangements. Examples of such arrangements are found in Chapter 6 on different models of energy renovation of houses and in Chapter 8 on energy transition in Wolfhagen, Germany, and in Chapter 12 on the use of a municipal website to engage different local communities in climate change mitigation.

Square 2 of the figure denotes arrangements initiated by a public agency that focus on different types of communities where the changes promoted require the support of a collectivity, or at least of a certain number of participants. Well-known examples of collective arrangements include environmental impact assessments relating to projects such as construction of wind turbines, national parks and power plants that impact landscapes or a neighbourhood. Examples of such arrangements are found in Chapter 8 on energy transition in Wolfhagen, Germany, in Chapter 6 on different models of energy renovation of houses and in Chapter 12 on the use of a municipal website to engage different local communities in climate change mitigation.

Square 3 of the figure denotes action initiated specifically by citizens themselves as individual actors. Citizens may reflect on and take action to mitigate climate change in their homes, at work, while shopping and transporting themselves and in numerous other ways. Many such daily choices are not made in response to temporary external interventions, but are based on the total knowledge, norms and values internalised by each individual throughout his/her life. Because individuals may try to save money at the same time as they try to conform to norms, respect legislation or be empathetic towards other living creatures, the motivations for such actions can be economic, social, legal and moral. Such individual actions can also depend on a number of socio-economic factors such as gender, age, income, education, values and political orientation, as discussed in Chapter 5 on environmental choices in everyday life.

Square 4 of the figure denotes arrangements/projects where the initiative comes from citizens or groups of citizens and are typically aimed at improving their local community or association. Arrangements in this square include, *inter alia*, food cooperatives, sustainable food clubs, carbon- neutral building blocks, communities or villages and sustainable islands. An example of the development of a low-energy neighbourhood is discussed in Chapter 6.

These four possibilities, which are arranged to illustrate both bottom-up/top-down agency and individual/collective targets, should be seen as ideal types. In practice, the two axes present themselves as continua, with most initiatives or projects situated somewhere in between the four extremes.

On the vertical axis, for example, even though local governments often take the initiative to launch environmental projects, they might do so under the pressure of public opinion, with the support of local politicians who wish to be re-elected in their constituency. Likewise, when citizens take the initiative to improve the local environment or reduce their carbon footprint, it is often difficult to distinguish between how much of this initiative responds (even if in part) to governmental stimuli such as information campaigns or economic incentives.

On the horizontal axis, even though collectivities are more than the sum of the individuals who constitute them, it is nevertheless through the actions of individuals that collectivities change. Inversely, individuals are social beings who have been socialised and are constantly influenced by others within a broader collectivity. Individuals and collectivities co-constitute each other, just as local government action and citizen initiatives are closely connected.

One of the lessons drawn from the studies presented in this book is that the traditional approach to influencing environmental behaviour, found in Square 1 and epitomised by information campaigns and economic incentives, cannot trigger the broad and deep behavioural changes required to reduce a sufficient amount of CO_2. Of course, it is easier for policy makers to work with individuals through the media or by taxation, but there is a limit to how much can be achieved this way, and there is an urgent need to complement approaches that focus on individuals with projects that target social groups and collectivities more explicitly. As discussed in Chapters 5 and 6, individuals who respond to information campaigns or economic subsidies are often those who already have a high environmental consciousness and are often relatively well-off. Thus, the 'additionality' of such campaigns (the extent to which they trigger changes that would otherwise not have happened had the project not taken place) needs to be questioned.

Several of our studies suggest that reaching sceptics will not be possible unless moral norms and values are changed, which would require a strong collective approach to environmental problems. People who do not want to change their behaviour to save money or for the sake of the environment are likely to reconsider their position once sound environmental behaviour becomes a dominant social norm. The multiplication of local collective projects that build on strong local commitments might reach a certain threshold and create new behavioural and consumption standards in the broader society, which, in turn, will trigger new legislation and political standards.

We come to a second lesson drawn from the present studies, namely that the engagement of citizens and their collaboration or interplay with various levels of government authority is crucial to addressing global warming successfully. Without citizen initiatives, political action is weaker, not only because it is less ambitious, but also because it appears less legitimate politically. Opinion surveys show that a majority of people support more environmental political actions (see Chapter 5). And yet, politicians continue to be hesitant about making bold decisions.

Therefore, local projects that mobilise different groups of citizens around common values can help trigger stronger environmental legislation. This is beginning to be understood in an increasing number of municipalities that are now trying new ways to encourage the emergence of local environmental associations. It is clear that the collaboration between local initiatives and municipal governments (and from there, higher levels of governments) is one of the keys to reducing the carbon footprint of our societies.

Traditional approaches to climate change mitigation are often driven from above and focus on individuals. This book suggests that new approaches be applied to climate change mitigation projects that emphasise the interplay between public agents and citizens and harness the full potential of working with social groups, collectivities and networks. Only then will we be able to trigger widespread behaviour change to mitigate climate change.

References

Bang H (ed.) (2003) *Governance as Social and Political Communication*, Manchester University Press, Manchester, UK.

Healey P (1997/2006) *Collaborative Planning Shaping Places in Fragmented Societies*, Palgrave Macmillan, Houndsmill, UK.

IPCC (2014) *Climate Change 2014 Synthesis Report. Summary for Policymakers*, Intergovernmental Panel on Climate Change (IPCC), Geneva. (www.ipcc.ch/pdf/assessment-report/ar5/syr/AR5_SYR_FINAL_SPM.pdf) Accessed 4 February 2015.

Joiner B and Josephs S (2007) *Agility: Five Levels of Mastery for Anticipating and Initiating Change*, Jossey-Bass, San Francisco, CA.

2 The conundrum of calculating carbon footprints

Bjarne W. Strobel, Anders Christian Erichsen and Quentin Gausset

Introduction

The awareness of climate change and its link with human activities is growing. This awareness is nursed by the gradual change in weather conditions experienced worldwide and an increase in the occurrence of extreme events such as heatwaves and floods. However, despite overwhelming scientific evidence that climate change is anthropogenic (IPCC 2013), there is still widespread scepticism and a wide knowledge gap between what science predicts and what people know and understand about climate change.

Mitigating the effects of climate change depends on reducing drastically the world production of carbon dioxide (CO_2) and other greenhouse gasses (GHGs). So far, the international community has been working towards limiting the increase in world average temperature to 2°C as compared to pre-industrial levels. (In the past 150 years of industrialisation, the global average temperature has increased by about 0.8°C). To reach this goal, the world community needs to reduce accumulated GHG emissions over the coming 90 years by 80 per cent (Erichsen and Arnskov 2010).

There are wide disparities in GHG emissions among countries. Average CO_2 emissions per capita in the EU is 50–100 times that of most Sub-Saharan countries (World Bank 2013). If one applies the principle of environmental justice, i.e. that each human should have the right to emit an equal amount of CO_2, then citizens from industrialised countries would have to reduce their emissions by much more than 80 per cent, while citizens from developing countries should be allowed to increase their level of emissions.

Corrective justice, or the principle of 'Common But Differentiated Responsibilities' (CBDR) was stated in the 1992 Rio Declaration and reaffirmed in the 1997 Kyoto Protocol. This principle recognises that industrial states bear a much bigger responsibility for having created the current environmental crisis and must therefore bear a much higher share in reducing their GHG emissions. Thus, early industrialised countries should reduce emissions even more drastically than other countries (Harris 1999; Rajamani 2000; Stone 2004; Cullet 2010).

In view of the fact that the international community has failed to date to reach ambitious global agreements, actors at lower levels (the EU, nations,

municipalities and individuals) are increasingly filling the gap by taking important initiatives to reduce their emissions. The EU 2020 Climate and Energy
Package wants to raise the share of the EU energy consumption produced from
renewable resources to 20 per cent by 2020. Formal talks at the EU are underway
to increase this share to 30 per cent (European Commission 2010).

Some countries have more ambitious goals. Denmark, for example, wants to
be at the forefront of environmental policies, and is committed to raising its
share of energy consumption produced from renewable resources to 33 per cent
by 2020, and to be 'free of fossil fuel' in 2050 (Regeringen 2011). At the local
level, many Danish municipalities have also developed plans to become CO_2-
neutral in the near future, as demonstrated in several chapters in this book (see
Hoff and Strobel 2013; and in this book: Baasch; Møllenbach and Hornbæk;
Tjørring and Gausset).

The majority of the chapters in this book address social technologies to
increase climate change mitigation, i.e. by reducing consumption and insulating
houses, among others. But how much do these actions contribute to climate
change mitigation? Will these actions be sufficient? Some studies argue that up
to 72 per cent of GHG emissions are related to household consumption, with
food accounting for 20 per cent of that figure (Hertwich and Peters 2009). Other
studies claim that Danish households account for only 28 per cent of total energy
consumption (Energistyrelsen 2012).

But how are these figures calculated? What do they include and exclude? How
much can be reduced by individual behaviour change and how much is due to
structural mechanisms over which individuals have very little control? Answers
to these questions require tools that allow actors to measure the impact of the
different options available to them and allocate differentiated responsibilities
among them. GHG emissions (CO_2) calculators are the most commonly used
tools for this purpose. But one can find a variety of calculators based on different
principles that produce very different carbon footprints for the same household
(Kenny and Gray 2009).

The greenhouse effect

The greenhouse effect consists of greenhouse gases in the atmosphere that reflect
long wavelength heat radiation emitted from the Earth's surface. It reduces the
amount of heat loss to the outer atmosphere and keeps the heat in the lower
atmosphere near the Earth's surface. The most important GHGs in terms of
climate change are carbon dioxide (CO_2), methane (CH_4) and nitrous oxide
(N_2O). In calculations, all GHGs are converted into CO_2 equivalents in order to
compare their greenhouse effect more easily. In this chapter, we discuss CO_2, or
carbon emissions, as generic terms and refer more broadly to GHGs.

During the past 100 years, the CO_2 concentration in the atmosphere has
increased from 280 parts per million (ppm) to over 400 ppm, a concentration
that was surpassed for the first time in May 2013. Since life on Earth evolved, the
climate has been changing (several ice ages and warm periods have occurred, for

example) and will continue to change. However, no climate change era in the past can compare to the speed and abruptness of the present change (see Figure 2.1). The problem is that the rapid increase of GHGs in the atmosphere since the beginning of the industrial revolution, accompanied by a rapid increase of the Earth's average temperature, can seriously challenge our welfare and the way human societies are organised.

If the concentration of CO_2 reaches 450 ppm, as will soon be the case, this would be 50 per cent more than the highest concentration found in pre-industrial times and would lead to an increase in the global average temperature of approximately 2 degrees (IPCC 2013). This temperature increase would affect continental areas much more than oceans. Thus, although the average temperature for the entire planet will rise by 2 degrees, the temperature rise of the ocean surfaces (covering approximately 70 per cent of the Earth's surface) is expected to be +0.1 to +0.3 degrees and the average temperature rise over the continents is expected to be +5 to +6 degrees (IPCC 2013).

Moreover, the continental temperatures will not be evenly distributed. Some regions, especially near the equator, might see very little change, while the temperature is expected to increase by 8–10 degrees in the Polar Regions (IPCC 2013). In large areas, the temperature increase will be barely detectable, while in

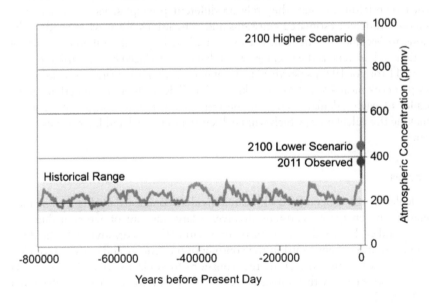

Figure 2.1 Atmospheric CO_2 concentration in the past 800,000 years

Source: US Global Change Research Program 2014, based on data from Tans 2008 and Lüthi *et al.* 2008.

other parts of the Earth it will be noticeable and will have dramatic consequences. Most scenarios predict that the concentration of CO_2 will not stabilise at 450 ppm and will reach between 550 and 900 ppm by the year 2100, which would lead to a global average temperature increase estimated to be between 2.5 and 5 degrees (IPCC 2013).

It can be difficult for individuals to notice such changes on a yearly basis since the weather we observe locally this year (or that we remember from the past few years) might be in contradiction to the weather experienced in other locations or observed globally. For example, arctic air from the Barents Sea cooled Europe in 2012–2013 by approximately a one-degree colder winter average, while at the same time Greenland experienced a very warm winter and record glacier and sea ice melting. It is therefore very difficult for individuals experiencing local climate variations to get a global picture of global warming. Variations such as these can create scepticism about scientific predictions, which can become an important obstacle to behaviour change.

Since GHG emissions circulate the global atmosphere within a few weeks, we all share the impact of emissions regardless of their source. Local actions have a global impact: we all have a shared responsibility to change behaviour so as not to harm other people. Carbon footprint calculators that measure the 'load' imposed upon nature by a given population can help people understand how their actions and consumption habits impact the global climate and help them adopt greener behaviour.

However, the variety of existing calculators may confuse people and increase their scepticism. Because they rely on different principles, various calculators produce different estimated emissions and conclusions about what needs to be done to become CO_2-neutral. For example, based upon the different results of various calculators, is the average CO_2 imbalance produced by a Danish citizen 6 tons, 11 tons or 19 tons per year? Is the average carbon footprint of one kilogram (kg) of pork meat 4 kg, 28 kg or 50 kg CO_2? It all depends on the underlying principles of each calculator and on the criteria taken into consideration when making the calculation, which will be discussed in more detail later in this chapter.

Scopes

Calculating the CO_2 emitted while an individual conducts daily life is a complex matter: the energy we consume involves a large amount of actors at different levels and each actor directly controls only part of the energy invested. The three scopes (sources of emission) in the consumption of energy and emissions of CO_2 are: 1) Direct emissions, 2) indirect emissions from electricity and heat and 3) activity associated with indirect emissions (GHG Protocol 2001), as illustrated in Figure 2.2.

Scope 1 applies to all direct GHG emissions resulting from the actor's own activity. In practice, this often amounts to the direct consumption of fossil fuels (such as coal, oil and gas) while heating the home, or the fuel burnt while driving

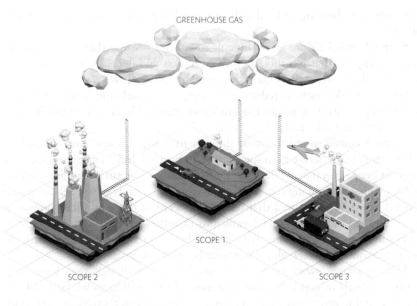

Figure 2.2 Emission of CO_2 from activities in three scopes: 1) actor's direct emissions, 2) indirect emissions from purchased electricity and heat, and 3) indirect emission from activities and products outside the actor's control

a private car. The producer of these emissions controls them: s/he can reduce his or her consumption.

Scope 2 applies to all indirect GHG emissions originating from the consumption of purchased energy such as electricity and district heating. These emissions are produced at power plants from which the consumer buys the energy. The actor controls Scope 2 emissions only indirectly. S/he cannot force the energy company to produce green energy, but can replace the supply company with a greener one.

Scope 3 applies to indirect GHG emissions coming from the public infrastructure, which surrounds the production chain, or from sub-contractors whose products are purchased to produce goods. Specific examples of public infrastructure include schools, roads and hospitals. Individual actors have little influence on Scope 3, apart from requesting from sub-contractors a minimal level of environmental friendliness, or voting for political parties that support strong environmental agendas and greener infrastructures.

Someone interested in reducing his or her carbon footprint would logically begin with Scope 1 emissions. As they are emitted directly by that person, he or she can reduce them without having to discuss the issue with anyone else. Rather, it is simply a question of burning less energy or replacing fossil fuel with renewable energy (and also driving less, reducing room temperatures in houses or switching from heating with oil to heating with renewable wood pellets, among others).

Scope 2 emissions are more difficult to control because they come from an energy company that has thousands of customers and depends on a large infra-structure that cannot be changed overnight. Nevertheless, there are a few options available, such as reducing consumption (insulating houses, reducing room temperatures) or producing one's own renewable energy (including e.g. wind energy and solar panels).

Scope 3 emissions are the most difficult to reduce because they depend on other actors (they derive from someone else's Scope 1 and 2 emissions). Yet it is often in Scope 3 emissions that one finds the largest potential for the reduction of CO_2 emissions (Huang *et al.* 2009). For example, a study of 491 sectors in the United States (US) showed that only 26 per cent of the total GHG emissions were captured by Scope 1 and 2 emissions (Matthews *et al.* 2008). It is only by addressing Scope 3 emissions that one can hope to reduce emissions by the 80 per cent required to keep global warming below +2 degrees.

Making people aware of Scope 3 emissions even though they have little control over them can help raise awareness of the challenges we face and can trigger a higher environmental consciousness. People can then lobby politicians or political parties to promote ambitious environmental goals, or they can request lower carbon footprint of the goods they consume. This can bring large-scale and long-lasting changes, even though they happen in the longer run.

Two approaches to calculating carbon footprint

The carbon footprint refers to the cumulative CO_2 emitted through the life-cycle of a product or through the total consumption of an individual or institution (Hertwich and Peters 2009; Weidema *et al.* 2008). It is not to be confused with the concept of ecological footprint that converts the burden imposed upon nature by a given population in terms of the equivalent land area necessary to sustain current levels of resource consumption and waste discharge by that popu-lation (see, for example, Wackernagel and Rees 1996, 1997). We focus here on carbon footprints and measure the load imposed on nature in CO_2e (or CO_2 equivalents), although we have chosen to write CO_2 for simplicity.

There are two broad approaches to calculating the carbon footprint. The first is a consumer-based model that calculates the total CO_2 emissions linked to the life cycle of a product (from its source to its ultimate consumption and disposal, including all scopes). The sum of the product consumed can thereby constitute the carbon footprint of the consuming unit, such as an individual. It is impossi-ble to reduce CO_2 emissions to zero with this model. Regardless of how much we reduce our emissions, we will always consume a minimal amount of basic goods (food, clothing, shelters, education, and health care, among others) that will always emit some CO_2.

The second approach is a geographically based model that calculates the total energy and CO_2 emissions produced and captured within a geographically circumscribed area (typically a municipality or a nation). The carbon footprint is calculated by adding all CO_2 emitted within the geographical unit and subtracting the emissions substituted by all renewable energies produced within the same boundaries, regardless of whether that energy is consumed locally or exported. If enough renewable energy is exported out of the geographical unit, then the carbon footprint of this unit can be said to be neutral or can even be negative. With this model, it is therefore possible for an actor (a company, a municipality or a country, for example), to claim to be CO_2-neutral simply by transferring CO_2 emissions to someone else's carbon footprint.

Consumption-based carbon footprints

Consumption-based carbon footprints of products are calculated by adding the CO_2 emitted throughout the production chain, and including all scopes, while the consumption-based carbon footprints of individuals are based on the total sum of all carbon footprints of all the products and services consumed by that individual.

What makes these calculations difficult is the fact that each product (and each sub-part used to make that product) combines different scopes. For example, when a farmer produces pigs, he uses Scope 1 energy (the fuel used in his engines or in heating his building) as well as Scope 2 energy (the electricity that he buys to light his buildings and to make his electric equipment work). Scopes 1 and 2 emissions represent around 4 kg CO_2 per kg of pork (which is carcass weight, including skin and bones, and which actually equals 6.6 kg CO_2 per kg meat). But this does not take into account the amount of emissions coming from the broader infrastructure that makes pig production possible (fodder, veterinary interventions, official controls, education of the farmer, road infrastructure, among others), all of which could be counted in the carbon footprint of one kg of meat (Chrintz 2012).

The pig is bought by a middleman (let's say a butcher or a supermarket), who also uses Scope 1 and 2 energy while transporting the pig to a slaughterhouse, lighting and heating the butchery or supermarket, paying salaries to employees (who will use part of it on transport from home to work) and processing the meat. Like the farmer, a butcher indirectly produces CO_2 depending on the energy provider. And finally, he has Scope 3-related CO_2 emissions related to the materials and the emissions from sub-contractors that he uses. It takes energy to produce butcher knives, buildings, packaging material, and butchers have very little control on how much CO_2 is produced in these activities. Moreover, like the farmer, the butcher depends on a well-functioning infrastructure of transport, education and health. The three scopes of the butcher significantly increase the carbon footprint of one kg of meat product.

The story continues: the meat is sold to a consumer. Scope 1 and Scope 2 are present in the form of the energy consumed to do the shopping, keep the meat in the refrigerator and cook it. The consumer is in direct or indirect control of these aspects and can choose to shop by bicycle rather than by car, buy a low-energy refrigerator and adopt environmentally-friendly cooking habits. Scope 3 includes, once more, the pot, water, road, education and health infrastructure that make it possible to buy and consume meat.

By the time the consumer eats the meat, the total carbon footprint of all scopes and all actors' amounts to 28 kg CO_2 per kg of pork meat, which is much more than the amount of CO_2 produced in Scope 1 and 2 at the farm. If the meat has been processed even further to produce pâté or sausages, for example, and handled several times more, the total carbon footprint can easily be up to 50 kg CO_2 per kg of meat product served at dinner. This means that waste at the end of the chain of users is much more damaging to the environment than waste at the beginning of the chain. If a pig dies at the farm the day before being sent to the slaughterhouse, the emissions represent 4 kg CO_2 per kg of pig wasted; if a consumer throws out pâté or sausage because the expiry date has been passed or left over from the dinner, then the CO_2 emission wasted can be more than 10 times higher (Chrintz 2012).

Figure 2.3 illustrates how the output from one industrial sector becomes the input of another sector, and how someone's Scope 1 emissions can become someone else's Scope 3 emissions (see Matthews *et al.* 2008; Wiedmann 2009). In addition, Figure 2.3 illustrates how the emissions change over time as actors change subcontractors. This makes it difficult to precisely define the carbon footprint of a product.

Another example: the carbon footprint of travelling by air (another important source of GHGs) is also controversial. The airline companies that currently inform customers about the carbon footprint of their air flights usually use Scope 1 figures based exclusively on the amount of fuel consumed per passenger and per trip. But one should not forget the energy spent on building aircrafts, airports, control towers, controlling passengers, selling tickets and building offices for the employees and travel agencies. Thus, in reality, the carbon footprint of traveling by air announced by airline companies represents only a small fraction of the total carbon footprint of travelling by air.

Taking Scope 3 emissions into consideration can cause dilemmas for customers, who have to choose between keeping an old item that has high energy consumption and replacing it with a newer and more efficient item. For example, is it a good idea to replace an old refrigerator with a high-energy consumption by a new A+++ refrigerator? Or, is it a good idea to replace an old fuel-consuming car with a new energy-efficient or electric vehicle? The manufacturing of a new refrigerator or smart car causes additional CO_2 emissions. While in use, the smart car or the refrigerator emits less CO_2 per kilometre (km) or per hour, but its higher energy efficiency has to compensate for the emissions produced during the manufacturing of the car, too. In order to optimise CO_2 emissions, climate-friendly purchases of more energy-efficient equipment should generally occur when the old equipment is worn out. However, if the end goal is the raising of environmental awareness instead of the absolute amount of reduced CO_2 emissions, then promoting the replacement of old equipment can play a significant role in the motivation for green technology.

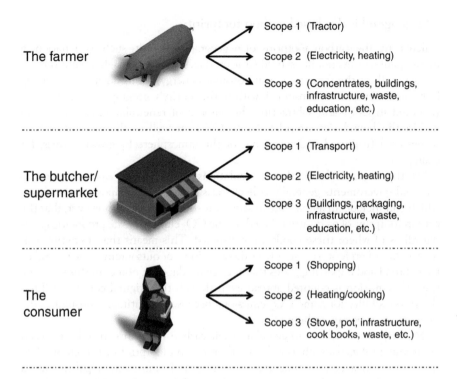

Figure 2.3 Scopes and actors in the chain from production to consumption of pork meat

The advantage of calculating the carbon footprint of a product in a consumer-based approach is that it can help them make environmentally conscious choices when they buy products, which can indirectly trigger environmentally friendly changes in the production chain. But it is difficult to use such tools directly in order to encourage the reduction of the carbon footprint of a product, since the responsibility for the carbon footprint is spread over the large number of people involved in its production, transformation and marketing. Moreover, the scope involved depends on the actors involved: while the energy used to produce aircrafts is a Scope 1 activity for the aircraft manufacturer, Scope 3 is applicable to the airlines flying the aircrafts. Calculators trying to evaluate GHG emissions linked to consumption seldom include all scopes, and when they do, they are complicated and difficult to understand. Encouraging people or companies to reduce their individual carbon footprint might therefore require another type of CO_2 calculator, which is called the geographically based carbon footprint.

The geographically based carbon footprint

Calculating the carbon footprint of a geographical unit, such as a nation, a municipality, or even a household (if it produces energy through a wind turbine or solar cells at the same time as it consumes energy), boils down to adding up how much energy is consumed within the entity's geographical boundaries (counted in CO_2) and subtracting the amount of renewable energy produced within the boundaries (translated into CO_2), as well as the amount of CO_2 sequestered (captured and taken out of the atmosphere by growing trees, for example).

At the national level, these calculations are relatively easy to make, as national governments generally collect statistics of energy imports and exports, which can include all actors and all scopes. It should be noted, however, that the carbon footprint of a country is based on the CO_2 emitted while producing goods regardless of where these goods are consumed. This means that a country can reduce its carbon footprint simply by delocalising – or outsourcing – heavy industries abroad and importing goods that it once produced at home. In this scenario, the CO_2 emission is counted abroad even though the original country still has the responsibility for some CO_2 emissions because it continues consuming the same goods as before, at home.

Municipalities also try to calculate their carbon footprints in order to reach environmental goals, such as reducing their carbon footprint or becoming CO_2-neutral within a certain time frame. In Denmark, most municipalities use a calculator developed by the country's National Association of Municipalities, which creates uniform carbon budgets, an overview of emissions by each municipality and assesses the largest carbon sinners. The calculator estimates carbon emissions within a defined area, including both the direct emissions of the given municipality, as well as the emissions generated by citizens and various sectors such as industry and agriculture.

Input data to the calculator are overall figures, including the number of citizens, livestock, type and size of industry and the municipal source of heating and electricity over a certain span of years. A number of Scope 3 services are included in these accounts, including libraries, municipal roads, hospitals, schools and local production. Hence, these calculators do provide an overview of the entire life cycle of products and total GHG emissions. However, producing an energy account for an entire municipality is not an easy task and there is no standard procedure for doing it. Calculations rely largely on gathering data from energy companies about energy production and consumption, on gross estimates of industrial and agricultural production and on using average consumption statistical data, despite the fact that there can be great disparities between the consumption of different social segments (see Jones and Kammen 2011).

When a municipality or a country intends to become CO_2-neutral, its strategy relies upon changing behaviour and reducing consumption. But even more important, its strategy also relies upon its producing renewable ('climate change-neutral') energy, often encountered as the equivalent to CO_2-neutral energy. For example, burning wood, straw or biofuels is considered CO_2-neutral because one assumes that the CO_2 released into the atmosphere will be captured again by growing trees or crops. This is despite the fact that there can be significant Scope 3 emissions related to the production of wood, and that converting non-farm land to crop-based biofuels or forest bioenergy production can create a heavy 'carbon debt' by releasing more CO_2 than would be gained annually by the displacement of fossil fuel (Fargione *et al.* 2008; Searchinger *et al.* 2008; Mitchell *et al.* 2012).

Moreover, in energy calculations, any CO_2-neutral energy produced within a certain boundary but sold outside that boundary is counted negatively (subtracted) in the CO_2 account of the producing unit, and is counted positively (added) in the CO_2 account of the purchasing geographical unit. In practice, this means that a municipality (or country) can become CO_2-neutral solely by exporting wind or solar energy without having to reduce its own consumption and/or without having to change its old practices. For example, in the strategy of the municipality of Copenhagen to become CO_2-neutral by 2025, the production of surplus wind power in its harbour and the export of CO_2-neutral district heating to neighbouring municipalities totals two-thirds of the expected reduction of the carbon footprint (Københavns Kommune 2012).

The district heating system of the municipality of Copenhagen produces high-pressure steam in a large incinerator. The steam is distributed to residential homes and industrial buildings for heating and industrial processes. The steam is recovered from waste energy produced in large industrial plants burning coal, in large electric power plants and by burning waste from households and industries. The district heating produced from burning waste or recovering energy spillages from electricity production is claimed to be CO_2-neutral because the CO_2 emitted is included in the carbon footprint of the electricity company or in the consumer's footprint relative to the buying and disposing of goods.

Thus, the current accounting system allows a district heating plant to declare itself CO_2-neutral even though it releases large amounts of CO_2, simply because it sends the CO_2 bill to the consumer who has thrown waste in the garbage or to the company that produces electricity. The accounting system also allows a municipality to declare itself CO_2-neutral even though it produces large amounts of CO_2 through transport, heating and agriculture, among others, simply because it can 'send' the CO_2 bill to neighbouring municipalities that buy wind energy or so-called 'CO_2-neutral' district heating.

Obviously, these accounting tricks can work only as long as there are buyers for wind energy or district heating in neighbouring municipalities, and as long as one is allowed to keep the account within the narrowly defined boundaries of the municipality. Moreover, this system discourages efforts to reduce consumption and improve the recycling of waste products, since the CO_2 neutrality of the district heating system depends upon a large and regular supply of waste to be burned. (For example, the municipality of Copenhagen has a very wide network of district heating and a rather archaic system of waste recycling). Even though district heating works effectively to trigger important CO_2 reductions at the municipal level, the system clearly has important limitations.

Different accounting tricks can also be used at the level of private companies. The University of Copenhagen, for example, prides itself for having reduced its energy consumption by 18.3 per cent and its CO_2 emissions by 24.1 per cent between 2006 and 2012 (Copenhagen University 2012). But this result is calculated per full-time student and employee (Copenhagen University 2012). In reality, the total electricity consumption has increased by 6.2 per cent in that period; real CO_2 emissions have indeed been reduced, but by only 8.2 per cent, not 24 per cent. The University has invested important resources in energy savings, and this has had a certain impact, but it has also enrolled more students and hired more staff (a total increase of 18.5 per cent for both categories in six years), which account for the lion's share of the energy and CO_2 reduction when counted per head. Had calculations been made per square metre occupied, the picture would have been gloomier, because the University total 'stock of buildings' decreased slightly between 2006 and 2012. If air flights had been counted as part of the University's CO_2 emissions, the picture would probably have been even less flattering: a significant proportion of its employees are frequent flyers to conferences and research sites all over the world.

Another way to reduce one's emissions on paper without changing one's behaviour and without reducing global emissions is to buy CO_2 caps by using an Emission Trading System (ETS). This can be done by individuals who want to offset the carbon emissions of travel by plane, for example, as well as by companies (or municipalities) who wish to reduce their carbon footprints. The first ETS was created by the EU in 2005 and regulates a wide range of factories, power stations and other installations that are collectively responsible for about half of the EU's emissions of CO_2. Each of the installations participating in the ETS is allocated a cap of how much CO_2 they are allowed to emit. If the installation emits less, it can sell its excess quota of CO_2 to an installation that emits more than the allocated cap and has to purchase 'unused' CO_2 emissions on the ETS market (Wagner 2004; Schleich and Betz 2005; Hufbauer *et al.* 2009).

In theory, buying CO_2 caps on the ETS should force industries to reduce their own emissions or prevent them from emitting as much CO_2 as they do. In practice, however, one buys someone else's right to emit CO_2 instead of buying or financing a CO_2 reduction, unless the money is invested in, for example, a project of reforestation or carbon sequestration. Buying emission permits thus allows someone to get rid of an excess of CO_2 by transferring it onto someone else's carbon footprint. This type of system can work only as long as one finds people willing to take on waste for money. When nobody is willing to do this, the system collapses and there is no alternative than to deal directly with one's own waste or unsustainable practices.

It is only when making calculations at the global level that accounting tricks no longer work and consumer- and geographically based calculations coincide. Figure 2.4 illustrates global emissions defined by both sectors and by end-use/ activity (WRI 2009). Producing a CO_2 budget with a CO_2 calculator at a scale below the global level implies making choices regarding which sectors to include or leave out. The advantage of making such calculations at the global level is

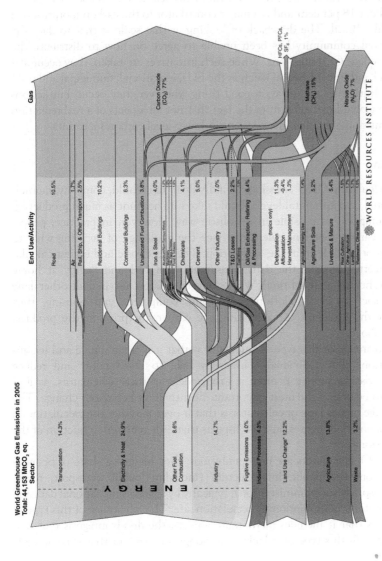

Figure 2.4 World GHG Emission. The flow chart is divided into sectors, end-users/activity and GHG production. Notice that when moving from left to right, sectors change depending on end-users/activities

Source: WRI 2009.

that everything is taken into account; one cannot delocalise part of the account (or deny the responsibility for CO_2 emissions) onto a neighbouring actor.

Furthermore, what seems to be a governing factor on a worldwide scale might not be that significant when defining a nation-wide scaled budget. For example, whilst deforestation does not play a major role in Denmark, where most forests were removed centuries ago, the removal of tropical forests impacts the global CO_2 by about 18 per cent and is a major contributor to the carbon footprint of a country like Brazil. The drawback of looking at that scale is that to date the international community has been unable to agree on how to distribute the efforts to reduce CO_2 emissions. When such initiatives are taken, they occur at a lower level, either continental (such as the EU), or national, municipal and even personal. Initiatives are always a good thing wherever they occur, but actions below the global level suffer from the fact that not all aspects of a real reduction of CO_2 emission are taken into account in lower-level carbon footprints.

Discussion

Ideally, calculating GHG emissions at individual, household, company, municipal, national or continental levels should take into account as much production and consumption as possible in a holistic way. However, in practice, people designing carbon footprint calculators face the challenge of deciding what to include in or exclude from the calculation. The most basic and easiest calculations concern primarily the daily consumption of fuel and energy at home (transport, heating and lighting). While some calculators also include other daily products such as food, clothing, electronic equipment and housing, they encounter the problems of calculating the carbon footprint of the products discussed above.

The advantage of this type of calculator is that it is fairly simple and recommend actions that individuals can easily take to save energy and reduce emissions. Saving money is often a strong focus of these calculators, as it is believed to be one of the most important incentives for behaviour change. The disadvantage of this type of calculator is that it oversimplifies the calculation of CO_2 emissions, and focuses on a few aspects that only represent a fraction of the total emissions.

Other CO_2 calculators are more ambitious: they include a share of Scope 3 deriving from the public infrastructure (including public transport, roads, schools, hospitals and administration), typically by aggregating national data and by dividing total consumption by population size. The advantage of this type of calculator is that it includes many more aspects; the disadvantage is that it is impossible with this type of calculator to adopt a behaviour that is completely CO_2-neutral.

Even people who live in a self-made wooden hut, walk every day, never buy clothes and eat only what they produce still have the responsibility for the public infrastructure that can upset their CO_2 balance. On the one hand, this can prove fairly discouraging for people who would like to change their behaviour. On the other hand, this can trigger a stronger political engagement, because the CO_2 balance deriving from the share of the public infrastructure can only be improved systemically, for example, by petitioning political decision makers for greener policies.

As we have seen, choosing one calculating method always implies including some things and excluding others. This can lead to very different carbon footprints for the same individual. For example, what is the carbon footprint of an average Dane? When the Danish government launched a national campaign in March 2007 under the heading '1-tonne-less' as part of its preparation for the 15th Conference of the Parties (COP15) Summit in 2009, it developed a simple calculator that focused on the personal consumption of Danes and established a yearly average CO_2 emission of six tons per person. This included Scope 1 (2 tons from fuel), Scope 2 (2.5 tons from heat and electricity) and some Scope 3 emissions (1.5 tons from food and goods) (Miljøministeriet 2007).

The *MapMyClimate.com* website adopted a similar concept for a carbon footprint calculator that allows individuals to estimate their personal carbon footprint online. It chose to include some Scope 3 emissions from non-food, governmental activities and infrastructure development over which individual citizens have no direct control, which increased the average carbon footprint to 8 tonnes per capita in 2010 (Erichsen and Arnskov 2010). This number is close to the carbon footprint calculated by the World Bank for 2010 (8.3 tons, or 15 per cent less than in 1990), calculated on the basis of the burning of fossil fuel and the manufacture of cement (World Bank 2013).

According to Denmark's national statistics, when applying the standards defined by the Kyoto Protocol (including Scope 3 from goods manufactured within the country), the carbon footprint is 9.5 tons per capita in 2007 (2 per cent less than in 1990) (Gravgård et al. 2009a, 2009b; Gravgård 2013). When including CO_2 equivalents from CH_4 and N_2O, the carbon footprint becomes 10.8 tons in 2010 (see Figure 2.5), a decrease of about 20 per cent when compared to 1990 (Færgeman 2012, 2013).

But these numbers do not take into account the goods that are produced abroad, imported and consumed in Denmark. While emissions calculated within the national boundaries have dropped since mid-1990s, this is mainly due to the delocalisation of heavy industries to other countries (Chrintz 2012; Færgeman 2012), a trend that is also found in other industrialised countries (see for example Weber and Matthews 2008; Druckman and Jackson 2009; Minx et al. 2009). Globally, imports account for about 40 per cent of regional carbon footprints (Andrews et al. 2009; Wilting and Vringer 2009).

When including imports of all goods consumed in Denmark (and subtracting exports), as shown in Figure 2.5, the average Danish carbon footprint per capita is between 18.4 and 19 tons in 2010, an increase of about 10 per cent since 1990 (Chrintz 2012; Færgeman 2012). Finally, when biomass and international transports are included in the calculation (Denmark has an important shipping sector that makes a significant contribution to the gross national product), then the carbon footprint jumps to a staggering 24 tons per capita in 2007, which is 65 per

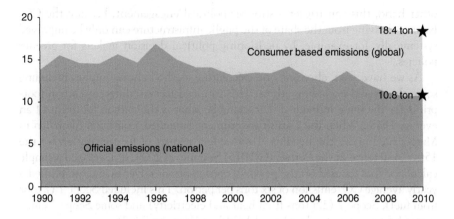

Figure 2.5 Consumption-based calculation of the CO_2 emission (tonnes per year per person) for an average Danish citizen with emissions produced within Denmark (dark grey) and emissions from production outside Denmark (light grey)

Source: Modified after Færgeman 2013.

cent more than in 1990 (Gravgård *et al.* 2009a, 2009b; Gravgård 2013). This ranks Danes as having one of the highest ecological footprints in the world, just behind Kuwait, Qatar and the United Arab Emirates (WWF 2014).

Thus, the calculation of the average carbon footprint of a Dane depends on the calculation method, the types of activities and scopes included, the span of years taken into consideration and whether it is calculated on the basis of production, consumption or economic activities. One needs to consider how imports and exports are included, whether the numbers are exact or normalised values and whether they are corrected for the import and export of electricity. The average carbon footprint calculation also depends on whether it includes the CO_2 equivalent of all GHGs, e.g. N_2O and CH_4, emissions from biomass and sequestration from carbon sinks (forests, agriculture and soil), whether the method corrects for the cumulative wind speed of the year and so on. All of these parameters are subject to some uncertainty; the accumulated uncertainty is even bigger and varies with the span of years used as the basis for the calculations. All this must be kept in mind when discussing and using calculated carbon footprint.

We must pause here and ask some questions. Have Danish CO_2 emissions declined by 20 per cent or increased by 65 per cent between 1990 and 2007–2010? Is Denmark one of the greenest countries on Earth or one of the countries with the highest carbon footprint per capita? Can Denmark become CO_2-neutral in 2050? It all depends on how carbon footprints are calculated and which part of the total CO_2 emissions is included or excluded. The lack of standards for calculating GHG emissions causes contradictory figures, and the lack of clarity about the method used and the complexity of the technical aspects make it complicated to compare.

Yet, calculating CO_2 emissions remains important for at least three reasons. First, quantifying emissions makes them visible, which is extremely useful since most people do not have much of a clue about how much CO_2 they emit or where it originates. Second, it creates a benchmark upon which one can measure progress made in reducing emissions, even though the reduction can happen just on paper simply by delocalising production elsewhere. Third, it attributes the responsibility for emissions (and the responsibility to reduce emissions). For all these reasons, CO_2 calculators are social technologies that are central to tackling global warming.

In Denmark alone, one finds a variety of different calculators, most of them accessible online. Some websites, such as *CO2-Guide.dk* or *husetsweb.dk*, concentrate on private energy consumption at home, but might also include transport and daily shopping (*CO2-guide.dk*), and focus at least as much on saving money as on reducing CO_2 emissions. (These two goals are at times contradictory, since the money saved can be spent on a plane travel abroad, for example, which can end up releasing more CO_2 than what was reduced). These websites refer to tangible consumption and behaviour and provide specific advice on how to reduce CO_2 emissions and save money at the same time. One of their drawbacks, however, is that they seldom advertise possibilities that will reduce CO_2 emissions but will cost something instead of saving money (for example, the longest 'payback time' promoted for investments made is 30 years).

MapMyClimate.dk takes the same point of departure, but adds a few Scope 3 emissions. Its aim here is to educate people and make them realise the seriousness of the threat posed by global warming, with the hope that they would use their new knowledge and consciousness to influence policy makers to make bold decisions with regard to infrastructure and social changes. The drawback of this approach is that it can appear to demotivate individuals when they realise that they do not have much control over a large part of their CO_2 emissions.

For example, when a beta-version of the *MapMyClimate* calculator was tested, it was assumed that if people did not use their own car for transport, they would use public transport, with the consequence that people could never reach zero emission even if they set all the cursors in the website's programme (for transport, heat and daily shopping) to zero. Including some Scope 3 emissions did not make sense to the people testing the site (see also Papazu and Scheele 2014): This was changed in the later version of the website calculator. One finds other calculators that include Scope 3 emissions (such as the 'smartbudget' on *nykredit.dk*, which is the homepage of a bank) that end up giving a very high average CO_2 emission per capita, regardless of how little individuals using the calculator consume in their daily life. The aim of such type of information is more to raise awareness and possibly trigger political changes in the longer run, since little can be done to address these problems here and now at the individual level.

Conclusions

Asking citizens to change behaviour presupposes that they know the consequences of their behaviour and can act accordingly. CO_2 calculations are social technologies that inform users and allow them to calculate their individual production of GHGs or, in other words, their carbon footprint. Calculating the carbon footprint of products can help consumers make environmentally conscious choices when they buy goods; calculating the carbon footprint of actors can also help them prioritise their reduction strategies according to the sector in which the reduction potential is the biggest, or the scope in which the control is the highest and where change is easiest.

Because the information that the footprint calculator provides can change citizens' behaviour, all types of calculators can play an important role in reducing our carbon footprint. But calculators are only useful if they are used with the genuine intent to reduce CO_2 emissions. If, on the contrary, they are used as a means for green-washing to deceptively give the impression that an organisation or product is environmentally friendly, they might be counterproductive. Having the goal of becoming CO_2-neutral by 2050 can be a powerful incentive for change, but only if it translates into a genuine reduction of emissions. Merely transferring emissions to someone else's account by delocalising production, exporting green energy to compensate for the brown energy consumed at home and taking as benchmarks the criteria that will make our progress appear in the most favourable light can create the misleading impression that we are on the right track to reduce our emissions. Whilst carbon footprint calculators are as good as the criteria that they take into account and the convention that makes them work, they should be regarded critically for no more than what they really are: a man-made social technology designed to shed some light on our emissions and inform us about what we want to know – as well as to keep us ignorant of what we don't want to hear.

Calculators targeting individuals and focusing on Scope 1 and Scope 2 emissions tend to save little CO_2 in absolute figures, while calculators used at the municipal or a higher level that include Scope 3 emissions tend to have a much bigger impact. Yet, it might be argued that the change at the individual level might require more sacrifice than the changes performed at the municipal level. Reducing the consumption of meat and dairy products, selling one's car to use public transport or bicycle, spending one's holiday at home instead of in an exotic country and changing daily habits require genuine, conscious effort that might be even more difficult to make than the decision to change a municipal infrastructure.

By triggering behaviour changes that require sacrificing some comfort, calculators can contribute to raising awareness, changing mentalities and social norms and ultimately influence politicians to make bold moves and adopt ambitious environmental policies. In this sense, calculators can have even wider consequences than the individual amounts of CO_2 emissions that are reduced at Scope 1 or Scope 2. The value of energy calculators as social technologies lies at least as much in their potential to raise awareness and trigger more profound long-term changes in society as in their potential to directly reduce emissions in the here and now.

References

Andrew R, Peters G P and Lennox J (2009) Approximation and Regional Aggregation in Multi-Regional Input-Output Analysis for National Carbon Footprint Accounting, *Economic Systems Research* 21(3) 311–335.

Chrintz T (2012) *Carbon Footprint – den ideelle opgørelse og anvendelse*, Concito, København (http://concito.dk/files/dokumenter/artikler/rapport_gcfr_ endelig.pdf) Accessed 10 April 2014.

Copenhagen University (2012) *Grønt regnskab 2012 for Københavns Universitet* (http://klima.ku.dk/groen_campus/voresresultater/groenneregnskaber/b_2012/Gr_nt_Regnskab_2012.pdf) Accessed 1 March 2013.

Cullet P (2010) Common but Differentiated Responsibilities, in Fitzmaurice M, Ong D M and Merkouris P (eds) *Research Handbook on International Environmental Law*, Edward Elgar, Cheltenham, UK, 161–181.

Druckman A and Jackson T (2009) The Carbon Footprint of UK Households 1990–2004: A Socio-Economically Disaggregated, Quasi-Multi-Regional Input-Output Model, *Ecological Economics* 68(7) 2066–2077.

Energistyrelsen (2012) *Energistatistik 2012 Data, tabeller, statistikker og kort*, Copenhagen Energistyrelsen Denmark.

Erichsen A C and Arnskov M M (2010) MapMyClimate: Between Science, Education and People, *Journal of Education, Informatics and Cybernetics* 2(1) 43–48.

European Commission (2010) *Analysis of Options to Move Beyond 20% Greenhouse Gas Emission Reductions and Assessing the Risk of Carbon Leakage* (http://eur-lex.europa.eu/LexUriServ/LexUriServ.do?uri=COM:2010:0265:FIN:en:PDF) Accessed 3 March 2014.

Fargione J, Hill J, Tilman D, Polasky S and Hawthorne P (2008) Land Clearing and the Biofuel Carbon Debt, *Science* 319(5867) 1235–1238.

Færgeman T (2012) *Annual Climate Outlook 2012 Hovedrapport Frederiksberg*, Concito, København (http://concito.dk/files/dokumenter/artikler/aco2012_endelig_0.pdf) Accessed 10 April 2014.

Færgeman T (2013) *Annual Climate Outlook 2013 Anbefalinger Frederiksberg*, Concito, København (http://concito.dk/files/dokumenter/artikler/aco2013_hovedrapport.pdf) Accessed 10 April 2014.

GHG Protocol (2001) *What is the Difference Between Direct and Indirect Emissions? Greenhouse Gas protocol* (www.ghgprotocol.org/calculation-tools/faq#directindirect) Accessed 5 March 2014.

Gravgård O (2013) *Grønne nationalregnskaber og det grønne BNP*, Copenhagen Danmarks Statistik.

Gravgård O, Olsen T and Rørmose P (2009a) *Greenhouse Gas Emissions from the Danish Economy*, Copenhagen Danmarks Statistik.

Gravgård O, Olsen T, Rørmose P and Kristensen B H (2009b) Dansk økonomis udslip af drivhusgasser, in *Statistisk tiårsoversigt 2009*, Copenhagen Danmarks Statistik, 5–19.

Harris P G (1999) Common but Differentiated Responsibility: The Kyoto Protocol and United States Policy, *The New York University Environmental Law Journal* 7 27–48.

Hertwich E G and Peters G P (2009) Carbon Footprints of Nations: A Global, Trade-Linked Analysis, *Environmental Science and Technology* 43(16) 6414–6420.

Hoff J and Strobel B W (2013) A Municipal 'Climate Revolution'? The Shaping of Municipal Climate Change Policies, *The Journal of Transdisciplinary Environmental Studies* 12(1) 3–14.

Huang Y A, Lenzen M, Weber C L, Murray J and Mathews H S (2009) The Role of Input-Output Analysis for the Screening of Corporate Carbon Footprints, *Economic Systems Research* 21(3) 217–242.

Hufbauer G C, Charnovitz S and Kim J (2009) *Global Warming and the World Trading System*, Peterson Institute for International Economics, Washington, DC.

IPCC (2013) *Climate Change 2013 The Physical Science Basis: Contribution of Working Group I to the Fifth Assessment Report of the Intergovernmental Panel on Climate Change* [Stocker T F, Qin D, Plattner G-K, Tignor M, Allen S K, Boschung J, Nauels A, Xia Y, Bex V and Midgley P M (eds)] Cambridge University Press, Cambridge, UK.

Jones C M and Kammen D M (2011) Quantifying Carbon Footprint Reduction Opportunities for US Households and Communities, *Environmental Science and Technology* 45 4088–4095.

Kenny T and Gray N F (2009) Comparative Performance of Six Carbon Footprint Models for Use in Ireland, *Environmental Impact Assessment Review* 29 1–6.

Københavns Kommune (2012) *KBH 2025 Klimaplanen – en grøn, smart og CO_2-neutral by*, Copenhagen Municipality Denmark.

Lüthi D, Le Floch M, Bereiter B, Blunier T, Barnola J-M, Siegenthaler U, Raynaud D, Jouzel J, Fischer H, Kawamura K and Stocker T F (2008) High-Resolution Carbon Dioxide Concentration Record 650,000–800,000 Years Before Present, *Nature* 453(7193) 379–382.

Matthews H S, Hendrickson C T and Weber C L (2008) The Importance of Carbon Footprint Estimation Boundaries, *Environmental Science and Technology* 42 (16) 5839–5842.

Miljøministeriet (2007 *1-ton-mindre* [1-tonne-less] (http://web.archive.org/web/20070609090502/www.1tonmindre.dk/beregner_start.asp?m=1) Accessed 29 May 2014.

Minx J C, Wiedmann T, Wood R, Peters G P, Lenzen M, Owen A, Scott K, Barrett J, Hubacek, K Baiocchi G, Paul A, Dawkins E, Briggs J, Guan D, Suh S and Ackerman F (2009) Input-Output Analysis and Carbon Footprinting: An Overview of Applications, *Economic Systems Research* 21(3) 187–216.

Mitchell S R, Harmon M E and O'Connell K E B (2012) Carbon Debt and Carbon Sequestration Parity in Forest Bioenergy Production, *Global Change Biology Bioenergy* 4 818–827.

Papazu I and Scheele C E (2014) (De-)Localising the Climate: The Production of Uncertain Agencies Through Climate Websites, *STS Encounters* 6(1) 1–34.

Rajamani L (2000) The Principle of Common But Differentiated Responsibility and the Balance of Commitments under the Climate Regime, *Review of European Community and International Environmental Law* 9(2) 120–131.

Regeringen (2011) *Energistrategi 2050 – fra kul, olie og gas til grøn energi*, Copenhagen Klima- og Energiministeriet Denmark.

Schleich J and Betz R (2005) *Incentives for Energy Efficiency and Innovation in the European Emission Trading System* ECEEE [European Council for an Energy Efficient Economy] Paper presented at the ECEEE Summer Study, Mandelieu, France, 1495–1506.

Searchinger T, Heimlich R, Houghton R A, Dong F, Elobeid A, Fabiosa J, Tokgoz S, Hayes

D and Yu T-H (2008) Use of US Croplands for Biofuels Increases Greenhouse Gases Through Emissions from Land-Use Change, *Science* 319(5867) 1238–1240.

Stone C D (2004) Common but Differentiated Responsibilities in International Law, *American Journal of International Law* 98(4) 276–301.

Tans P (2008) *Trends in Atmospheric Carbon Dioxide*, Mauna Loa NOAA Earth System Research Laboratory (ESRL) (www.esrl.noaa.gov/gmd/ccgg/trends/) Accessed 29 May 2014.

US Global Change Research Program (2014) *Climate Change Impacts in the United States: The Third National Climate Assessment* (www.globalchange.gov/browse/multimedia/atmospheric-carbon-dioxide-levels) Accessed 2 December 2014.

Wackernagel M and Rees W E (1996) *Our Ecological Footprint: Reducing Human Impact on Earth*, New Society Publishers, Gabriola Island, BC.

Wackernagel M and Rees W E (1997) Perceptual and Structural Barriers to Investing in Natural Capital: Economics from an Ecological Footprint Perspective, *Ecological Economics* 20 (1) 3–24.

Wagner M (2004) *Firms, the Framework Convention on Climate Change and the EU Emissions Trading System: Corporate Energy Management Strategies to Address Climate Change and GHG Emissions in the European Union*, Lüneburg Centre for Sustainability Management (CSM).

Weber C L and Matthews H S (2008) Quantifying the Global and Distributional Aspects of American Household Carbon Footprint, *Ecological Economics* 66(2–3) 379–391

Weidema B P, Thrane M, Christensen P, Schmidt J and Løkke S (2008 Carbon Footprint: A Catalyst for Life Cycle Assessment? *Journal of Industrial Ecology* 12(1) 3–6

Wiedmann T (2009) Carbon Footprint and Input-Output Analysis: An Introduction, *Economic Systems Research* 21(3) 175–186.

Wilting H C and Vringer K (2009) Carbon and Land-Use Accounting from a Producer's and Consumer's Perspective: An Empirical Examination Covering the World, *Economic Systems Research* 21(3) 291–310.

World Bank (2013) CO_2 *Emissions (metric tons per capita)* (http://data.worldbank.org/indicator/EN.ATM.CO2E.PC) Accessed 1 April 2014

WRI (2009) *World Greenhouse Gas Emissions in 2005* World Resources Institute (www.wri.org/publication/world-greenhouse-gas-emissions-2005) Accessed 5 March 2014.

WWF (2014) *Living Planet Report 2014 Species and spaces, people and places* World Wide Fund for Nature, Gland Switzerland (www.worldwildlife.org/pages/living-planet-report-2014) Accessed 2 December 2014.

3 'Think globally, act locally'

Climate change mitigation and citizen participation

Jens Hoff

Introduction

From its inception as a separate policy field in the 1960s, the issue of the environment has been connected to citizen participation (see e.g. Connelly et al. 2012, 354ff). Since then, green movements with different orientations have formulated what has been called the 'green discontent' of the 1960s (Tatenhove and Leroy 2009). This period in the evolution of the green movement eventually led to the institutionalisation of different forms of citizen participation – public hearings, citizen meetings, policy network creation, interactive policy-making and others – during the 1970s and 1980s in many Western European countries, most notably the United Kingdom (UK), Germany, the Netherlands and Scandinavian countries.

While most green movements and parties realised long before the Rio Earth Summit in 1992 that many environmental problems are of a transnational or global character (nuclear power, air pollution and climate change are cases in point), most of their activities have been directed at the national or local level. The rationality behind this orientation seems to be that the key to the successful resolution of global environmental problems is change in individual or local community behaviour and consumption patterns, something best accomplished through local initiatives and community processes (Sale 1985; Ward 1996). This thinking is condensed in the green slogan 'think globally, act locally'.

In much green thinking, this orientation to the national and local is intertwined with ideas about participatory democracy, the central argument being that (local) participatory democracy is the political form most conducive to the expression of citizens' environmental concerns (Ward 1996, 150). There are many advocates for why this should be so. Some argue that the corrosive effects of self-interest on the environment are best controlled by political processes operating at the community level (Ostrom 1990). Others suggest that smaller-scale economic processes centring on relatively self-sufficient communities is a necessary pre-condition for establishing sustainable societies. The latter argument was the position of Die Grünen in Germany in the 1980s, who also stated that such decentralised communities should have extensive autonomy and rights of self-government, and that citizens should be participating directly in decision making (Die Grünen 1983, 8). While still alive, this line of thinking is not represented in a pure form in any of the major sustainability movements today.[1]

At the global level, the role of local governments and communities in more systematic action on sustainable development was recognised with the adoption of the Agenda 21 Convention at the 1992 Rio Earth Summit. The Convention recognised that because local government is the level of government closest to the general population, its functions and ability to mobilise support are seen as essential to any move towards a sustainable future. In fact, at the time of the Summit it was estimated that over two-thirds of Agenda 21 could not be delivered without the commitment and cooperation of local government (Connelly et al. 2012, 364). Agenda 21 also stressed the need to strengthen the role of social groups in articulating and implementing environmental policies. These groups include women, indigenous populations, non-governmental organizations (NGOs), workers and trade unions, businesses and industries and partnerships between these groups and local authorities.

The fate of Local Agenda 21 (LA21) seems to have been very different in different countries, depending both on the financial and political support it has received from local and regional authorities and on whether local initiatives on sustainability had been put in place before the Agenda. However, there seems to be general agreement – at least in the research community – that both the rhetoric and practice of LA21 has gradually died out (Feichtinger and Pregering 2005; Kern et al. 2007). This does not mean (as we shall see below) that local authorities are no longer engaged in action on sustainability or have not taken on the challenge of climate change. It simply means that engagement in climate change issues today is only in a few cases conducted under the rubric of LA21.

Local governments in Western Europe and many other parts of the world are actively pursuing actions on sustainability and climate change; they often take the lead in developing innovative practices in this area, and in pressuring and lobbying other levels of government and international organisations to develop more environmentally sustainable policies. However, it is probably fair to say that after Rio and the signing of the Kyoto Treaty in 1997, the media, researchers and the public have paid more attention to developments at the international and global levels. After the signing of the Kyoto Protocol, much attention concentrated on the annual United Nations (UN) Conference of the Parties (COP) meetings, and the positions of major international actors in relation to these negotiations. This focus was reinforced after the COP meeting at Bali in 2005 and during the build-up to COP 15 in Copenhagen in 2009, where hopes were high for a new global agreement on climate change.

After the Copenhagen COP failed to produce an agreement, many actors became disillusioned; interest in the issue of climate change no longer appeared at or even near the top of the public agenda. However, the inability of global institutions to come to an agreement on climate change also seems to have spurred a renewed focus on the capacity of local governments and locally focused organisations and movements to make a difference in climate change (Hoff and Strobel 2013).

It is this 'reorientation towards the local' that is the theme of this chapter. After a discussion of a definition of citizen participation, the chapter argues that citizen participation in environmental policies in general, and in climate policies in particular, has moved through four phases from the early 1960s until today. Each phase is marked by different policy regimes; i.e. a changing role of the state, emphasis on different policy instruments, different dominant political discourses and different citizen and expert roles. Special attention is paid to the last phase of this development, which began after 2009, when new forms of climate change governance appeared. Some have called these new forms of collaboration between local government and citizens 'culture governance' or 'post-normal governance' (Blaxekjær 2014); we pay special attention to the effects of these new forms on the steering capacity and democratic functioning of local government.

This chapter attempts to answer the following two research questions: 1) what is the precise content of this 'reorientation towards the local' after 2009 in terms of citizen participation? 2) how can this 'reorientation' be understood using a governance steering perspective and a democratic perspective respectively?

This analysis places a special focus on climate change mitigation efforts on the local level in Denmark and cases drawn from the country's Citizen Driven Environmental Action (CIDEA) project,[2] which has investigated how to best engage and motivate citizens to reduce their CO_2 footprint through a case-based approach.

In the course of this discussion, we remain within the theoretical traditions that have already dealt with citizen participation and environmental policies from various angles, i.e. democratic theory (Dryzek 2005), ecological modernisation theory (Hajer 1995; Mol *et al.* 2009), institutional theory (Ostrom 1991; Fisher *et al.* 2009), and governance theory (Hajer 2009). The discourse below draws implicitly on these theories; we shall return to their usefulness in the discussion below.

Defining citizen participation

We define citizen participation in climate change mitigation as:

> The participation of citizens in any type of collaborative activities with public agencies to either formulate, decide on, and/or implement measures that have to do with climate change mitigation.

The citizen involvement discussed here normally takes place at the local level and can be anything from citizens participating in the formulation of local climate change mitigation plans and/or the design of mitigation projects to citizens carrying out such projects or becoming actively involved in climate change mitigation activities.

As explained in the introductory chapter to this book, the initiative for such collaborative arrangements can occur 'top-down', as in the case of LA21, or move 'bottom-up', as in the case of Transition Towns or similar initiatives. The involvement of both local authorities and citizens in such initiatives reflects a continuum of 'very little' to 'a lot'; however, in our definition of citizen participation, there is always an element of involvement, however minor, of local authority.[3] Also, these collaborative arrangements can concern citizens as individuals, as well as citizens as members of different types of communities. This reflects another continuum of going from individual, family, social networks to village, association or 'community' (see Figure 1.1. in Chapter 1).

Our analysis of citizen participation in climate change concerns the activities of citizen initiatives, green movements and green parties insofar as they engage in some form of collaboration with local public authorities. Such collaborative arrangements, which are discussed in greater detail below, can have many different forms, from local authorities with little manpower or money simply facilitating civil society processes to more formal arrangements such as the implementation of specific LA21 activities. Using this definition of citizen participation also indicates that we have no intention of telling the comprehensive story of green movements or parties; we focus solely on what we call 'collaborative arrangements' (Healey 1997/2006).

Phases in citizen participation

An earlier attempt at describing the different phases of citizen participation in environmental policies is made by Tatenhove and Leroy (2009), who take as their point of departure the development of the relations between state, market and civil society, and the ensuing dominant discourses of government. Tatenhove and Leroy distinguish analytically between three phases of citizen participation in the green movement, which they label as *early*, *anti-* and *late modernisation* (cf. Alexander 1995). Each of these phases is discussed as dominated by certain policy practices (or arrangements).

Early modernisation, used as a characterisation of the social order and policies from at least the 1920s until the mid-1960s carried with it a great optimism concerning the state's capacity to solve societal problems by rational policy making and comprehensive planning. *Anti-modernisation* (mid-1960s to around 1980) was characterised by scepticism and even severe criticism of the optimism and the one-dimensional character of early modernisation, and of the external effects of its different political decisions on, among other things, the environment and the Third World. Much of this criticism was precipitated by the new social movements of the late 1960s and early 1970s that focused on issues like inequality, emancipation, democracy and participation. *Late modernisation* (1980 until now), as described variously by Beck (1992, 2003) and Giddens (1992), presumes neither a synoptic rationality nor an omnipotent 'system' which must be criticised and fought. Rather, they stress that the side-effects and unforeseen consequences of modernisation, such as global risks, are factors that increasingly structure society and politics. These risks, they argue, cannot be dealt with effectively by the classical, state-centred system of industrial society.

What we are seeing today is a decreasing centrality of the state as political actor, and an increasing politicisation of other spheres of society. Thus, *late modernisation* assumes an increasing interweaving of state, market and civil society, and an increasing cooperation between their respective agencies. Policy problems are defined, and policy solutions are designed in cooperation between these agencies, and become part of the policy making process. Today, this is reflected in a variety of participatory, interactive and deliberative patterns of policy making in much of contemporary Europe (Tatenhove and Leroy 2009, 192–193).

Tatenhove and Leroy attach two important provisos to their theory. First, they stress that there is a gradual transition between the phases, and second, they emphasise that their own empirical research has demonstrated that there is no clear evolutionary path of development concerning the policy instruments used in each of the phases. Thus, while the idea of a unilinear evolution consisting of consecutive phases can be seductive, these phases should rather be seen as 'ideal types', rather than as real historical policy arrangements. Also, different areas of environmental politics might occur in different phases: some may be more traditional in terms of citizen participation, while others may be more advanced.

In the following narrative, we use Tatenhove's and Leroy's three phases as a point of departure for our description of citizen participation in environmental politics and policies. However, our phases deviate somewhat from theirs, as we focus especially on the issue of climate change from the time when the issue began to gain public recognition. We pay special attention to the role of the state/public authorities, the policy instruments used, the dominant environmental policy discourse and the roles into which citizens and experts are cast.

First phase: Institutionalisation of citizen participation in environmental policies, 1960s–1980s

Tatenhove and Leroy argue (2009, 195–196, and following Lauwers 1983) that from the first emergence of environmental issues in the 1960s, they have been closely associated with citizen participation. They use the concept of 'green discontent' to frame this coupling. Green discontent is seen as having two sources. First, criticism grew in the 1960s of the ignorance of the political and economic establishment about the environmental effects of industry (hazardous waste), transport (air pollution) and energy (nuclear power). Second, criticism also grew about the way in which decisions about these problems were being made, i.e. without properly informing the people concerned, and, in many cases, dismissing and overruling protests out of hand. Tatenhove and Leroy see this criticism as a part of what they call 'a larger anti-modernist discourse', and link them to those of other new social movements such as the civil rights movement in the United States (US), and the student and anti-Vietnam war movements.

This criticism also paved the way for the gradual development and institutionalisation of environmental policies. Environmental policy departments were established in many national governments, including the Environmental Protection Agency (EPA) in the US in 1972 (which reflects the leading role of the US in environmental politics at that time). Environmental standards were set in various areas and implemented in a series of permits and environmental planning procedures. In addition, such features as environmental impact and technology assessments were introduced.

The green movement's criticism of the lack of transparency and participation in environmental politics led to a long string of protests over the siting of hazardous industries, infrastructure and nuclear power plants, among others. How much effect these protests had is debatable, but eventually public authorities set up different procedures for consultation and participation.

The first policy field in which such procedures were institutionalised was physical planning. While these procedures opened up new opportunities to involve citizens and environmental action groups in decision making processes, they were still largely bound to local processes, and were limited to a restricted number of environmental issues. However, many environmental problems were not entirely local or very specific – nuclear power is a case in point.

For this reason, the forces of green discontent continued their criticism in directions that took various forms in different countries. In Germany, for example, the radicalisation of the environmental movement led to the establishment of the Green Party in the late 1970s. In the Netherlands, in an expression of the country's consensus tradition in political life, the environmental movement was frequently consulted by the Dutch political establishment, and became what Tatenhove and Leroy call 'a natural ally of the Ministry of the Environment' (2009, 98). In the multi-party Scandinavian countries, the green agenda was adopted quite early by the centre-left parties, leaving little room for specific green parties. However, in Sweden, a Green Party (*Miljöpartiet*) was established in 1981, gained representation in Parliament in 1988, and has been permanently represented in Parliament since 1994.

In terms of citizen participation in environmental politics, one can conclude that developments in the 1960s and 1970s led to the introduction of a number of participatory features into the environmental policy domain. However, these were in large part supplements to the dominant (liberal) representative democracy, and did not affect the roles and power positions of other agencies or actors very much. Thus, parliament and the state bureaucracy were still in control of policy making and implementation, and citizens and civil society still very much the objects of steering by governmental agencies. The dominant discourse was one of 'social engineering', with decision makers and bureaucrats (mainly lawyers and engineers) still very optimistic about the ability of (national) public authorities to effectively solve environmental problems.

Second phase: Development of instruments for citizen participation, 1980s–1992

There is a general consensus in the literature that the 1970s and 1980s witnessed an erosion of the power bases of the nation-state and the emergence of a diversity of alternative policy arrangements (Scharpf 1993) There is also a general consensus about the causes for this development, namely the globalisation of economic, social, political and cultural relationships (Scholte 2005).

These transformations are often captured in terms of a shift from 'government' to 'governance', and are seen as an indication of a movement away from hierarchical and well-institutionalised forms of government towards less formalised practices of governance. These practices allow a wide variety of actors, including corporations, civil society organisations, political and bureaucratic actors to coordinate their agendas and solutions in dealing with a range of societal problems (Pierre 2000). The shift is also seen as a movement away from what used to be the central locus of democratic politics – the nation-state – towards subnational and transnational arenas.

In order to come to terms with the impact of this development on citizen participation in environmental policies, Tatenhove and Leroy (2009, 198ff) distinguish between the societalisation and the marketisation of environmental politics. Societalisation marks the changing relationship between public authorities and civil society actors. Public authorities who recognise the erosion of their steering capacity are under pressure to find solutions to complex societal problems with scarce resources. As a result, they increasingly invite civil society actors to communicate proactively with them about policy proposals during all stages of the policy process, from the formulation of problems to decisions and implementation. These new arrangements, ranging from policy network creation and management to co-production and interactive policy making, reflect the principles of coordination and self-governance. These non-codified political practices are found all over Europe. There is great variety among them; how much they are integrated into policy-making differs in different areas and in different countries (Akkerman *et al.* 2000).

Marketisation marks the changing relationship between public authorities and market actors. In this period, we see a shift from laws and permits towards more market-based types of regulation, including taxes, levies and subsidies aimed at putting a price on the environment as a common good. These are supplemented by more sophisticated measures such as 'tradeable' emission permits. We also see in this period a delegation of responsibilities and competencies towards either (new) autonomous or private (privatised) agencies, a trend that was inspired by the period's New Public Management philosophy. This is the case in such areas as energy, water management and waste management (see Chapter 11 in this book). Apart from this contracting out of public assets and thereby activating market actors and mechanisms, there were also numerous attempts to better coordinate policies with market stakeholders. Examples of this target group policy – where certain groups of polluters (agriculture, transport and electricity among them) are invited to be co-responsible for setting and implementing environmental standards – can be found both at national and EU levels. Covenants and other types of flexible policy instruments are also used; they are called new environmental policy instruments, or NEPIs (see Fisher *et al.* 2009, 144).

Whilst all of these new types of policy arrangements with their different types of citizen and stakeholder participation appear in this period, they were not institutionalised until the next phase of citizen participation. For example, the Model Plan for Public Participation formulated by the EPA in the US was passed in 1996. In 1998, four directives were passed by the EU mandating public participation in environmental decisions, including the Water Framework Directive, which mandates consultation with and 'active involvement' of the public (Fisher *et al.* 2009, 147). Also in 1998, the UN endorsed the Aarhus Convention, which created increased access for justice, transparency and public participation in environmental decision making (Connelly *et al.* 2012, 275).

To summarise, this second phase of participation is characterised by a huge expansion of citizen involvement in all stages of the policy process. Many new arenas for citizen participation were created because state/public authorities increasingly realised that the resources and cooperation of citizens are necessary in order to create effective and acceptable policy solutions. However, many of the arenas and occasions created for citizen participation were still at an experimental stage; even though a track for participation was established, citizen participation in the environmental area did not become institutionalised until the late 1990s.

Third phase: Citizen participation in a global governance perspective, 1992–2009

The Rio Earth Summit in 1992 marked a watershed in many respects. It has already been noted how the agreement on LA21 emphasised the role and importance of local government, and also underscored the need to strengthen the role of different social groups and NGOs in order to establish more systematic action on sustainable development. Of similar importance was the agreement on the Convention of Biological Diversity and the Convention on Climate Change at the Summit. The latter brought the issue of global warming to prominence, and marked a shift in the discourse on the environment from individual environmental problems towards a greater understanding of the interconnectedness of different environmental challenges. This interconnectedness was also stressed by the Rio Declaration itself, which coupled both environmental and development challenges (Connelly *et al.* 2012, 270ff).

Whilst this interconnectedness was a point of departure in the Bruntland Report from 1987, and lay behind the Report's famous definition of sustainability, the Rio Declaration is nonetheless outstanding in the sense that it reflects both the growing acknowledgement of the global character of many environmental problems, and a belief in the possibility of establishing global solutions to these problems. Climate change is certainly a good illustration of both the global character of environmental problems, and of the belief in global solutions. Indeed, climate change is what Jänicke and Jörgens (2009, 157) have called a 'persistent environmental problem'.[4]

Persistent environmental problems have four characteristics:

•   Their sources lie outside the traditional domain of environmental policy and are the product of the 'normal' functioning of other sectors of the economy and society. There is no quick fix – solving them requires lasting change in the operating logic of the sectors that cause them;

- They cross sectors and sectoral policies in such areas as energy, building, transport and agriculture. These sectors are vital to the economy, and contain many 'heavy' actors and political veto points;
- They are highly complex, and manifest themselves as creeping forms of degradation with substantial delays between cause and effect; and
- They are global in nature. Problem solving of environmental problems has to take place on many levels and involve international agreements in order to be effective. In the case of climate change, this has been accomplished by the setting up of the IPCC (Intergovernmental Panel on Climate Change) in 1988, creation of the UN Convention on Climate Change (UNFCCC) signed by over 150 nations at the Rio Summit in 1992, the establishment of the Kyoto Protocol at the COP3 meeting in Kyoto in 1997, which included legally binding targets for CO_2 reductions for highly industrialised countries and a subsequent series of COP meetings.

The attempt to establish a global regime on climate change has been very difficult. Critical roadblocks to international climate change accords include the refusal of the US to sign the Kyoto Protocol and the inability of nations to agree to a successor to the Protocol at COP15. However, what is interesting is that the EU used the issue of climate change to surpass the US as the global leader on environmental policy during this phase. In fact, prior to negotiations on the UNFCCC in 1992, the European Commission launched an ambitious climate change strategy, and the EU was also actively engaged in pushing forward the 1997 Kyoto Protocol process.

Since 2000, the EU has stepped up its measures to meet its Kyoto commitments and preserve its international leadership position (Connelly *et al.* 2012, 304). Most significant among these measures are the European Climate Change Programme, a major output of which was the Emissions Trading Directive. In January 2007, the European Commission adopted a proposal seeking EU greenhouse gas emissions (GHGs) reductions of at least 20 per cent (based on 1990 levels) by 2020. The proposal also introduced mandatory targets across the EU of 20 per cent renewable energy consumption and 10 per cent of transport fuels from biofuel sources. Both the European Parliament and Council accepted this strategy, and the Commission drafted specific measures to meet these targets.

In 2013, these so-called '20-20-20' targets were replaced by the more ambitious '30-20-20' targets, and the malfunctioning Emissions Trading System was tightened by the 'backload' of quotas (reducing the total number of quotas to boost their price). Both these measures ramped up the EU's position as the global leader on environmental policies. The EU was not very active on local level action (cities, regions, municipalities) on climate change in this phase, even though it was active on the subject of citizen and stakeholder participation in other environmental areas, as we saw above. However, after 2009, the EU stepped up its measures to involve the local level in action on climate change to a greater extent.

As noted above, the 'top-down' strategy of LA21 has been successful, but only to a certain extent. Even though LA21 generated a great deal of enthusiasm in the post-Rio era, it is an open question how much its activities have moved beyond what Stoker and Young (1993) have called 'business as usual' and 'superficial tokenism' to an actual 'holistic policy approach' in which local councils start to systematically develop state-of-the-environment reports and sustainability strategies, among others. The pioneering nations concerning LA21 seem to have been Sweden, the UK and the Netherlands (Connelly *et al.* 2012, 367). It is a bit surprising that otherwise environmentally active nations such as Norway and Denmark engaged with LA21 relatively late. However, this is probably explained by the fact that local governments in these countries were already involved in many environmental projects, and therefore did not see LA21 as a lever in this respect.[5]

Even in countries where the national level has been very reluctant to take action, local governments have responded to the issue. The prime example of this is the US, where a number of states and cities have tried to take on a leadership role in climate governance despite the hostile federal agenda under the 2001–2009 George W. Bush administration. In Europe, many local governments have used the window of opportunity opened by the climate change agenda to restructure their policies and practices in ways that override the normal distinctions between such policy areas as environment, energy and employment (see Chapter 6 in this book). This has opened up new opportunities for local governments to have dialogues with actors other than the 'usual suspects', and to become policy innovators and exporters of environmental norms and practices. Several transnational networks have aided in this development and helped build local capacity in this area, most notably the International Council for Environmental Initiatives, *now* Local Governments for Sustainability (ICLEI) through its Communities for Climate Protection (CCP) programme (Betsill and Bulkeley 2007; Hoff 2010; and Chapter 9 in this book), such networks as the C40 Cities network and the EU Mayors Covenant. National climate change networks among local governments also exist in a number of European countries.

However, even though many local governments have taken action on climate change, it is important to recognise the limitations of these actions. In many cases, plans are not systematically followed up and evaluated, meaning that outcomes have been difficult to measure and are possibly modest (Granberg and Elander 2007). Also, the lack of support or guidance from the national level has left some local governments operating in a void (Hoff and Strobel 2013). This is corroborated by a number of studies, which have tried to tease out the factors that affect local responses to climate change policy. While the amount of support from national government is clearly an explanatory variable, other explanatory variables are the policy, fiscal independence and competencies of local authorities and a given local authority's previous approach to the environment and sustainable development (Collier 1997; Granberg and Elander, 2007). The presence of climate policy champions in key positions within local administrations also seems to be an important explanatory variable (Wilson 2006; Hoff and Strobel, 2013).

This 1992–2009 phase of citizen participation can be seen as a peak period in many respects. Hopes were high for global solutions to global environmental problems such as loss of biodiversity and climate change, and citizens were appealed to as cosmopolitans who were ready to take on global responsibilities through local action. This thinking is reflected in the hitherto unseen institutionalisation of citizen and stakeholder participation at both global and transnational levels. At the global level, this was the case with the passing of the Convention on Agenda 21, and the LA21 statutes. At the EU level, this was the case with the Model Plan for Public Participation passed in 1996, and four directives passed in 1998 mandating public participation in environmental decisions in EU member states.

Apart from these more formal arrangements, the climate change agenda spurred an enormous number of activities at the local level, not only in countries normally known to be in the forefront of environmental activities, but also in countries such as Mexico, South Africa, Brazil and India. These activities were in many cases supported by transnational local government networks, and local networks used to transmit ideas and knowledge on plans and actions (Betsill and Bulkeley, 2007; Bulkeley and Newell, 2010). Many of these activities involved citizens and other stakeholders in new constellations with local government, and a considerable amount of policy innovation was (is) taking place. Some examples of this are described in the next paragraph.

Fourth phase: From global to local – citizens as policy agents, 2009–?

The year 2009 marked yet another watershed in terms of citizen participation in sustainability and climate change mitigation. Even though hopes were initially high for securing a follow-up agreement to the Kyoto Protocol at the 2009 COP15 meeting in Copenhagen after months of pre-negotiations, the final outcome – the Copenhagen Accord – was a weak and non-binding agreement that disappointed most actors. It was drafted by the US, China, India, South Africa and Brazil, some of the main emitters of CO_2, and seems to reflect the national interests of these countries and their internal politics. This expression of *real-politik* effectively diminished the leadership position of the EU, leaving wide open the question of who is now the global environmental hegemon.

For international NGO's (INGOs), national NGOs and other environmental social movements and local climate change initiatives, the fiasco of the Copenhagen summit was a huge blow (see e.g. Connelly *et al.* 2012, 282). However, after the initial disappointment, the lesson these organisations, movements and initiatives seem to have drawn from the event is that we can no longer rely on the actors at the global level to deliver any 'silver bullets' that will redeem us from the effects of climate change. Because 'there is no planet B', as one of the slogans from the public demonstrations at the Copenhagen Summit puts it, local organisations and initiatives have affirmed their belief that working at the local level is the only way forward. Interestingly, but quite logical, this reorientation towards the local is now increasingly supported by actors at the national and international levels. The EU, for example, is now seeking to cultivate greater local level action through its 'A World You Like – with a Climate You Like' campaign[6] that seeks to spread citizen-driven innovations in the area of climate change mitigation. In addition, climate change researchers are now recognising that the local level is an important component of any future solutions to the challenge of climate change. An example of this is Steve Rayner's (2010) idea about 'clumsy solutions', i.e. seeing future commitments to GHG reductions as a patchwork of agreements at different levels.

The fact that many different actors are looking increasingly to the local level for initiatives concerning GHG reductions has placed local authorities in a conspicuous position. As the level of government closest to the citizens, local authorities are increasingly expected by both national governments and citizens to initiate, orchestrate and/or facilitate citizen initiatives concerning GHG reductions. For example, most Danish municipalities have taken on this challenge for political, economic or more altruistic reasons. Relatively ambitious climate change plans have been passed by 72 per cent of all Danish municipalities. Most of these plans set concrete GHG reduction goals that cover at a minimum the municipalities' own activities; a good 75 per cent of these plans also cover the municipality as a geographical unit (Hoff and Strobel 2013). A similar pattern can be seen in the UK, Germany (Bulkeley and Kern 2006) and in the Scandinavian countries.

For municipalities, the task of initiating or facilitating citizen action concerning climate change mitigation involves the development of new policy instruments. As action in this field in many cases affects the everyday lives of citizens, people's everyday activities, homes and workplaces have increasingly become 'sites of public involvement' (Marres 2010, 18). In parallel with solving other persistent public problems in areas such as health (e.g. obesity), people's homes are increasingly seen as suitable sites for 'doing one's share' (see Marres 2011, 511).

This development requires a hitherto unseen degree of sophistication on the part of public authorities in their engagement of citizens, as citizen support is absolutely necessary if such policies are to be successful and legitimate. This requires the deployment of considerable scientific knowledge on the part of public authorities. They are also called upon to use fields such as public relations, marketing, behavioural psychology, anthropology and policy implementation, thus marking a new phase in the way public authorities approach citizen participation. Such a level of sophistication can be seen clearly in the action plans of the UK Department of Environment, Food and Agriculture (DEFRA 2007) and in the supporting work by Tim Jackson that deals with environmental behaviour and motivation (Jackson 2005).

The following are three examples of the new policy instruments used in this phase of citizen participation. All examples are drawn from the CIDEA project (see above), and are examples that are placed differently on the public authority–citizen axis and/or the individual–community axis.

Example #1: The Climate Family Project in the municipality of Ballerup

Ballerup is a typical suburban municipality located just outside Copenhagen with approximately 50,000 inhabitants. Following the disappointment of the COP15 Climate Summit in Copenhagen, the municipality launched a plan to reduce the CO_2 emissions of the municipality as a geographical unit by 25 per cent (compared to 2006 levels) by 2015. Five per cent of this reduction is to be achieved through the efforts of citizens, which means that they need to reduce their CO_2 emissions by 26 per cent by 2015.

To address this challenge, Ballerup initiated a project called 'The Climate Family Project', which began in 2009, ran for three years and involved 20 families. These families were to be role models and a showcase of a more CO_2-sensible way of living that would communicate a message of sustainability and change to the citizens of the municipality (see Chapter 4 in this book).

The families had to engage in two types of activities: the first was a six-month carbon accounting regime; the second was the use of a toolbox of green devices (a shower duck timer and bicycle gear, among others), which the families received from the project. This introduction of green devices is an example of 'nudging' – an approach much hyped in recent years (see Thaler and Sunstein 2009).

The project was very successful: the families involved reduced their CO_2 emissions significantly (20–25 per cent). Two factors seem to have been particularly important for the success of the project. One was the early involvement of the families in the project, and their role as co-developers of the project process. The other was that the project succeeded in turning the families into communicators of the project's success in achieving CO_2 reductions in the families' everyday lives. The families organised events and made appearances at town fairs and the like, often with the Mayor in tow, who wanted to be associated with such active citizens.

In terms of policy instruments, what is interesting in this case is how the material devices of the carbon-accounting form and the toolbox of green devices allowed the authorities to enter deeply into the private homes of individual families, changing identities and creating engagement as the material devices were put to practical use. These changing identities, appearing as new 'green identities', were created through what the families themselves called the 'hard work' of carbon accounting and use of the green devices. The project represents an interesting case for a governmentality-oriented analysis, which we shall briefly touch on below.

Example #2: Energy renovation in Danish municipalities

The second example of the use of advanced policy instruments and the increased use of expertise in sustainability policies are projects addressing energy renovation in private households that have been conducted in several municipalities in Denmark (see Chapter 6 in this book).

Apart from the citizens, the two main actors involved in reducing energy consumption at the household level are energy companies and the municipalities themselves. The Danish government compels energy companies to reduce their customers' energy consumption, which amounts to the companies helping their customers save on conventional energy by either investing in green energy and/or by reducing their energy consumption.

It has been estimated that the greatest potential for reducing energy consumption in private households is to retrofit houses by improving insulation and changing the source of heating in particular. In order to significantly reduce their energy consumption, citizens must be convinced of the wisdom of investing in such retrofits.

The municipality of Middelfart has been at the forefront of setting up such schemes. It introduced the Energy Service Company (ESCO) concept[7] to Denmark, which made it possible for municipalities to energy retrofit municipal buildings without having to use municipal funds. Building on these experiences, the municipality set up a project called *MyClimatePlan* in 2009, which offered a free energy check of homes to any group of a minimum of 10 citizens living in the same neighbourhood. An energy advisor from the local energy company, a representative from the municipality and two builders visited and evaluated each house. The energy advisor then sent an energy report to each household, and the builders sent an offer estimating the costs of the recommendations suggested in the report. In order to convince households to do the work, they were offered a 15 per cent cost reduction by the builders under the condition that the retrofitting be done at the same time as that of the other members of the group.

Whilst the MyClimatePlan appeared to be well planned, it was slow to get going. A major problem was the cost of the energy consultation, which the municipality had to pay. It was replaced by the so-called 'ESCO-light' project in 2011, in which the municipality, in collaboration with the local energy companies, began training builders in energy counselling. After this training, the builders could now deliver the necessary energy counselling to the customers, and if they decided to have the work done, the builder could then help customers sell their energy savings to the energy company. From the customers' perspective, this project provides both free and qualified energy counselling, as well as a subsidy to those who choose to retrofit their house. Indeed, it has been the idea of the project to create a win-win situation for all involved. The builders increase their knowledge about energy renovation, energy companies outsource to builders some of the burdens of generating energy savings in private households and the municipality realises CO_2 reductions and more revenue because more jobs in the building industry are created.

This project, and the similar ZeroHouse project in southern Denmark, has been very successful in generating numerous energy renovations in private households. However, what is also clear is that they depend on an intricate mix of interventions in order to develop a new policy instrument. The instruments involved are: a public–private partnership (municipality–energy company), training courses, subsidies (the possibility for private customers to sell their energy savings), information to citizens about the possibilities and the actual energy counselling. Recently, local banks have also become involved, as they have been prompted by the municipality to develop products to finance private energy renovations.

Example #3: The computer game 'Urgent Evoke'

A third example of a sophisticated policy instrument aimed at both the individual and communities is the computer game Urgent Evoke (UE) (see Chapter 13 in this book). UE is one of several so-called Games for Change or 'Serious Social Games' that are meant to facilitate citizen-driven innovation and action in relation to wicked social problems such as poverty, migration and climate change. The game was developed by the World Bank Institute; it is an online game that is free to play via a computer, tablet or smartphone. The game is open for players of all ages and can be played from anywhere in the world. It is a social network game, meaning that the game concentrates the players' engagement simultaneously on one platform, and is structured to instigate collaboration and co-creation between its players. The last mission the players are asked to complete is to write a detailed and innovative plan of how the player will tackle a self-chosen socio-political challenge in the physical world after the game has ended. The UE calls such plan an 'Evokation'.

In her evaluation of the game, Wichmand (Chapter 13) demonstrates that the '1 per cent rule of thumb' is valid for UE, meaning that only around 1 per cent of the active players ended up submitting an Evokation. However, many more players are involved in creating the output: even non-players contribute in various ways, including 'liking' and 'hearting' the work of the active creators. But, taken together with the efforts made by non-players, these 'micro-contributions' were found to have important effects. Wichmand concludes that even though not every citizen (player) is ready to go all the way and make the effort it takes to become a social innovator, a large number of citizens (players) are interested in socio-political issues and willing to contribute to the development of a greater good if they can do so in a light and easy way. As Wichmand noted, 'The challenge is therefore not to create social innovative game winners, but to design games that facilitate and acknowledge even micro-contributions as a legitimate form of participation and thereby make it possible to cultivate social innovative communities'.

The seriousness of an approach like this is underlined by the fact that Ms. Wichmand's Ph.D. research is co-sponsored by a number of Danish municipalities that are considering using computer games in their approach to wicked problems, among these climate change. For example, computer games have already been used for energy-saving purposes in Sweden; other social media, as well as more traditional websites, are also used for these purposes. An example of this is described in Chapter 12 of this book, where Møllenbach and Hornbæk present *Klimafesten*, which is a digital platform rewarding citizens (groups) behaving in environmentally sustainable ways with the intention of inspiring others to follow. The experiences with the first iteration of the intervention were so positive that a second iteration was run in the fall of 2013.

In summary, this fourth phase, which is ongoing, is characterised by a new surge of citizen engagement and initiatives following the failure to reach significant global agreements on climate change mitigation. This reorientation towards the local constitutes a big challenge for local governments, as national and global actors as well as citizens increasingly expect municipalities to encourage and facilitate such initiatives. In order to be able to produce results that deliver on CO_2 reductions and satisfy the expectations of all stakeholders involved, policy instruments have become increasingly sophisticated. Increasing amounts of expertise have been brought to bear in order to produce the much wanted 'green identities' of citizens.

An overview of the four phases of citizen participation in climate change mitigation/environmental regulation is provided in Table 3.1.

Table 3.1 The four phases of citizen participation in climate change mitigation/ environmental regulation

Period:	1960s–1980s	1980s–1992	1992–2009	2009–
Role of public authorities	Regulator	Innovator	Mediator	Facilitator
Dominant discourse on policy solutions	Social engineering	Common responsibility	Global responsibility	Citizen responsibility
Policy instruments	Laws, permits	Policy network creation, co-production, self-regulation, interactive policy making, environmental taxes, tradeable permits	Global treaties, Local Agenda 21, EU Model Plan for Public Participation, four Directives concerning citizen participation	Ad hoc arrangements to cope with citizen initiatives and projects, 'Nudging' (artefacts and techniques to affect behaviour)
Type of experts used	Engineers Lawyers Biologists	Engineers Lawyers Biologists Social scientists Stakeholders	Engineers Lawyers Biologists Social scientists Stakeholders NGOs 'Citizen experts'	Engineers Lawyers Social scientists Psychologists PR Consultants Stakeholders NGOs 'Citizen experts' Lay people
Role of citizens	Objects of steering/ protesters	Co-producers, stakeholders	'Cosmopolitans' (objects/ participants in global action)	'Future makers' ('do it here and now')

Discussion: How should we understand the reorientation towards the local from a steering perspective and a democratic perspective respectively?

On the basis of the analysis above it could be tempting to frame the development of the four phases of citizen participation in environmental policies/climate change mitigation as a Foucauldian story. The increasingly sophisticated techniques of governance used to convert disengaged or uninformed citizens into 'green bodies' subject to a low-carbon diet can lead to the conclusion that the new policy instruments strengthen the power of public authorities by making more effective policy implementation possible.

However, in our view this is not the whole story. In the story of the creation of new 'green identities', the Ballerup case highlights the point that it was only possible to engage the 20 families in the project because they were involved in the project very early and given a huge say in the development of the project. In other words, citizens eventually assumed a large share of the responsibility for the project. While this can be seen as yet another steering technique, it nonetheless means that (in this case) the municipality also released control of the project. Just as public authorities enter deeply into the private homes of families, so do the families enter into the inner workings of the public authority. We are presented with a precarious balance: public authorities are obliged to 'do more with less control', so to speak, or to release control in order to gain governability.

Bang (2003) has framed this form of steering as 'culture governance', which works by changing perceptions and identities. In a similar vein, others have argued that this development of policy instruments is a part of a bigger trend or even a 'paradigmatic shift' in the field of public policy, reflecting the increased complexity and sheer numbers of social problems that public authorities are now expected to deal with (Kickert et al. 1997; Blaxekjær 2014).[8] The main points in this argument is that this shift warrants an increased involvement of citizens in public policies, both in order to effectively solve problems, but also in order to legitimise policies, and an increased use of science and scientists in the development of policies and policy instruments.

While we accept this analysis, the point we want to make here is that the public 'loss of control' also creates a space for citizen-instigated or citizen-directed initiatives that might work in directions not anticipated by public authorities, and that might challenge their preferred policies in the area.

An example of this is the housing cooperative AB Søpassagen in Copenhagen, which encompasses several apartment buildings with a total of 90 apartments. AB Søpassagen boast of being the first CO_2-neutral housing cooperative in Denmark, a status that has been achieved through the hard work of its board of directors and its occupants. On their own initiative, occupants began to install solar panels on the roof, insulate buildings, phase out clothes dryers, replace all conventional light bulbs, buy CO_2 credits to offset remaining CO_2 emissions and more. In doing this, the association sought the help and advice of the municipality of Copenhagen, which was hard put to find the ways and means to help this citizen-driven initiative. Thus, the municipality developed its own policy in this area, and re-configured methods to subsidise such initiatives.

Looking at the reorientation towards the local from a democratic perspective, we are faced with the same ambiguity as in the case of the steering perspective. On the one hand, it is necessary to realise that there is nothing inherently democratic about citizen participation, even though this is often assumed by practitioners as well as by academics. Citizen participation has in many instances become a tool or policy instrument used in more or less sophisticated ways by public authorities confronted with new or complex problems. The attraction of using citizen participation as a policy instrument is aptly formulated by the pragmatic tradition within citizen participation theory (Reed 2008).

In the pragmatic tradition, one can distinguish between substantive and instrumental arguments for citizen participation. The *substantive argument* focuses on the substance of the policy output. When discussing why citizens should participate, theorists refer to the improved quality, substance and robustness of the policy output. In improving the substance of the output, *knowledge* is seen to play a pivotal role, especially the knowledge of lay actors (Wright and Fritsch 2011, 2269). This local knowledge is thought to contribute insights that are outside or under the radar of experts.

Through these insights, which are based on local conditions, solutions are then developed in collaboration between public and local actors that are better adapted to the particular setting and have a better chance for success. The assumption is that:

> those who are closest to the problem develop the best understanding of it ... [which is why] it seems plausible that environmental decisions can profit from the factual knowledge that local actors have about the environmental issues concerning them.
>
> (Kastens and Newig 2008, 28)

Furthermore, citizen participation is also seen to *reduce the uncertainty* connected with scientific knowledge. Even though the knowledge of lay actors does not in and of itself contribute significantly to the scientific knowledge base, the participation of lay actors often means that more ideas and perspectives are represented in the decision making process. This increases the likelihood of addressing local problems and priorities, because the information of decision makers will be more complete (Reed 2008, 2420). The substantive argument of authors writing in this tradition is that citizens should participate in policy discussions and implementation because this will add more perspectives to the process, improve the knowledge base and reduce uncertainty, which will – all things being equal – lead to better decisions and a better policy output.

The *instrumental arguments* for citizen participation focus on how participation can improve the implementation of a given decision (Wright and Fritsch 2011, 2268). If citizens feel excluded from decisions or implementation, they can obstruct current as well as pending law-making and implementation (participation of stakeholders is also said to have a conflict-reducing effect). Central concepts in this tradition are *accept, confidence* and *ownership*. By effectively engaging stakeholders, it is possible to increase the understanding and acceptance of a given decision. This cannot help but have a positive effect on implementation (Wright and Fritsch 2011, 2269).

Confidence and *learning* are also posited as central arguments for engaging citizens as stakeholders in decision making and implementation processes because such integration is said to transform antagonistic relations between actors. If confidence and learning is increased, a broad coalition behind a given policy can be formed, which can give the policy longevity and lead to better implementation (Reed 2008, 2420). Healey (1997/2006) deals at length with these processes, and suggests that:

> '... a collaborative episode may be able to combine creative innovation with effectiveness ... to achieve a better problem-solving capacity than other policy making modes', and that 'developing the systematic use of collaborative processes to address policy issues helps to make them more legitimate'.
>
> (Healey 1997/2006, 332 and 334)

Finally, when they become involved, citizens can take on ownership, which can only improve implementation (Reed 2008, 2420):

> If goals are developed through dialogue...between participants, they are more likely to take ownership over the process, partnership building will be more likely, and the outcomes are more likely to be more relevant to stakeholder needs and priorities, motivating their ongoing active engagement.

While these are all good arguments for why a public authority entertains the idea of citizen participation, one also has to realise that citizen protest, initiatives and engagement in sustainability issues have led to changes in democratic institutions and/or democratic procedures, which have institutionalised such participation. Cases in point exist in the work of LA21, which has been given a formal role in a number of participatory processes in Denmark, including, among others, complaint boards with representatives from environmental organisations and hearing procedures where citizen groups and (local) NGOs are automatically included.

In addition, bureaucratic cultures have changed in many local governments in Western Europe; bureaucratic thinking about citizen participation in a given issue has become part of the course of doing one's work when planning new initiatives or delivering services to citizens. Thus, a certain democratisation has taken place, even though the form it takes is quite far from the idea of decentralised communities with extensive autonomy and rights of self-government once imagined by Die Grünen in Germany (see above).

Such developments can be interpreted as more in line with the normative tradition within citizen participation theory. This tradition explicitly takes its point of departure from literature and ideas about democracy, in particular those related to participatory democracy (see e.g. Pateman 1970; Barber 1984). Central to this tradition is that the purpose of participation is as much the process itself and its participants as it is the results of the process. The focus of the writers in this tradition is on the *civic potential* of the individual citizen. Pateman (1970), for example, talks about citizen participation as a 'school in democracy'. Other early writers in this tradition stress the empowerment dimension of participation, but still with a focus on the benefits of the individual citizen or group of citizens. An example of this is Arnstein's famous definition of citizen participation, which states that:

> citizen participation is a categorical term for citizen power. It is the redistribution of power that enables the have-not citizens presently excluded from the political and economic processes to be deliberately included in the future.
>
> (Arnstein 1969, 216)

Newer developments within democratic theory, such as the deliberative democracy approach, (Dryzek 2002; Held 2006) emphasise the democratic process itself and its potential for developing the capacities of the individual citizen through deliberation about public matters. Such deliberation is not only seen to improve the democratic capabilities of citizens. It is also seen to improve public decision making because private interests are scrutinised publically, which transforms initial preferences to positions able to stand the test of public debate. In this tradition, participation is also linked to the decisions and the output of the process, even though this is not the main concern of the theory.

These ideas from the normative tradition are echoed by some contemporary academics writing about citizen participation in environmental politics. Priscoli (2004), for example, in an article about management of water, stresses the educating and informing aspects of involving citizens and considers these aspects as prerequisites for a democratic culture. Referring to classic democratic theory, she states that '*those who are affected by a decision should have a say in decisions that affect their lives, because in doing so they become better citizens*' (Priscoli 2004, 224). Others draw on the deliberative democratic tradition, coupling their commitment to citizen participation with considerations about efficiency. This is true for Blackstock *et al.* (2007), who write that participation results in '*increased understanding of complex systems, more durable and equitable solutions and increased capacity for active citizenship*' (Blackstock *et al.* 2007, 727). There is here a simultaneous emphasis on improved capacities for citizens and better policy output.

Whether it is in fact possible to have both – increased efficiency and more democracy – seems, as in the case of steering above, to be very dependent on the context. One can say that at least in the current conjuncture it is impossible to make sweeping generalisations concerning these balances. The best we can do at the moment is to follow the recommendation of Flyvbjerg (2001) and produce exemplary case studies, which can enrich our understanding of these complicated processes as they are played out in relation to climate change policies. Seen in this light, the structure and content of this book seem well-placed.

Finally, it is also worth noting that most of the existing theories, including institutional theory and ecological modernisation theory, which are used to study sustainability and climate change policies, do not seem well-suited to the study of context-specific micro-politics of citizen-driven climate change action. To this end, such theories as actor-network theory or practice theory might be a better match. (This is illustrated in some of the following chapters.)

Conclusion

This chapter has tried to answer two research questions: 1) what is the precise content of the reorientation towards the local after 2009 in terms of citizen participation in climate change mitigation, and 2) how can this reorientation be understood by using a steering perspective and a democratic perspective?

In order to answer the first question, it was necessary to illustrate how citizen participation in environmental/climate policies has moved through four phases since the early 1960s, each of which is characterised by different policy regimes.

An original emphasis on local action and local participatory democracy was institutionalised globally with the adoption of the Agenda 21 Convention at the Rio Earth Summit in 1992. However, both the rhetoric and practice of LA21 gradually died out towards the millennium; after the signing of the Kyoto protocol and the beginning of the COP meetings, most attention from media, academics and practitioners was concentrated on the global level.

The disappointment after the COP 15 meeting in Copenhagen 2009 spurred a renewed focus on the capabilities of locally focused environmental organisations and movements and prompted a challenge for local governments to work harder on the issue of climate change mitigation. This constituted a reorientation towards the local.

The reorientation towards the local has placed local authorities in a conspicuous position: they are increasingly expected by both national governments and citizens to initiate, orchestrate or at least facilitate citizen initiatives concerning GHG reductions. Coping with this task in many cases affects the everyday life of citizens in order to motivate and convince them to reduce their carbon footprint. Policy instruments have been developed, which to a hitherto unseen degree turn people's lives, homes and workplaces into sites of public involvement.

Due to the complexity of this task, policies must be innovative. Examples of such innovative policies are provided in this chapter, the most complex probably being the ESCO-light project intended to motivate home owners to retrofit their homes. The project involves private–public partnerships, including banks who finance energy renovations, training courses, subsidies to private energy customers, information for citizens about the possibilities and actual energy counselling.

While the complexity and fine-tuning of the policy instruments is remarkable and is growing, an increasing amount of scientific expertise is needed in order to develop and orchestrate policies. Whilst environmental policies at the local level were once handled by biologists, engineers and lawyers, local governments now hire or employ social scientists, communication experts, psychologists or 'citizen experts' (Bang and Dyrberg 2003).

In answering the second research question, the most important lesson learned is the ambiguity connected with evaluating the fourth phase of citizen participation in a steering perspective as well as in a democratic perspective. In terms of steering, the increasingly sophisticated techniques used to try to turn disengaged citizens into 'green bodies' can easily be interpreted in a Foucauldian frame. In such a frame power relations are expressed through the self-discipline citizens are exercising when they subject themselves to a life on a low-carbon diet.

However, our case studies tell us that this is not the whole story. In many cases, citizens take the initiative or 'demand' ownership of projects, putting local authorities in a situation where they must release control in order to remain able to govern. Rather than concluding that the new policy instruments have strengthened the power of local authorities vis-à-vis citizens, it is more correct to say that there has been a qualitative shift in the way this relationship is being played out, and that the jury is still out on how these power relations should be interpreted.

In terms of democracy, the situation is much the same. The pragmatic tradition within citizen participation theory lists many good arguments for why citizens should participate in public policies. Citizen participation contributes local knowledge to the policy process, it reduces uncertainty and it delivers *acceptance, confidence* and *local ownership* to the policy process. However, while these are all arguments designed to create a smooth policy process without changing existing democratic procedures too much, we also notice how citizen protests and initiatives have led to changes in democratic institutions and/or democratic procedures, and thus have institutionalised such participation. Seen from the perspective of local authorities, working with citizen participation holds no guarantees of being able to keep the game within well-established democratic boundaries. Unforeseen developments might suddenly challenge these, transforming citizen participation into the 'school in democracy' that Pateman dreamt about (Pateman 1970).

When we consider where the post-2009 policy regime in climate politics on the local level has taken us relative to steering and democracy, we can say that the successful use of the new policy instruments depends on precarious balances between governability and control and between democracy and efficiency. No sweeping generalisations are possible; the best we can do at the moment is to produce exemplary case studies that can enrich our understanding of the complex political challenges posed by the 'super wicked' problem (Lazarus 2008) of climate change.

Notes

1 However, see Connelly *et al.* (2012, 123–125) for an extended discussion of Transition Towns. The Transition Town movement was initiated by permaculture

designer Rob Hopkins in 2004. The movement aims at developing local community resilience against peak oil and climate change through developing ' road maps' to a sustainable future involving issues such as energy production, health, education, economy and agriculture. The first known example of a Transition Town is Totnes in the UK. As of September 2013 there were 1,130 registered Transition Town initiatives in 43 countries.

2   CIDEA is an acronym for 'Citizen Driven Environmental Action', which was a cross-disciplinary and cross-sectoral research project funded by the Danish Council for Strategic Research. It ran for four years (2010–2014), and used an interactive research method to help municipalities carry out concrete, citizen-driven climate change mitigation projects such as low-energy villages, car-free schools and energy renovation clusters (www.cidea.dk).

3   Jänicke and Jörgens (2009, 174) point to the fact that citizen participation presupposes an 'enabling state', and is, in fact, highly demanding on public authorities, because 'using' citizens as an added resource demands a system of incentives and an infrastructure of rights and information for citizens.

4   Along with problems like biodiversity loss, urban sprawl, soil and groundwater contamination and use of hazardous chemicals.

5   Nonetheless, a clause making it compulsory for Danish municipalities to set up an Agenda 21 committee to produce a strategic plan for municipal sustainability was inserted into the Law on Planning in 2000.

6   See http://ec.europa.eu/clima/citizens/aworldyoulike/index_en.htm

7   ESCO means Energy Service Company. The ESCO concept is a financing model in which a company conducting energy renovation in bigger buildings can guarantee a certain level of energy savings. The payment of the renovation is directly financed by the energy savings realised. In this way, municipalities are able to renovate their buildings (offices, schools, old age homes) without having to increase their budgets. After the payback period (typically 2 to 15 years), the municipality reaps the full benefit of the energy savings.

8   This is in line with Fischer et al. (2009, 149), who argue that in order to obtain the necessary reductions in GHG emissions, changes in energy systems as well as in human behaviour are required on a scale that implies 'deep paradigmatic changes'.

References

Akkerman T, Hajer M and Grin J (2000) *Interactive Policy Making as Deliberative Democracy? Learning from New Policy-making Practices in Amsterdam.* Paper presented at the Convention of The American Political Science Association, 31 August –3 September 2000, Washington, DC.

Alexander J C (1995) *Fin de Siécle Social Theory: Relativism, Reductionism, and the Problem of Reason*, Verso, London.

Arnstein S R (1969) A Ladder of Citizen Participation, *Journal of the American Institute of Planners*, July 1969.

Bang H P (ed.) (2003) *Governance as Social and Political Communication*, Manchester University Press, Manchester, UK.

Bang H P and Dyrberg T (2003) Governing at Close Range: Demo-Elites and Lay People, in Bang H P (ed.) 2003 *Governance as Social and Political Communication*, Manchester University Press, Manchester, UK, 222–240.

Barber B (1984) *Strong Democracy, Participatory Politics for a New Age*, University of California Press, Berkeley, CA.

Beck U (1992) *Risk Society*, Sage, London.

Beck U (2003) *Individualization, Institutionalized Individualism and Its Social and Political Consequences*, Sage, London.

Betsill M and Bulkeley H (2007) Looking Back and Thinking Ahead: A Decade of Cities and Climate Change Research, *Local Environment* 12(5) 447–456.

Blackstock K L, Kelly G J and B L Horsey (2007) Developing and Applying a Framework to Evaluate Participatory Research for Sustainability, *Ecological Economics* 60(4) 726–742.

Blaxekjær L (2014) *Global Climate Governance Practices*, Unpublished PhD thesis, Department of Political Science, University of Copenhagen, Denmark.

Bulkeley H and Kern K (2006) Local Government and the Governing of Climate Change in Germany and the UK, *Urban Studies* 43 2237–2259.

Bulkeley H and Newell P (2010) *Governing Climate Change*, Routledge, London.

Collier U (1997) Sustainability, Subsidiarity and Deregulation: New Directions in EU Environmental Policy, *Environmental Politics* 6(2) 1–23.

Connelly J, Smith G, Benson D and Saunders C (2012) *Politics and the Environment: From Theory to Practice* (3rd edn), Routledge, New York.

DEFRA (2007) *A Framework for Pro-environmental Behaviours* [Report], Department for Environment Food and Rural Affairs, UK.

Die Grünen (1983) *Programme of the German Greens*, Heretic Books, London.

Dryzek J S (2002) *Deliberative Democracy and Beyond: Liberals, Critics, Contestations*, Oxford University Press, Oxford, UK.

Dryzek J S (2005) *The Politics of the Earth: Environmental Discourses*, Oxford University Press, Oxford, UK.

Feichtinger J and Pregering M (2005) Imagined Citizens and Participation: Local Agenda 21 in Two Communities in Sweden and Austria, *Local Environment* 10(3) 229–242.

Fisher D R, Fritsch O and Andersen M S (2009) Transformations in Environmental Governance and Participation, in Mol A P J, Sonnenfeld D A and Spaargaren G (eds) *The Ecological Modernisation Reader: Environmental Reform in Theory and Practice*, Routledge, London.

Flyvbjerg B (2001) *Making Social Science Matter: Why Social Inquiry Fails and How It Can Succeed Again*, Cambridge University Press, Cambridge UK.

Giddens A (1992) *Modernity and Self-identity, Self and Society in the Late Modern Age*, Polity, Cambridge, UK.

Granberg M and Elander I (2007) Local Governance and Climate Change: Reflections on the Swedish Experience, *Local Environment* 12(5) 537–548.

Hajer M (1995) *The Politics of Environmental Discourse: Ecological Modernization and the Policy Process*, Oxford University Press, Oxford, UK.

Hajer M (2009) *Authoritative Governance, Policy Making in the Age of Mediatization*, Oxford University Press, Oxford, UK.

Healey P (1997/2006) *Collaborative Planning: Shaping Places in Fragmented Societies*, Palgrave Macmillan, Basingstoke, UK.

Held D (2006) *Models of Democracy*, Stanford University Press, Stanford, CA.

Hoff J (2010) *Local Climate Protection Programmes in Australia and New Zealand: Results, Dilemmas and Relevance for Future Actions*, CIDEA Project Report no 1 Det Samfundsvidenskabelige Fakultets Reprocenter, University of Copenhagen Denmark.

Hoff J and Strobel B W (2013) A Municipal 'Climate Revolution'? The Shaping of Municipal Climate Change Policies, *Journal of Transdisciplinary Environmental Studies* 12(1) 4–16.

Jackson T (2005) *Motivating Sustainable Consumption: A Review of Evidence on Consumer Behaviour and Behavioural Change*, A report to the Sustainable Development Research Network Centre for Environmental Strategy University of Surrey, UK.

Jänicke M and Jörgens H (2009) New Approaches to Environmental Governance, in Mol A P J, Sonnenfeld D A and Spaargaren G (eds) *The Ecological Modernisation Reader: Environmental Reform in Theory and Practice*, Routledge, London, 156–189.

Kastens B and Newig J (2008) Will Participation Foster the Successful Implementation of the Water Framework Directive? The Case of Agricultural Groundwater Protection in Northwest Germany, *Local Environment* 13(1) 27–41.

Kern K, Koll C and Schophaus M (2007) The diffusion of Local Agenda 21 in Germany: Comparing the German Federal States, *Environmental Politics* 16(4) 604–624.

Kickert W J M, Klijn E-H and Koppenjan J F M (eds) (1997) *Managing Complex Networks: Strategies for the Public Sector*, Sage, London.

Lauwers J (1983) Het groene ongenoegen, *Tijdschrift voor Sociologie* 4 431–449.

Lazarus R J (2008) Super Wicked Problems and Climate Change: Restraining the Present to Liberate the Future, *Cornell Law Review* 27(3) 220–230.

Marres N (2010) Frontstaging Nonhumans: Publicity as a Constraint on the Political Activity of Things, in *Political Matter Technoscience, Democracy, and Public Life*, Minnesota University Press, Minneapolis, 177–210. Goldsmiths Research Online (http://eprints.gold.ac.uk/6229/1/Marres_frontstaging_nonhumans.pdf) Accessed 20 August 2012.

Marres N (2011) The Costs of Public Involvement: Everyday Devices of Carbon Accounting and the Materialization of Participation, *Economy and Society*, 40(4) 510–533.

Mol A P J, Sonnenfeld D A and Spaargaren G (eds) (2009) *The Ecological Modernisation Reader: Environmental Reform in Theory and Practice*, Routledge, London.

Ostrom E (1990) *Governing the Commons: The Evolution of Institutions for Collective Action*, Cambridge University Press, Cambridge, UK.

Ostrom E (1991) Rational Choice Theory and Institutional Analysis: Towards Complementarity, *American Political Science Review* 85 237–243.

Pateman C (1970) *Participation and Democratic Theory*, Cambridge University Press, Cambridge, UK.

Pierre J (ed.) (2000) *Debating Governance: Authority, Steering and Democracy*, Oxford University Press, Oxford, UK.

Priscoli J D (2004) What is Public Participation in Water Resources Management and Why Is It Important? *Water International* 29(2) 221–227.

Rayner S (2010) How to Eat an Elephant: A Bottom-Up Approach to Climate Policy, *Climate Policy*, 10 615–621.

Reed M S (2008) Stakeholder Participation for Environmental Management: A Literature Review, *Biological Conservation* 141(10) 2417–2431.

Sale K (1985) *Dwellers in the Land*, Sierra Club Books, San Francisco, CA.

Scharpf F W (ed.) (1993) *Games in Hierarchies and Networks: Analytical and Empirical Approaches to the Study of Governance Institutions*, Campus Verlag, Frankfurt am Main.

Scholte I (2005) *Globalization: A Critical Introduction*, Palgrave Macmillan, Basingstoke, UK.

Stoker G and Young S (1993) *Cities in the 1990s*, Longman, Harlow, UK.

Tatenhove J P M and Leroy P (2009) Environment and Participation in a Context of Political Modernisation, in Mol A P J, Sonnenfeld D A and Spaargaren G (eds) *The Ecological Modernisation Reader: Environmental Reform in Theory and Practice*, Routledge, London.

Thaler R H and Sunstein C R (2009) *Nudge, Improving Decisions About Health, Wealth and Happiness*, Penguin, London.

Ward H (1996) Green Arguments for Local Democracy, in King D and Stoker G (eds) *Rethinking Local Democracy*, Macmillan, London, 130–157.

Wilson E (2006) Adapting to Climate Change at the Local Level: The Spatial Planning Response, *Local Environment* 11(6) 609–625.

Wright S A I and Fritsch O (2011) Operationalising Active Involvement in the EU Water Frame Directive: Why, When and How? *Ecological Economics* 70 2268–2274.

4 On the materialisation of participation in a municipality near you

Irina Papazu

Introduction

With reference to Jens Hoff's Chapter 3 in this book, we currently find ourselves in a new phase of citizen participation in the area of climate change. This phase is characterised by a hitherto unknown higher degree of involvement in citizens' everyday lives, homes and workplaces, which are increasingly perceived as 'sites of public involvement' (Marres 2010a). This development requires a great deal of sophistication on the part of public authorities in their efforts to engage citizens in solving major societal problems. This chapter picks up where Hoff's chapter left off, and details how this intensification of citizen participation may be achieved and how we might make sense of the development theoretically by exploring which theories might aid us in the analysis of this new phase of citizen participation in climate change mitigation.

Following the capsized 2009 United Nations (UN) Conference of Parties 15 (COP 15) climate summit in Copenhagen, the municipality of Ballerup, which has 50,000 residents and is situated just outside Copenhagen, launched a plan to reduce the carbon dioxide (CO_2) emissions of the municipality as a geographical unit by 25 per cent by 2015 as compared to 2006 levels. Five per cent of this reduction was to be achieved through the efforts of the citizens of the municipality, which means that they had to reduce their CO_2 emissions by 26 per cent by 2015.

In order to address this challenge, the municipality of Ballerup initiated a project called 'The Climate Family Project', which ran for three years and, according to the 20 participating families, 'made a huge difference' (Papazu, 2012, 72). The families were to constitute a 'miniature Ballerup' and be a showcase of a more CO_2-sensible way of living that communicated a message of sustainability and change to other citizens of the municipality. Notable reductions in CO_2 were achieved in this project; it is generally understood to be a success. How do we understand such a municipality-initiated and -facilitated process of change that is situated deep within the realm of the privacy of the participating citizens' everyday lives?

Our analysis does not take as its starting point abstract ecological discourses 'out there' in society, nor does it take as its vantage point the different levels (be they local, national, global, regional or individual) on which change is (or is not) taking place. By taking a particular, local, singular climate project as the vantage point of analysis, a bigger picture of climate change mitigation begins to come into view. Furthermore, we need a theory that does not stop at the front door of the citizen's home, but penetrates that conceptual barrier, just as it dissolves the traditional level-thinking of theoretical perspectives such as ecological modernisation theory and governance theory, which social science researchers of climate change initiatives so often resort to.

Climate change in and of itself is a level-defying and -dissolving challenge; a hybrid of politics, culture, science and nature, and at the same time arguably a social reality of our daily lives (Latour 1993, 19–20; Blok 2010, 898). This chapter argues that we need a theory that reflects this complexity, i.e. a theoretical and methodological framework equipped to take the complexity of the climate change problematic into account. Ballerup's Climate Family Project poses questions about citizen participation and the achievement and creation of individual and public engagement with the climate. This chapter illustrates that consideration of the body of work collectively referred to as Science and Technology Studies (STS)[1] enlightens the analysis of the project and increases our understanding of the complicated processes at work when citizens are involved in climate mitigation projects.

More specifically, analytical sensitivities and concepts derived from actor-network theory (ANT) and post-ANT are also applied to the analysis of The Climate Family Project, while at the same time attending to the broader research question: *What value might STS perspectives add to analyses of citizen participation in the policy area of climate change?*[2] Furthermore, readers interested in how to work on the practical level with citizen engagement in local environmental initiatives will hopefully gain something from reading about the lessons learned in the case of the Ballerup climate families.[3]

The chapter focuses on this broader question, and uses empirical and analytical insights from the Ballerup project as illustration. The analysis of the project was conducted for my master's thesis. Its data consist of qualitative in-depth interviews with the families who participated in the project, expert interviews with the municipal project manager, who was my point of entry into the field and the head of the environmental and technical administration and a focus group interview with the climate project families and the project manager, who was my point of entry into the field.

The analysis of The Climate Family Project falls into two parts that illustrate the two fronts on which the citizens are involved in the climate agenda through their participation in the project. One part consists of meetings between the families and the project manager that were orchestrated primarily by the project manager. In the project's second part, the work of *involvement* involves a range of 'green' technologies: the families are presented with a 'climate toolbox' designed to make their transition to less CO_2-intensive lives easier. By following the families' use of this toolbox, we are brought into the homes and everyday lives of the climate families. The main focus of this chapter is on the roles of these green artefacts and the carbon accounting that the climate families went through.

The chapter proceeds as follows: first, an overview of STS approaches to the study of public participation is provided. The Ballerup Climate Family Project is then analysed with a view to how the participating citizens are simultaneously engaged in the project and in the issue of climate change. The chapter's conclusion highlights how STS approaches may enlighten our understanding of public participation in climate change mitigation management.

An STS-informed perspective on citizen participation

In this section, we suggest a way for researchers to engage with the issue of public involvement in climate change as seen through the lens of STS. This is not to claim that the STS literature contains an actual 'theory' of citizen participation. In STS, theories and explanations arise through concrete empirical analyses; they are not laid out *ahead of* the empirical work (Law 2004, 8). Each explanation and new concept in STS is considered to be to a large degree context-dependent and cannot be expected to apply to supposedly similar situations (Gad and Bruun Jensen 2010, 76).

Still, we believe that STS adds valuable insights and has the potential to strengthen our understanding and grasp of this proposed 'new era' of citizen participation in the environmental area (cf. Hoff). The account here is by no means exhaustive; as Mol puts it: 'The art is not to build a theoretical stronghold, but to adapt the theoretical repertoire to every new case' (Mol 2010, 256). Our hope is simply to point the way and add some new tools to the analytical toolbox for researchers interested in analysing the new conditions for citizen involvement brought on by the challenge of climate change.

We begin on a high note by briefly discussing the *why* of citizen involvement in climate change management. We then move on to the more practical *how*, pointing out analytical avenues and tools for the researcher to follow and employ when analysing questions relating to citizen involvement in climate change policies and projects.

Taking the idea of embodied knowledge as her starting point, Isabelle Stengers puts the point succinctly in her contribution to the anthology *Making Things Public*, edited by Bruno Latour:

> ... there is no knowledge that is both relevant and detached. It is not an objective definition of a virus or a flood that we need, a detached definition everybody should accept, but the active participation of all those whose practice is engaged in multiple modes with the virus or with the river.
>
> (Stengers 2005, 1002)

It follows from this that those who are ontologically implicated in an issue (Marres 2005, 2007) must participate not only in its solution but also in the definition of the problem. The goal of policy making is not to obtain a level of objectivity, but rather to address the issue concretely, publicly and, most importantly, in a way that is consistent with the perceptions of the problem and the needs of those implicated.[4] This calls for a high degree of citizen involvement at all levels of the policy process, not least in the problem definition and policy development phases.

According to Noortje Marres, one of the leading scholars in the area of STS, such a degree of public involvement 'cannot be adequately handled within existing frameworks of knowledge production and policy making' (Marres 2005, 7). She characterises the climate as belonging to a type of challenge that calls for new types of policy processes and solutions:

> Simple, 'manageable' problems can be expected to be taken care of by existing institutions, and by the social groupings that encounter them. For 'foreign entanglements' [such as the climate], this is not the case. They require something else if they are to be taken care of: a public.
>
> (Marres 2005, 7)

Thus, an experimental approach to public involvement in issues is needed (Marres 2011, 526), an approach that pays special attention to involving citizens at all levels of the policy process.

Such an experimental approach demands new thinking and openness on the part of policy makers as well as researchers. A theory is needed that can handle these new developments *and* move into the private sphere of citizens because what goes on within the home becomes of political relevance. The home, where life is lived, is where citizens get involved and engaged through their experience of being concretely involved in different issues (Marres 2011). In the face of climate change, the dividing lines between the private, the public and the political are torn down – perfectly in line with the field of STS's general distaste for pre-established distinctions. Because we are not able to discuss both citizen involvement in more formalised political processes and citizen involvement in concrete policies and projects in this chapter, we focus on the latter. This is in keeping with Marres's analytical focus, as we shall see later.

The site and scope of politics has traditionally been conceived of as 'a quite restricted space – limited to ideas, decisions and exchange – whereas mundane and material realities were left outside' (Asdal *et al.* 2008, 5). In other words, the traditional dividing line between the political and the non-political cannot be upheld when the focus of policy making (and research) moves to the home and the mundane, down-to-earth everyday practices of the citizen (Marres 2011), and turns the previously private home into a 'site of politics' (Asdal *et al.* 2008, 5).

It is in everyday life, and in the changes to its daily rhythms and routines, that the citizen experiences her implication in and involvement with climate change and the environmental agenda. This implication often becomes concrete and embodied through the introduction of new material devices into the home and everyday life, a point to which we return shortly. An STS-inspired understanding of public involvement in climate change management may thus be deemed a *down-to-earth approach* (Asdal 2008), as public engagement is 'located in everyday practices such as cooking and heating' (Marres 2011, 510).

In this literature, democracy is neither processual nor abstract; considerations of democracy and public involvement do not hinge on what democracy *is* or ought to be. What is important is how democracy is carried out in practice, that is, how, where, with what and by whom it is *done* or *performed* (see e.g. Mol 1999).[5] People become involved in politics because of the *content* of the issue at stake, not because they strive to be 'good, democratic citizens' (Marres 2005, 14). With reference to Foucault, who can be said to share with STS a concern with the citizen[6] (Asdal *et al.* 2008, 6), it can be said that 'government is to be understood as a point of contact where techniques of the self [the citizen] interact with techniques of domination or power [the authorities]' (Asdal 2008, 23).

Towards a material theory of public participation in climate change mitigation

Moving from the *why* to the *how to* of our examination of STS's contribution to the field of citizen involvement in climate change mitigation, we move closer to the not-so-private sphere of the citizens (Marres 2010a), because people tend to get engaged in issues that are not 'radically distinct from the things that people have to deal with as part of daily life' (Marres 2005, 14). When analysing public participation in climate change mitigation efforts, Marres turns her attention to those instruments of the everyday that, if successful, can be said to materialise participation and engagement with the climate issue (Marres 2011, 510). These instruments range from 'the environmental teapot' (a teapot that tells you how much water to use and when to boil it) (Marres 2012), carbon accounting devices (Marres 2011), green internet blogs (Marres 2009, 2010b) and 'eco-homes' (Marres 2008) to 'bins, bulbs, and shower timers' (Hobson 2006). The focus of these analyses is what these green devices do (or don't do) with regard to strengthening engagement with and participation in the climate issue.

STS draws attention to 'the sub-political quality' of things (Lezaun and Marres 2011, 495) and how publics are constituted by not only people, but also things. These things are mundane, everyday and often low-tech artefacts that possess the ability to generate new forms of citizenship (Lezaun and Marres 2011, 492) and thus function as 'tools of democracy' (Asdal 2008, 22) in that they enable processes of public participation in salient issues.[7]

So how do these mundane artefacts work? While each green technology has its own distinct workings, one way of approaching this analysis is to ask whether and how a green device such as an environmental teapot 'enables the de-composition and re-composition of everyday action' (Marres 2011, 516). Does the device challenge the way we live by forcing us to act consciously with regard to concrete everyday practices? By changing these practices, be it our practices of heating our homes, making tea or getting around in traffic, does the device strengthen our sense of engaging, practically and concretely, with the climate? Or do the devices do all the work for us, thus enacting what Dona Haraway called 'the change of no change' (Marres 2011, 517) by 'facilitating a mode of participation that requires only a minimum of effort' (Marres 2011, 517)?

An example of minimal engagement is energy-saving light bulbs which, after having been installed, do not draw attention to themselves until they need changing. On the other hand, installing a geothermal heating system in the front garden of a small house or rigorously accounting for every aspect of one's home's energy use are examples (both from Papazu 2012) of a different logic. This more intense engagement in energy-saving measures brings carbon into an individual's life through three avenues, following Marres: 1) the effort involved, 2) the monetary costs incurred (and possibly saved) and 3) the disruptive modifications of habitats and habits (Marres 2011, 526). In this way, hitherto separate spheres of the home, everyday life and the environment are brought together or *co-articulated*: innovation, technology, the future of the planet, personal finances, even social life. In this process, participation is co-articulated as *work* (Marres 2011, 528). Simply doing the work reminds people that if they willingly make an effort for the climate, they are involved in the issue; it also underscores that their involvement with climate to this degree is not easy – it is challenging and can be disruptive.

If such green devices are supplied by the local authorities, or if new practices, e.g. carbon accounting, are initiated by political initiatives or projects, acknowledging the often disruptive consequences to citizens' everyday lives and identities of such measures raises questions of power. Such measures are what Rose, developing Michel Foucault's governmentality framework, refers to as 'technologies of government' (Rose 1999). The implication is that by supplying families with shower timers, for example, the authorities are, by extension, virtually moving into the bathroom with the showering citizens, and promoting a certain politically desired citizen identity.

At the same time, as constantly stressed by actor-network theory (ANT) from within the STS literature, neither humans nor non-humans have inherent qualities. Rather, the character of the individual actor is determined by relationships with other actors with which he/she/it engages (see e.g. Latour 2005). It follows that there is no determinism to this thinking and each actor – citizen or green home device – may function or react in unpredictable ways to the situation staged by the authorities. It is this multiplicity of practices that may arise from just one climate project that gives citizen participation in the environmental area its experimental character and which makes it difficult to say anything general about the field. For every new case there is a new story and a new explanation.

In the following section, we revisit these considerations in more detail, employing empirical insights from the Climate Family Project to enhance our understanding of what an STS-informed approach to public participation in climate change might look like in practice.

The Climate Family Project

The Climate Family Project challenges the researcher in at least two important areas, and poses the following questions that are investigated in the remainder of this chapter:

1   How is the mobilisation of hitherto unengaged citizens in the notoriously unrelatable issue of climate change achieved (see e.g. Jasanoff 2010)?
2   How do the authorities manage to enter the private sphere of the participating citizens where the reductions in CO_2 are to take place, and how are new citizen identities shaped in the process?

Mobilisation

With the help of STS, we can approach the first question – achieving mobilisation – by stressing how climate change and its entities, most notably CO_2, need not be global phenomena. Rather, the globalisation of a given phenomenon is a condition achieved through the hard work and concerted actions of numerous human and non-human actors (such as satellite pictures and scientific models) involved in networks relating to the phenomenon (Blok 2010, 902). It is in this way that the globality of a phenomenon such as climate change can be achieved, and it can be made *local* in much the same way. The Climate Family Project managed to do just this: it brought climate change down-to-earth for participating citizens (20 families) by teaching them that their everyday actions relate to considerations of CO_2. It also situated their engagement with the climate in two concrete venues: the municipality, where they held project meetings, and in homes, where they worked to reduce their CO_2 emissions.

Most of the families who signed up for the project were not looking for a way to become engaged in the issue of climate change. They were looking for a way to become engaged with their municipality: 'We wanted to give something back to the municipality'; 'We wanted to show our support for a municipal project' (Papazu 2012, 51). Climate change offered the families an opportunity to interact more closely with their municipality, something which was especially important to the families who lived on the outskirts of Ballerup and felt detached from life in the community. In this way, climate change and the municipality became intimately interconnected. Since most of the families did not have climate change in their lives prior to entering the project, the issue was like modelling clay in the hands of the municipality, and the families were like blank slates upon which the manager of the project could impose her and Ballerup Municipality's idea of climate change. The fundamental belief that underscored the municipality's climate action plan and its CO_2-reduction goal was that a reduction of 26 per cent could be achieved over a span of six years through 'changed habits and behaviour' in citizens' daily lives (*www.ballerup.dk*).

Two further aspects of the project design were central to the mobilisation of the families around the issue of climate change. First, the families were involved in the project at a very early stage and were invited to co-develop the project in the spirit of direct citizen participation. For example, the municipality sought citizen engagement in deciding which activities were to be part of the project and which areas of energy consumption were to be targeted. This was a risky move by the project manager, who early in the process had to deal with frustrated families who could not understand why all they did at project meetings was sit around and talk. The families wanted to act, and instead they experienced a 'chaotic' (Papazu 2012, 52) municipal process that fuelled the prejudices of the families (most of whom worked in the private sector) about the workings of the public sector. However, the project manager's tactic – involving the families in the design of the process – proved to be a bold one. Instead of giving up on the project, the families eventually tired of talking and began to establish some ground rules for the process. In this way, they assumed responsibility – the process not only ended up successfully linking them to the project, it strengthened their sense of engagement in the climate issue.

Second, the project succeeded in mobilising the participants around the issue of climate change by turning the families into communicators of the message of the project's success at achieving CO_2 reductions in the realm of the everyday (a theme to which I return shortly). The families organised events and made appearances at town fairs and the like, often with the town mayor in tow, who wanted to be associated with these active citizens and the solution-focused, constructive approach to the issue of climate change mitigation. By championing and making visible their recently acquired CO_2-conscious lifestyles, the families – dressed in rainwear and bike helmets sporting the project's logo – became standard-bearers of a green identity, the specific Ballerup-brand of 'being green', thus strengthening their attachment to the project.

The municipality never managed to build the website or 'climate portal' that had been intended to communicate the families' successes to the rest of Ballerup's citizens; at least one family was dissatisfied and disappointed with the municipality's failure to communicate the families' experiences to a wider circle of citizens (Papazu 2012, 80). However, these details do not change the fact that the mobilisation of hitherto disengaged citizens around the issue of climate change was extremely successful.

Greening citizen identities

Two essential parts of the project were not up for debate: the carbon accounting regime the families engaged in for six tough months and the toolbox of green devices which each family received from the project in order to get a head start with their new, sustainable practices. This project focus on actions and devices cannot be ascribed to an innovative local administration: the project manager was just as concerned with 'attitudes', 'habits' and 'behaviour change' as any public official (Shove 2010).[8] The device-centred approach was simply cheaper and easier to manage than planning workshops, sponsoring lectures and paying experts for their time.

The carbon accounting regime was a crucial tool to secure the families' continued support of the project, since, as one participant remarked 'To me it's not a result that I show up at the meetings' (Papazu, 2012, 55). This was also a critical aspect of the project from the municipality's perspective. The project required calculations about family energy use, including conversion of kilowatt hours, kilometres and the number of toilet flushes into CO_2-equivalents. These calculations, called 'registrations', would tell the municipality how much CO_2 had been reduced by the families over the project period. This was the main message of the project, the message that the families would later try to communicate to other citizens of Ballerup.

Registering the energy consumption of the families' homes and lives, thus engaging them in the 'hard work' (Papazu, 2012, 80) of accounting for every energy-related daily activity, brought with it a 'materialisation' and concretisation of the families' engagement with the climate. It made their project participation, along with the climate itself, tangible and physical to them. For the first time, the consequences of climate change became part of the families' reflections on their everyday practices. The accounting regime turned them into 'climate families': they began to feel that they were finally 'making the *difference*' they had dreamt of when they joined the project.

Each day the families had to fill out an extremely complicated schedule, which at first only existed in physical form, hung up as wallpaper in their small detached houses. These schedules, shining bright with distinct colours, detailed the different areas subjected to the regime: transportation (kilometres covered by which vehicles of transportation), water consumption (how many large and small toilet flushes, the length of showers, how long the water tap ran in the kitchen or bathroom) and other consumption (how many light bulbs of how many watts were turned on for how many hours and what food had been eaten or thrown out).

Later on, one of the men in the project turned the paper-based schedule into an Excel spreadsheet. He found the registrations 'annoying and boring' (Papazu 2012, 57), but was eager to show his engagement in the project and keep his place in the network. As annoying as he found the task, he took it on voluntarily and made sure his connection to this crucial part of the project was secured. He also strengthened his attachment to the CO_2 calculations, the pivotal point of the registration period. By contrast, his wife enjoyed the challenge of registering every aspect of everyday life: it was a concrete piece of work that had to be done, and with the help of the devices of the toolbox and the heightened awareness that came with the project, results were achieved. Whilst the families were clearly challenged by this new practice of accounting, they found that it was *doable* (Papazu 2012, 57).

According to some views of public engagement (see Marres 2011), involvement has to be made easy in order to succeed and not scare off the citizens, i.e. shaping engagement along the lines of doability. In this view, authorities cannot demand more than a minimal investment of effort (Papazu, 2012, 510).[9] This project, however, never claimed that going green is easy. Instead, the aspects of the project that were perceived as hard work was emphasised by the families when I talked to them – there was an element of pride expressed in the families' storytelling. They had made it! They made it through the tough registrations and, as in a rite of passage, emerged as new, green citizens. What we witness in the case of the climate families is, in Marres's words, 'the co-articulation of participation as work' (Marres 2011, 528).

When commenting to me about the green devices of the toolbox that were supposed to kickstart the families' new, green practices, the man of one family enjoyed telling the story of their 'shower duck':

> One of the things from the toolbox that we had a lot of fun with in my family was the shower duck, which by the way is still hanging on the wall in the bathroom. In principle it was a small timer, an egg timer in the shape of a shower duck that you could attach to the bathroom mirror. You could then time the length of your shower. And in my family we had a lot of fun with that, we tried to reduce our shower times. We started out with ten minutes, then we tried five, and in the end we got down to three, that's where we met our tolerance level, especially the female members of the household. But it was a fun instrument because it wasn't placed where you could reach it from the shower, so when it started beeping, you had to get out and turn it off.
>
> (Papazu 2012, 68)

In effect, the shower duck reminded the family members of the time and water consumption connected to showering, thereby problematising the practice of showering and making it a part of their growing and evolving climate engagement and new green identities. The duck brought the family members together in fun and challenging competitions over the length of showers because of its material design – the beeping, its ironic duck-like appearance and the fact that it can only stick to the surface of a mirror, so it needed to be placed some distance from the shower cubicle. This simple device allowed the families to engage with the climate while showering and thus effectively reconfiguring this daily routine. This, again, is not engagement made easy, but it is engagement made visible and tangible through work *and* play.

Another example from the toolbox that is efficient but not necessarily fun are electricity-saving devices such as LED light bulbs, which to the families were 'all right and everything, but boring' (Papazu 2012, 69). While these devices do represent the environmental costs of everyday life, they offer the opportunity to mitigate these costs without forcing the user to change her actions.

In summary, Ballerup's Climate Family Project, a network consisting of the participating families, the project manager and an array of carbon-reducing devices was successfully designed and conducted with the concerted efforts of all actors involved.

Conclusion

This local Danish climate project managed to reach its official goal of reducing the participants' CO_2 emissions significantly while also successfully installing in these participants a hard-won new sense of engagement with the climate. The overriding reason for analysing this project here is to illustrate the usefulness of STS approaches to the study of citizen participation in climate change management. Without the STS-inspired sensitivity to the power of materialisation and the significance of *grounding*, *localising* and *(re)constructing* climate change and CO_2 as entities to be taken into account in everyday practices, the project's success may not have been assured.

Climate change is a challenge to be handled where people *are*, in all those local places where CO_2 is being emitted. It is a policy challenge that demands the participation and engagement of lay citizens. In order for citizens to become engaged, the climate needs to be placed firmly within the setting of our lives. And we need the down-to-earth devices of everyday life to help us achieve this movement, this scaling downward of the climate from 'up there' to 'down here'. For these reasons, perspectives from the STS literature are suited to addressing this academic challenge.

At the same time, more practical lessons may be derived from the analysis of the project to light the way for future projects to come. The single most important lesson is the potential for delegating responsibility to and sharing the workload with green devices in all shapes and forms. This delegation of responsibility from authorities to material devices allows local authorities to enter deeply into the private homes of individual families, thereby changing identities and creating engagement as they are put to practical use in the household. The work that these public devices carry out in private homes are an interesting subject for a more governmentality-oriented analysis than the one presented here, because issues of power and control are invariably evoked in the process of engaging citizens through everyday devices provided by the authorities.

It is the accomplishment of engaging the families *where they are* that is somewhat puzzling about the case of The Ballerup Climate Families. These families were not *ontologically implicated* in the issue of climate change prior to joining the project. Consequently, and contrary to Stengers' point earlier in this chapter, they had not felt the consequences of climate changes on their own bodies – they had experienced no floods, no droughts, no life-changing events. In fact, they were not particularly interested in climate change and did not even follow the news media's coverage of the issue prior to joining the project. For a host of other, non-climate-related reasons, they decided to sign up for the project, they started to engage with it and through that with the climate. They started to *work*, and climate engagement began to evolve and grow.

Surprisingly, the most climate-clueless families to join the project were the families who ended up the most engaged in the project. Perhaps they were blank slates: they entered the project without a clue about the climate and allowed the project to construct their new, climate-conscious identities. And they were enthusiastic! They were the families who cherished the hard work of the accounting regime the most, just as they were the ones who lamented the project's end the most. But once the project ended, they did not have the figurative and non-figurative tools to continue exploring their relation to the climate on their own. So they developed new hobbies; one of the families even bought a puppy. Thus, whilst their engagement was great, the character of their engagement was fleeting. This, needless to say, is a great weakness of these types of projects. When the project network dissolved, the families' engagement also dissolved because there was nothing concrete to keep their attention captured any longer.

However transient, the climate families' engagement still challenges the view that to be engaged in an issue one must be concretely and personally implicated. Analysis suggests that engagement may occur through other avenues and for other reasons; the issue need not be of intrinsic importance prior to engagement in it. The very act of engaging with an issue in concrete ways in everyday life will create a sense of implication in the issue; once one stops enacting this implication, engagement will also slowly dissipate. This finding brings to mind Latour's point:

> There exists no society to begin with, no reservoir of ties, no big reassuring pot of glue to keep all those groups together. If you don't have the festival now or print the newspaper today, you simply lose the grouping, which is not a building in need of restoration but a movement in need of continuation.
>
> (Latour 2005, 37)

Finally, we see another lesson for policy makers and climate employees in the analysis of the Ballerup climate project. The delight the families took in the daily work of registering their energy consumption points to the fact that participation need not be contingent upon *doability*, i.e. participation need not be easy or painless for people to get involved. There may even be a point in the difficulties that the families encountered when working on changing their practices and reducing their CO_2 emissions. When you attempt to take the climate into account in all your doings, you will encounter 'the material, social, technical and economic relations of interdependence that constitute everyday life' (Marres 2011, 528). This renewed understanding of the complexity of daily life and the relationship between our lives and the climate challenge may provide us with a whole new idea of what the dual challenges of participation and climate change are all about.

Notes

1   Whether the field of STS may be termed a 'theory' is not the topic of this paper. Let me just refer to Michael Lynch's evasion of the same issue: 'STS "theory" (if I can be permitted to say there is such a thing)... .' (Lynch, 2008, 2).

2   This is not to claim that the application of an STS-inspired framework to current climate-related problems is the only way to go within the social sciences. Rather, the reader may understand the employment of theories from the STS repertoire as *one* direction (chosen in this chapter) out of a larger theoretical trend that takes the focus off the individual and places it on material artefacts, social practices and the like, thus contextualising the challenges we face.

3   Since it is outside of the scope of this chapter to provide an introduction to the central concepts of ANT and post-ANT, the analysis is written in such a way as to be accessible to a reader who is not familiar with the STS literature. Theoretically, it is the understanding of citizen participation within the field of STS studies that is the focus of the present chapter.

4   One might argue that citizens in the West have not yet been implicated in 'floods' or 'viruses' when it comes to climate change, and that for this line of thinking to apply we need to witness more direct consequences in our lives. This question cannot be answered definitively here, but we can point to such incidents as the cloudburst that hit Zealand and the Copenhagen area of Denmark on 2 July 2011, and the flooding that forced people out of their homes in the Czech Republic's capital of Prague in 2013.

5   This point is reflected in Bruun Jensen's (2004) claim that the constructivism of STS shifts focus from a representative to a performative approach.

6   Some readers, especially those who equate STS with actor-network theory (ANT), may find this concern with the citizen surprising, since ANT enjoys provoking its readers by levelling human 'actants' with non-human actants. Suffice it to say that when STS perspectives are merged with those of American pragmatism (especially Dewey) (cf. Marres) and Foucault (cf. Asdal), the human actor regains some of the territory it may have lost to ANT.

7   Contrary to Hoff's argument in the previous chapter that processes of citizen involvement need not be related to democracy, in STS it is typically understood that the involvement of citizens has implications for democracy, as such practical involvement *enacts* democracy or brings democracy to life. It is not within the scope of this chapter to go further into this debate.

8   As contextual theories, STS, along with social practice theory as represented by Elisabeth Shove (2010), stand in opposition to behaviouralist theories, which see the individual as a rational agent and view behaviour as something external to the individual, i.e. something that can be freely *chosen*. Authorities have traditionally taken a behaviouralist approach to behaviour change, which frequently involves information campaigns and the like.

9   Rutland and Aylett address this tendency when they state that 'the translation of interests, while it allows diverse goals to be furthered to some extent, always involves a kind of betrayal of the enrolled actants' (Rutland and Aylett 2008, 635).

References

Asdal K (2008) On Politics and the Little Tools of Democracy: A Down-to Earth Approach [in Moser I and Asdal K (eds) Special Issue on The Technologies of Politics], *Distinktion, Scandinavian Journal of Social Theory* 16 11–26.

Asdal K, Borch C and Moser I (2008) Editorial: The Technologies of Politics [in Moser I and Asdal K (eds) Special Issue on The Technologies of Politics], *Distinktion, Scandinavian Journal of Social Theory* 16 5–10.

Blok A (2010) Topologies of Climate Change: Actor-Network Theory, Relational-Scalar Analytics, and Carbon-Market Overflows, *Environment and Planning D Society and Space* 28 896–912.

Bruun Jensen C (2004) A Nonhumanist Disposition: On Performativity, Practical Ontology, and Intervention, *Configurations* 12(2) 229–61.

Gad C and Bruun Jensen C (2010) On the Consequences of Post-ANT, *Science, Technology & Human Values* 35(1) 55–80.

Hobson K (2006) Bins, Bulbs, and Shower Timers: On the 'Techno-Ethics' of Sustainable Living, *Ethics, Place and Environment* 9(3) 317–336.

Jasanoff S (2010) A New Climate for Society, *Theory, Culture & Society* 27 233–254.

Latour B (1993) *We Have Never Been Modern*, Harvard University Press, Cambridge, MA.

Latour B (2005) *Reassembling the Social: An Introduction to Actor-Network-Theory*, Oxford University Press, Oxford, UK.

Law J (2004) *Enacting Naturecultures: A Note From STS.* Center for Science Studies, Lancaster University, Lancaster, UK. (www.lancaster.ac.uk/sociology/research/publications/papers/law-enacting-naturecultures.pdf) Accessed 4 February 2015.

Lezaun J and Marres N (2011) Materials and Devices of the Public: An Introduction, *Economy and Society* 40(4) 485–509.

Lynch M (2008 *Ontography: Investigating the Production of Things, Deflating Ontology,* Oxford Ontologies Workshop, Saïd Business School, Oxford University (25 June 2008).

Marres N (2005) Issues Spark a Public Into Being, in Latour B and Weibel P (eds) *Making Things Public,* MIT Press, Cambridge MA.

Marres N (2007) The Issues Deserve More Credit: Pragmatist Contributions to the Study of Public Involvement in Controversy, *Social Studies of Science* 37 759.

Marres N (2008) The Making of Climate Publics: Eco-Homes as Material Devices of Publicity [in Moser I and Asdal K (eds) Special Issue on The Technologies of Politics], *Distinktion Scandinavian Journal of Social Theory* 16 27–46.

Marres N (2009) Testing Powers of Engagement: Green Living Experiments, the Ontological Turn and the Undoability of Involvement, *European Journal of Social Theory* 12(1) 117–133.

Marres N (2010a) Frontstaging Nonhumans: Publicity as a Constraint on the Political Activity of Things, in Braun B and Whatmore S (eds) *Political Matter Technoscience, Democracy, and Public Life,* Minnesota University Press, Minneapolis, MN, 177–210.

Marres N (2010b) What Kind of Space is the 'Sustainable Home'? A Comparative Analysis of Three Media Spheres on the Web, *Mapping Green* 49–55.

Marres N (2011) The Costs of Public Involvement: Everyday Devices of Carbon Accounting and the Materialization of Participation, *Economy and Society* 40(4) 510–533.

Marres N (2012) The Environmental Teapot and Other Loaded Household Objects: Reconnecting the Politics of Technology, Issues and Things, in Harvey P, Casella E, Evans G, Knox H, McLean C, Silva E, Thoburn N and Woodward K (eds) *Objects and Materials: A Routledge Companion,* London, Routledge.

Mol A (1999) Ontological Politics: A Word and Some Questions, in Law J and Hassard J (eds) *Actor Network Theory and After,* Blackwell Publishing/The Sociological Review, Oxford, UK, 74–89.

Mol A (2010) Actor-Network Theory: Sensitive Terms and Enduring Tensions, *Kölner Zeitschrift für Soziologie und Sozialpsychologie* 50(1) 253–269.

Papazu I (2012) *'Ballerup Kommune skal jo ikke redde den sidste pingvin!' Et speciale om Klimafamilieprojektet i Ballerup Kommune og om hvordan kommuner kan engagere borgerne i bekæmpelsen af klimaforandringer* ['It's not up to Ballerup Municipality to save the last penguin!' A Master's thesis about the Climate Family Project in Ballerup Municipality and about how municipalities can engage citizens in fighting climate change], Master's thesis, Department of Political Science, Copenhagen University (http://cidea.ku.dk/pdf/Cidearapport6SpecialeBallerupkommuneIrinaPapazu.pdf/) Accessed 4 February 2015.

Rose N (1999) *Powers of Freedom: Reframing Political Thought,* Cambridge University Press, Cambridge, UK.

Rutland T and Aylett A (2008) The Work of Policy: Actor-Networks, Governmentality, and Local Action on Climate Change in Portland, Oregon, *Environment and Planning D, Society and Space* 26(4) 627–646.

Shove E (2010) Beyond the ABC: Climate Change Policy and Theories of Social Change, *Environment and Planning A* 42(6) 1273–1285.

Stengers I (2005) The Cosmopolitical Proposal, in Latour B and Weibel P (eds) *Making Things Public*, MIT Press, Cambridge MA.

5   Environmental choices

Hypocrisy, self-contradictions and the tyranny of everyday life

Quentin Gausset, Jens Hoff, Christian Elling Scheele and Emilie Nørregaard

Introduction

There is a broad consensus today around the threat posed by global warming and the need to address the problem. A large percentage of carbon dioxide (CO_2) emissions come from consumption patterns found at the household or individual level. In 2011, transport accounted for 33 per cent of the total CO_2 emissions in Denmark (of which more than two-thirds come from private transport), and household energy consumption – mainly for heating houses – accounted for 22 per cent of total emissions (Energistatistik 2011).

Although Denmark's energy strategy to make the country independent from fossil fuel by 2050 focuses on systemic and infrastructure changes, it also relies on reducing citizens' energy consumption by 6 per cent by 2020, as compared to 2006 (Regeringen 2011). In the long-term perspective, this percentage probably needs to increase in order to reach a carbon-free society by 2050.

Such goals cannot be reached without citizens changing their environmental behaviour substantially. For this reason, this chapter looks at the factors that motivate people to reduce their CO_2 footprint in various areas of consumption, and the barriers that stand in the way of such reductions. We analyse these questions theoretically as well as empirically, using pooled survey data from 2,005 respondents in three Danish municipalities.

Theories on environmental behaviour change

There are a variety of primarily economic and socio-psychological theories and models that identify the factors that determine environmental behaviour. Many of these theories take *rational choice theory* as their point of departure. This theory, a central tenet of economic theory, assumes that individuals, when faced with the choice between two options, will choose the one that maximises their private benefits and minimises their costs.

The *expectancy value model* builds on this idea, stating that behaviour depends on how individuals believe they can gain the benefit that they seek, and on how they evaluate (positively or negatively) the outcome of the behaviour (Fishbein

1967, 1968; Fishbein and Ajzen 1974, 1975; Palmgreen 1984). The *theory of reasoned action* elaborates on the expectancy value model by adding norms to beliefs and attitudes, and by introducing intentions as an intermediary factor between these beliefs and attitudes and behaviour. Thus, according to the theory of reasoned action, an individual's behaviour depends on his or her intentions, which depend, in turn, on attitudes and beliefs towards the outcome of that behaviour (as in the expectancy value model), and on the subjective norms and normative beliefs (i.e. on their belief regarding how people will judge their behaviour) (Fishbein and Ajzen 1975; Ajzen and Fishbein 1980).

Over time, a third factor was introduced into the mix that focuses on whether individuals perceive that they can control behaviour and its outcome. This new model is called the *theory of planned behaviour* (Ajzen 1985, 1991). Emotions have also been identified as an important aspect of attitudes and beliefs, e.g. people might strongly react to fear (Jackson 2005, 35; Uzzell et al. 2006, 19). Even though emotions might not appear to be rational, this theoretical approach shares with other approaches (including the rational choice theory) the idea that behaviour choices are determined by the individual's own values and/or knowledge.

Although the theories of reasoned action and planned behaviour accept that norms and the social influence of others have a place in the discussion, they still focus very much on individuals and private benefits. Other scholars have attempted to shift the focus towards collective altruism and ethics, or towards social pressure as determinants for behaviour. For example, the model of the new environmental paradigm holds that people do not behave selfishly just to maximise benefits or to avoid social disapproval; they also behave for social and altruistic reasons according to what they believe is ultimately ethical and moral (Dunlap and van Liere 1978; Stern et al. 1995).

The *norm-activation theory* argues that two crucial aspects determining altruistic behaviour are whether people are aware of the consequences that their actions have on others, and whether they accept the responsibility for these consequences (Schwartz 1977). Stern attempted to merge the theories of the new environmental paradigm and norm-activation into a new *value-belief-norm model*. He argues that people who hold biospheric and altruistic values are the most aware of the consequence of their actions, take responsibility for them, change their personal norms and adopt environmentally friendly behaviour, whilst people holding egoistic values prefer to ignore the consequences of their actions and/or deny any responsibility (Stern 2000).

The focus on collective norms has been further refined by studies arguing that behaviour might depend less on private benefit or on the desire to do good and behave well than on social compliance and the desire to behave as others do (regardless of the material benefit for oneself or for others, and regardless of ethical considerations) (Cialdini et al. 1990). Using social networks can therefore be a crucial approach to anchoring identity and behaviour (Uzzell et al. 2006, 14). This approach links to political theories that study not just compliance to social norms, but also compliance to rules and regulations prescribing and proscribing certain behaviours, and to the study of the importance of citizen participation in decision making (see Chapter 3 in this book).

As we can see, there are two broad clusters of theories on environmental behaviour. On the one hand, theories developed around the rational choice theory focus on individuals who are presumed to behave in order to maximise their own benefit and welfare. On the other hand, theories focusing on social responsibility, social norms or social pressure focus on groups that influence individual behaviour. The first cluster of theories locates behaviour change within individual choices, while the second locates it within social relations. Although they differ in focus, these different models overlap and combine a limited number of recurrent factors. Therefore, in our survey, we selected the following seven factors that we think are the most influential in determining environmental behaviour:

1   *Economic considerations*: People adapt their behaviour and consumption patterns to the means they have at their disposal. They try to minimise expenses/costs and maximise benefits. Following this approach, environmental behaviour can be promoted by subsidising sound behaviour and taxing unsound behaviour.

2   *Values*: People behave according to a certain morals and ethics. They work to create a better world for their children and refrain from behaving in ways that harm others. But ecological or biospheric values can contradict each other and can compete with other sets of values (such as private and/or collective welfare). Environmental policy must therefore promote ecological values over others.

3   *Norms*: People adapt their behaviour to social expectations, i.e. to what they believe people expect from them. They conform to norms, behave like others or avoid behaving in ways that are considered to be anti-social, which would risk the disapproval of others. Large-scale behaviour change can be triggered when a certain critical mass of people (preferably role models) change their behaviour, pulling a larger part of the population along with them. In these cases, environmental policy can rely more heavily on role models and promote collective environmental action or collective green identities.

4   *Legislation*: People adapt their behaviour according to legislation, both out of a social and moral drive to avoid social judgement and ostracism (see point 2) but also to avoid the sanctions and penalties that might derive from contravening laws and regulations.

5   *Responsibility and empowerment*: People might be willing to change their environmental behaviour if it proves detrimental to their neighbours or to future generations (point 2). But they will only do so if they are aware of the consequences of their actions, and if they are convinced that changing their behaviour will have a direct and immediate impact on the well-being of others.

6   *Knowledge*: People's behaviour depends on the knowledge they have of the different costs and benefits of their behaviour and consumption patterns

(point 1), what is socially expected from them (point 3), legislation (point 4) and the consequences that their behaviour can have on themselves and on others (point 5). Providing information to the public can therefore be an important tool for triggering environmental behaviour change.

7   *Social categories*: Gender, age, income and political orientation can correlate with different needs or interests, types or levels of knowledge, sets of values and sense of responsibility or powerlessness (points 1–6) and can also be factors that determine behaviour.

Data and method

The results reported in this chapter are based on a survey of 2,005 adults over 18 years old from the Danish municipalities of Kolding, Køge and Herning Kommune. The survey was conducted by computer-assisted telephone interviews in April 2012. The respondents were selected on the basis of an extract from the Central Person's Register (CPR) (the Danish Government Register of all citizens) containing approximately 10,500 people, which sets the response rate of this survey at 19 per cent.

However, even though the survey's response rate was modest, the data are considered representative for the population in Denmark with respect to age and gender. Because the data were deemed representative, the dataset was not weighed. Although there are 2,005 respondents in the dataset, n ranges from 1,323–1,371 in the logistic regression analyses. Cases with missing values in any variable used in the analysis have been dropped (list-wise deletion). The survey contains information on environmental behaviour, environmental attitudes, knowledge, motivation to take action on climate change and socio-demographic questions.

Dependent variables

We used four parameters that track specific choices made by survey respondents. We asked if they:

- Look for eco-labels when shopping;
- Wash clothes at the lowest possible temperature;
- Own a car; and
- Travelled by plane for leisure and family visits (non-business flights) in the past year.

These factors cover different aspects of environmental behaviour relating to consumption and transport, and also cover both daily choices and choices that are made less frequently, e.g. plane travel. These choices have different impacts on carbon emissions. However, even choices that do not have a strong and direct implication with regard to carbon emissions, such as 'look for eco-labels when shopping', are relevant. This is because the behaviour is easy to adopt and denotes a certain awareness of and responsibility for environmental problems.

The survey contained more parameters, including the annual amount of electricity consumed, annual expenditures associated with domestic heating, the annual distance driven in private cars and a set of twelve self-reported questions concerning environmental habits. The questions, which called for a specific numerical answer, resulted in a high amount of 'don't know' answers, blanks and inconsistencies. We chose to leave them out of the analysis.

The twelve self-reported questions regarding environmental behaviour addressed whether respondents take action to protect the environment (e.g. buying seasonal fruits and vegetables produced locally, eating less meat, recycling). Responses included, 'I do it as much as I can', 'I am considering doing it more' and 'I don't do it and I am not considering doing it'. Items were re-coded in such a way that the answers 'doing it' and 'considering doing it more' scored with a value of 1 and the answer 'not doing it or not considering doing it' scored 0 (see the distribution of the variable in Table 5.1). Experimentation with index construction of behaviour through a factor analysis resulted in unsatisfactory Cronbach's Alpha values, indicating that there is a lack of co-variation between the variables. This demonstrated that the respondents do not behave in the same way across different climate-changing actions. Instead of using indices, we selected only two specific variables, washing clothes at the lowest temperature and looking for eco-labels when shopping, as indicators of climate-friendly behaviour. These items were selected because they turned out to be the most representative for shopping and for energy-saving actions in the home.

Independent variables

The seven factors hypothesised to determine environmental behaviour were operationalised in our questionnaire as follows:

1) and 2) *Economic considerations and values* (egoism and altruism): In our questionnaire, we asked informants what motivates them most when adopting an environmentally friendly behaviour: a) economic benefit, b) improving the health of the family, c) protecting threatened species, d) reducing climate changes, e) improving the resource base of future generations or f) having a good conscience. The first answer was coded as an egoistic dummy variable (0–1) and was taken as an indicator of economic considerations. In our analysis, this was equated to an indicator of egoistic values. Answers c), d) and e) were merged and

Table 5.1 Frequency of dependent variables, eco-labels, laundry, car and flight

	Looking for eco-labels when shopping		Washing clothes at lowest possible temperature		Own a car		Flew privately in the last year	
	No	Yes	No	Yes	No	Yes	No	Yes
N	673	1299	242	1686	246	1753	1043	962

coded as one altruistic dummy variable and were interpreted as an indicator of altruistic values.

3) *Norms:* To uncover normative behaviour in our survey, we asked whether respondents could be motivated to adopt more environmentally friendly behaviour if a) they were part of a group sharing the same environmental goals, or b) if they were encouraged to do so by friends, family members or colleagues. Responses were the degree of motivation coded into a dummy of 1 = 'it motivates me greatly' and 'it motivates me to some extent', and 0 = 'it motivates me poorly'.

4) *Personal responsibility:* The issue of awareness and empowerment is covered by a series of questions asking respondents whether it is worth changing behaviour in Denmark if a) the bigger nations do not move in the same direction, b) whether it is worth changing behaviour if others do not do the same, c) whether the effects of climate change are too far in the future to worry about today and d) whether the threats of global warming are exaggerated. These are four continuous variables with scores ranging from 1 to 5, with 5 = 'strongly agreeing' and 1= 'strongly disagreeing'.

5) *Legislation:* We asked respondents to what extent they agreed with the idea that the government should increase taxes so that people would pay the full environmental cost of travelling by plane or driving cars, and whether there should be more regulations to force people to adopt more environmentally friendly behaviour. These variables also have scores ranging from 1 to 5 (5 = 'strongly agreeing' and 1= 'strongly disagreeing', and are coded in the same way as the variables above.

6) *Knowledge:* We did not try to measure respondents' environmental knowledge; instead, we asked them to judge their own levels of knowledge about climate change in particular. The answers were recoded into a dummy variable with 'a lot' and 'some' coded as 1 and 'a little' and 'nothing' coded as 0.

7) *Social categories:* Six demographic variables were included to control for potential confounding (i.e. gender, age, education, household income, political orientation and a dummy variable for having children under 18 years of age in the household).

Method

We examined which factors influence environmental behaviour by analysing the data from the questionnaire. We addressed the magnitude of the relationship between different set of variables using Pearson correlations. We explained the differences in environmental behaviour through the four dependent variables covering different aspects of environmental behaviour.

For these dichotomous variables, we employed a binary logistic regression procedure that uses maximum likelihood estimation to estimate the probability of pro-environmental behaviour (see Table 5.2). To facilitate the interpretation, the odds ratio and standard errors are also presented as marginal effects.

Although not presented, a test of co-linearity between the independent variables was conducted by examining the VIF, tolerance and eigenvalues. No significant co-linearity was indicated. All of our analyses were run in STATA SE 12.0.

Table 5.2 (Binary) logistic regression, eco-labels, laundry, car and flight (dep.)

	Looking after eco-labels when shopping	Washing clothes at lowest possible temperature	Own a car	Flew privately in the last year
Egoism (economic motivation) (dichotomous)	0.68* (0.14)	1.05 (0.29)	1.04 (0.38)	0.86 (0.17)
Altruism (dichotomous)	1.27 (0.25)	1.67* (0.45)	0.93 (0.31)	0.98 (0.18)
Being leftist (dichotomous)	1.41** (0.19)	1.74*** (0.37)	0.77 (0.18)	0.82 (0.10)
Motivated by community (dichotomous)	1.37** (0.18)	1.45** (0.27)	1.13 (0.28)	1.07 (0.13)
DK is too small to make a difference	0.93 (0.05)	0.97 (0.07)	1.19* (0.12)	0.94 (0.05)
The effects of climate change are too far in the future	0.87** (0.06)	0.85* (0.07)	1.03 (0.12)	1.03 (0.06)
Not worth changing behaviour if others do not do the same	0.89** (0.05)	0.98 (0.07)	0.97 (0.09)	1.01 (0.05)
Plane travellers should pay the full environmental cost	1.09 (0.06)	0.98 (0.08)	0.96 (0.10)	0.72*** (0.04)
Increase environmental taxes	1.03 (0.06)	1.06 (0.09)	0.79** (0.08)	1.02 (0.06)
More environmental regulations	1.22*** (0.06)	0.92 (0.07)	1.02 (0.10)	1.20*** (0.06)
Climate knowledge (dichotomous)	1.58*** (0.21)	1.76*** (0.32)	0.62** (0.15)	1.21 (0.15)
Education	1.00 (0.03)	0.96 (0.05)	0.90* (0.05)	1.11*** (0.04)
Gender (dichotomous, woman=1)	1.26* (0.16)	1.31 (0.25)	0.88 (0.21)	0.74** (0.09)
Age	1.01** (0.00)	1.02*** (0.01)	1.03*** (0.01)	1.00 (0.00)
Income	1.04 (0.03)	1.02 (0.04)	2.26*** (0.18)	1.15*** (0.03)
Children (dichotomous)	0.80 (0.12)	1.17 (0.25)	2.24** (0.73)	0.56*** (0.08)
N	1356	1325	1369	1373
pseudo R^2	0.101	0.084	0.327	0.078
Log lik.	−776.84	−443.66	−282.92	−877.35
LR Chi-squared	173.92	81.04	275.34	148.56
Correctly classified	69.62%	88.15%	91.96%	63.15%

Notes: Odds ratio/Exponentiated B-coefficients. Standard errors in parentheses. * $p<0.10$, ** $p<0.05$, *** $p<0.01$.

Results

Generally speaking, all of the seven factors explained above do influence environmental behaviour. However, they do so in different and sometimes subtle ways.

1) Informants who declared that saving money is their primary motivation to change their environmental behaviour tend to exhibit less environmentally friendly behaviour than informants whose motivation to change environmental behaviour is not primarily economic. A total of 53 per cent of those primarily motivated by economic benefits look for eco-labels and 83 per cent wash clothes at the lowest temperature possible, compared to 71 per cent and 89 per cent respectively for those whose primary motivation is not economic (see Table 5.3).

When controlling for other variables, respondents primarily motivated by economic savings are less likely to look for eco-labels when shopping than those having another primary motivation (odds = 0.68, see Table 5.2), while the correlation with washing clothes in lower temperatures disappears. These results may seem puzzling, since environmentally friendly behaviour (buying non-food items with low-energy eco-labels, washing clothes at lower temperature or using public transport instead of private cars) often allows people to save money. The paradox is that people who declare to be primarily motivated by saving money tend in fact to save less money (or in any case, not more) than those who do not have economic factors as their primary motivation. If we interpret the motivation to save money as an egoistic and individualistic value, as opposed to an altruistic value, we might conclude that the behaviour of people holding egoistic values is less environmentally friendly than the behaviour of people holding altruistic values, and also that their behaviour is self-contradictory. This will be verified when discussing the next point.

Table 5.3 Value variables by four environmental behaviour determinants (cross-tabulation)

	Looking after eco-labels when shopping		Washing clothes at lowest possible temperature		Own a car		Flew privately in the last year	
	%	Sig.	%	Sig.	%	Sig.	%	Sig.
Egoistic values								
No	71	***	89	***	87	—	48	—
Yes	53		83		88		48	
Altruistic values								
No	57	***	84	***	87	—	46	—
Yes	73		90		88		49	
Political orientation								
Right	60	***	85	***	91	***	51	—
Left	75		92		85		47	

Notes: Chi-square significance test (H_0 the variables are statistically independent. H_A the variables are statistically dependent.) * $p<0.10$, ** $p<0.05$, *** $p<0.01$.

2) Altruistic values (declaring that caring for others, caring for nature, or caring for future generations is the primary driver of one's environmental behaviour) correlates positively with greener behaviour. A total of 73 per cent of respondents holding altruistic values look for eco-labels when shopping and 90 per cent wash clothes at lowest temperature, compared to 57 per cent and 84 per cent respectively for those who do not have altruistic values as their primary motivation (see Table 5.3). When controlling for other variables (see Table 5.2), people holding altruistic values are more likely to look for eco-labels (a result that is not statistically significant, however) and also more likely to wash clothes at the lowest temperature than respondents whose primary motivation is not altruistic (odds ratios = 1.27 and 1.67 respectively).

People who define themselves as leftists also tend to exhibit greener behaviour than others, and do so in a proportion comparable to people holding altruistic values (see Table 5.3, and note the high odds ratios of 1.41 and 1.67 in Table 5.2). In Denmark, when it comes to taxation and socio-economic policies, left-wing voters tend to give more support to state interventionism, the welfare state and community solidarity, whilst right-wing voters tend to support free market solutions and policies rewarding individuals for their personal achievements.

Schematically, one could say that left-wing voters hold more altruistic values while right-wing voters hold more egoistic values. Thus, political values can be a good indicator of egoistic/altruistic values, and therefore environmentally related values (there is a strong correlation between the two factors; see Table 5.6 below). People who generally put collective interests before individual interests are more willing to sacrifice some of their private benefit for the collective environmental benefit, whilst those who hold egoistic values might not be ready to sacrifice their comfort or welfare for the environment. (This is especially true when it is difficult to establish a clear link between individual local behaviour and its global and future negative consequences.)

3) Following social norms (behaving like others, or in a way that is approved of by others) can be an important motivation to adopt more environmentally friendly behaviour. When considering whether to adopt a greener behaviour, some informants are highly influenced by what others think or do. Our results show that 71 per cent of people who said they are influenced by their community look for eco-labels when shopping and 91 per cent wash at lowest possible temperature, compared to 58 per cent and 82 per cent respectively for those who declare they are immune to the influence of others (see Table 5.4). In our regression analysis, people who declare they are influenced by the community are more likely to look for eco-labels and more likely to wash clothes at the lowest possible temperature than other respondents (odds = 1.37 and 1.45, see Table 5.2). Because few people want to be perceived as 'environmental pigs', norms can be effective in inducing a behaviour change.

4) Legislation is an important tool for encouraging environmentally friendly behaviour. Legislators have the power to distribute economic rewards and to levy taxes on behaviour or consumption that is detrimental to the environment. A total of 45 per cent of our respondents support more environmental regulation

Table 5.4 Motivation by four environmental behaviour determinants (cross-tabulation)

Motivated by community	Looking after eco-labels when shopping		Washing clothes at lowest possible temperature		Own a car		Flew privately in the last year	
	%	Sig.	%	Sig.	%	Sig.	%	Sig.
No	58	***	82	***	89	—	48	—
Yes	71		91		87		48	

Notes: Chi-square significance test (H$_0$ the variables are statistically independent. H$_A$ the variables are statistically dependent) * p<0.10, ** p<0.05, *** p<0.01.

and 41 per cent support more environmental taxation, compared to 37 per cent and 39 per cent respectively who oppose such policies (the rest were undecided).

However, there are disparities among the different categories of informants. As Table 5.5 indicates, there are more supporters of an increase in environmental regulation and taxation among those who look for eco-labels when shopping and wash at lowest temperature possible than among others. Table 5.5 also shows that plane travellers tend to oppose paying the full environmental cost of plane

Table 5.5 Attitude towards legislation by four environmental behaviour determinants

	Looking after eco-labels when shopping		Washing clothes at lowest possible temperature		Own a car		Flew privately in the last year	
	%	Sig.	%	Sig.	%	Sig.	%	Sig.
Plane travellers should pay the full environmental cost								
Strongly disagree/ disagree	60	***	86	—	89	*	55	***
Strongly agree/agree	72		88		86		38	
Increase environmental taxes								
Strongly disagree/ disagree	58	***	85	***	89	—	48	—
Strongly agree/agree	73		90		87		47	
More environmental regulations								
Strongly disagree/ disagree	57	***	85	**	88	—	45	**
Strongly agree/agree	74		89		88		50	

Notes: Chi-square significance test (H$_0$ the variables are statistically independent. H$_A$ the variables are statistically dependent) * p<0.10, ** p<0.05, *** p<0.01.

travel, but, surprisingly, they also tend to support a more global approach to increasing environmental regulations. This is confirmed in our regression analysis (odds = 0.72 and 1.20 respectively, see Table 5.2).

Owning a car does not seem to make a big difference in terms of attitudes towards environmental taxation and regulations, but when controlling for other variables, car owners tend to oppose an increase in environmental taxes (odds = 0.79, see Table 5.2). This paints a mixed picture of attitudes towards more environmental regulations and taxation. On the one hand, people whose daily behaviour is environmentally friendly tend to support increasing environmental regulation, and also tend to support (or at least do not oppose) increasing environmental taxation. Car owners and plane travellers, on the other hand, tend to oppose increasing taxation but also tend to support (or at least do not oppose) increasing environmental regulation.

5) Some people are sceptical regarding the difference they can make as individuals. For example, 29 per cent of our respondents agree that it is useless for them to change behaviour if others do not follow suit, compared to 61 per cent who disagree and 10 per cent who are undecided. Likewise, 23 per cent of our respondents agree that it is useless to take action in Denmark unless the bigger countries (China, the United States) also take action, compared to 64 per cent who disagree and 13 per cent who are undecided.

Logically, the sceptics are also significantly less willing to adopt a greener behaviour (look at eco-labels, wash clothes at lower temperature and refrain from flying or owning a car) than those who believe that individual and national action does make a difference, even if others do not follow suit. In Table 5.6, for example, only 55 to 58 per cent of those who think that Denmark is too small to make a difference, that it is not worth changing behaviour if others don't do the same, and that the effects of climate change are too far in the future to be worried about look for eco-labels when shopping, compared to 70 to 72 per cent who think the opposite. These results are partially confirmed in our regression analysis, at least for climate changes in the future and for the idea that it is not worth changing behaviour if others do not follow (odds = 0.87 and 0.89 respectively, see Table 5.2). Surprisingly, people who fly non-work related flights tend to be less skeptical: 43 per cent of those who think Denmark is too small to make a difference or that the effects of climate change are too far in the future flew such flights in the past year, compared to 50 per cent of those who did not fly. However, when controlling for other variables these correlations disappear; one finds instead a correlation between car owners and the perception that Denmark is too small to make a difference (odds = 1.19, see Table 5.2). All this confirms the general picture that people who adopt environmentally friendly behaviour (in both home and transport habits) tend to 'think globally and act locally', e.g. they are more convinced than others that their own individual behaviour can or does make a difference on a larger scale.

6) Knowledge plays an important role in several theoretical models, whether it is knowledge to maximise benefit, to understand the consequences of one's action, knowledge about legislation and social norms/expectations or actual

Table 5.6 Personal and collective responsibility by four environmental behaviour
determinants

	Looking after eco-labels when shopping		Washing clothes at lowest possible temperature		Own a car		Flew privately in the last year	
	%	Sig.	%	Sig.	%	Sig.	%	Sig.
Denmark is too small to make a difference								
Strongly disagree/ disagree	71	***	89	***	87	*	50	**
Strongly agree/agree	58		82		90		43	
The effects of climate change are too far in the future								
Strongly disagree/ disagree	70	***	90	***	89	*	50	**
Strongly agree/agree	55		80		85		42	
Not worth changing behaviour if others do not do the same								
Strongly disagree/ disagree	72	***	89	**	88	—	49	—
Strongly agree/agree	55		84		87		45	

Notes: Chi-square significance test (H_0 the variables are statistically independent. H_A the variables
are statistically dependent) * $p<0.10$, ** $p<0.05$, *** $p<0.01$.

knowledge about climate change issues. A total of 65 per cent of the respondents
believe that they possess a good knowledge of environmental issues; these
informants do indeed exhibit a greener behaviour than those who think that
they have only a little knowledge.

For example, 70 per cent of those who think that they have a lot of knowledge look for eco-labels and 90 per cent wash clothes at lower temperature,
compared to 50 per cent and 83 per cent respectively for people who say they
have not much knowledge (see Table 5.6). People who say they have adequate
knowledge seem to fly more than others (52 per cent as compared to 42 per cent,
see Table 5.7), although this correlation disappears when controlling for other
parameters in a regression analysis (see Table 5.2). When it comes to owning a
car, however, a regression analysis demonstrates that people who say they have
adequate environmental knowledge are less likely to own a car than others (odds
= 0.68, see Table 5.2). This leads us to conclude that knowledge is one of the
most important factors in determining environmental behaviour.

The level of education does not have significant effect on either 'look for eco-
labels' or 'wash clothes at lowest possible temperature' in the logistic regression
analysis. However, education does correlate strongly with knowledge, and just as
knowledge does, it correlates negatively with owning a car and positively with

Table 5.7 Climate knowledge by four environmental behaviour determinants

	Looking after eco-labels when shopping		Washing clothes at lowest possible temperature		Own a car		Flew privately in the last year	
	%	Sig.	%	Sig.	%	Sig.	%	Sig.
Climate knowledge								
Small	58	***	83	***	87	—	42	***
Large	70		90		88		52	

Notes: Chi-square significance test (H_0 the variables are statistically independent. H_A the variables are statistically dependent). * $p<0.10$, ** $p<0.05$, *** $p<0.01$.

flying (see Table 5.2). This indicates that the level of education does indeed have an effect, even though it sometimes affects behaviour through specific knowledge of climate change issues, as illustrated in a path analysis (see Figure 5.1).

7) Social (or demographic) categories correlate with environmental behaviour in different ways. First, women perform more positively than men on all indicators of environmental behaviour, but especially when it comes to looking at eco-labels, buying local and seasonal fruits or owning a car (odds = 1.26 and 0.74 respectively) (see Table 5.2). Women are also more likely than men to be leftist and to hold altruistic values (see Table 5.8).

Second, the environmental behaviour of elderly people is significantly greener than the behaviour of younger people (see Table 5.2). But older people also tend to think that climate change is too far in the future to concern them and to oppose more environmental regulations (see Table 5.8). Their relatively sound environmental behaviour seems therefore to be more motivated by habits than by ideological reasons or a stronger environmental consciousness. (However, they are less likely to declare that money is their primary motivation to adopt more environmentally friendly behaviour.)

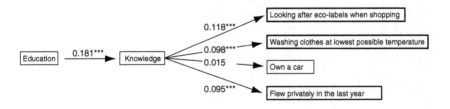

Figure 5.1 Path analysis of education

Note: Pearson's R correlations.

Table 5.8 Sociodemographics variables by climate engagement: Correlation matrix

	Egoism (economic motivation) (dichotomous)	Altruism (dichotomous)	Being leftist (dichotomous)	Motivated by Community (dichotomous)	DK is too small to make a difference	The effects of climate change are too far in the future	Not worth changing behaviour if others do not do the same	Plane travellers should pay the environmental cost	Increase environmental taxes	More environmental regulations	Climate knowledge (dichotomous)
Gender (dichotomous, woman=1)	-0.180***	0.164***	0.120***	0.040	-0.171***	-0.059***	-0.154***	-0.093***	-0.011	0.048*	-0.077***
Age	-0.086***	-0.014	0.049*	0.017	0.040	0.088***	0.026	0.138***	0.000	-0.093***	-0.034
Education	-0.002	0.067**	0.049*	-0.070**	-0.146***	-0.180***	-0.073**	-0.022	0.050*	-0.000	0.181***
Income	0.002	0.076**	-0.057*	-0.090***	-0.074**	-0.176***	-0.070**	-0.086***	0.013	0.023	0.128***
Children (dichotomous)	0.001	0.077***	-0.047	-0.032	-0.060**	-0.140***	-0.066*	-0.052*	0.030	0.083***	0.033

Notes: * p<0.05, ** p<0.01, *** p<0.001.

Third, wealthier people are more likely to have a car and to make holiday-related trips by plane than poorer people (odds = 2.26 and 1.15 respectively, see Table 5.2). Interestingly, income does not correlate with declaring that saving money is the primary motivation for changing behaviour (see Table 5.8). In other words, the desire to save money is not a characteristic specific to poorer respondents: it is a concern that cuts across all categories of income. Moreover, income does not correlate with a call for more legislation and eco-taxes (see Table 5.8), which means that poorer people are as likely to support eco-taxes as wealthier people. Another finding that has relevance for the issue of environmental justice is that poorer respondents tend to support the idea that travellers should pay the full environmental cost of plane travel, while wealthier people tend to oppose it (see Table 5.8), even though an increase in eco-taxes would probably strike poorer people harder.

Fourth, like knowledge, the impact of education is somewhat ambivalent. Although people who have higher levels of education are more likely to own a car or fly, when controlling for other factors (such as income or having children), higher education correlates negatively with owning a car (odds = 0.90) but still correlates positively with flying (odds = 1.11, see Table 5.2).

Fifth, almost all families with children at home own a car, but (when controlling for other factors) they also tend to fly less than families without children at home (odds = 0.56, see Table 5.2). This might be because it is cheaper and often more convenient for families with children to go on holiday by car rather than by plane. People with children also tend to be more altruistic, to disagree with the idea that the effects of climate change are too far in the future to be concerned and to support eco-taxes and more environmental legislation (see Table 5.8). This may indicate that parents are concerned about the consequences of global warming on their children and not just on themselves.

Discussion

Our survey clearly shows that environmental behaviour is multi-faceted, and that behaviours relating to daily consumption, i.e. looking for eco-labels or washing clothes at lower temperatures, differ from choices relating to transport. Daily consumption choices are influenced first of all by altruistic values, norms, feelings of personal responsibility and knowledge about climate change, while transport choices are influenced particularly by people's social identity (gender, age, education, income and family structure), even though knowledge, gender and age influence both types of behaviour. In general, we can say that our respondents are willing to change some of their behaviour as a result of increased climate knowledge or social pressure, but that when it comes to transportation, neither of these 'drivers' seem to do the job.

Parallel to this divide between daily consumption and transport, one finds a general divide between economic motivation on the one hand, and moral or social motivation on the other. If daily consumption behaviour can be influenced by the 'soft power' of social pressure and persuasion, it is much more difficult to

Table 5.9 Correlation matrix by climate engagement

	Egoism (economic motivation) (dichotomous)	Altruism (dichotomous)	Being leftist (dichotomous)	Motivated by Community (dichotomous)	DK is too small to make a difference	The effects of climate change are too far in the future	Not worth changing behaviour if others do not do the same	Plane travellers should pay the environmental cost	Increase environmental taxes	More environmental regulations	Climate knowledge (dichotomous)
Egoism (economic motivation) (dichotomous)	1										
Altruism (dichotomous)	−0.738***	1									
Being leftist (dichotomous)	−0.096***	0.081**	1								
Motivated by community (dichotomous)	−0.116***	0.085***	0.092***	1							
DK is too small to make a difference	0.107***	−0.127***	−0.207***	−0.036	1						
The effects of climate change are too far in the future	0.126***	−0.149***	−0.162***	−0.001	0.367***	1					

Table 5.9 continued

	Egoism (economic motivation) (dichotomous)	Altruism (dichotomous)	Being leftist (dichotomous)	Motivated by Community (dichotomous)	DK is too small to make a difference	The effects of climate change are too far in the future	Not worth changing behaviour if others do not do the same	Plane travellers should pay the environmental cost	Increase environmental taxes	More environmental regulations	Climate knowledge (dichotomous)
Not worth changing behaviour if others do not do the same	0.112***	−0.129***	−0.159***	−0.051*	0.334***	0.358***	1				
Plane travellers should pay the full environmental cost	−0.006	−0.001	0.102***	0.113***	0.002	−0.013	−0.014	1			
Increase environmental taxes	−0.062**	0.088***	0.176***	0.126***	−0.104***	−0.133***	−0.092***	0.397***	1		
More environmental regulations	−0.110***	0.097***	0.156***	0.157***	−0.060**	−0.090***	−0.076***	0.194***	0.320***	1	
Climate knowledge (dichotomous)	−0.040	0.059**	0.118***	−0.001	−0.082***	−0.149***	−0.064**	0.012	0.059**	0.016	1

Notes: * $p<0.05$, ** $p<0.01$, *** $p<0.001$.

convince people to change their transport choices, unless one relies on harder tools such as eco-taxes. But even eco-taxes might be insufficient if people are unwilling to save money because it goes against their comfort, their values, or because the savings realised are marginal with regard to their income.

Moreover, there is also a group of people who are sceptics, i.e. those who do not wish to or do not see the point of changing behaviour. These people tend to hold egoistic values, refuse taking responsibility for the collective consequence of individual behaviour, are more immune to social pressure and less inclined to believe that they possess the necessary knowledge regarding climate change.

One can read a certain 'bad faith' among environmental sceptics. They claim to be willing to change behaviour if it allows them to save money, but they nevertheless do not systematically choose the environmentally friendly options that allow them to save money. They claim that it is useless to change behaviour unless everyone else does the same, but they nevertheless are opposed to state intervention that would encourage everybody to change behaviour at the same time (see Table 5.9). They behave as if what mattered most was to be able to continue living as before, without changing anything in their level of current comfort or habits. When people are unwilling to reflect upon the consequences of their acts, are immune to social pressure and insensitive to rational calculations, when two-thirds of the people declare to have a fair knowledge of environmental problems (and are presumably uninterested in learning more) and when behaviour is determined in part by social identity rather than by deliberate choices, the best or only option left to trigger behaviour change might be new legislation, regardless of how unpopular this might be among sceptics.

On the other hand, there is also a core of informants convinced of the urgency of climate problems and the need to change behaviour. They tend to hold altruistic values, reflect upon the consequences of their actions and take responsibility for them, they respond to social pressure and believe that they have knowledge regarding climate change. This group plays an important role in redefining collective norms, encouraging others to change behaviour and petitioning policy makers to develop new environmental regulations and eco-taxes. They defend altruistic values as well as the personal responsibility of each and every person vis-à-vis the collective consequences of individual behaviour.

Conclusion

In general, our results give greater support to theories that stress the importance of altruism, social pressure, personal ethics and knowledge rather than to theories relying on the maximisation of private benefits when it comes to explaining people's climate-relevant behaviour. Thus, we found that altruistic values correlated positively with green behaviour in a number of areas. The same was the case for the motivation or social pressure brought about by friends, family, colleagues and/or local community.

Knowledge of climate change issues was also found to be an important factor in determining climate-friendly behaviour. However, all of these positive 'drivers' of behaviour change did not have an impact on people's transportation habits (car ownership and holiday-related plane travel). We conclude that the car–airline travel category is basically determined by people's social identity (here measured by gender, age, education, income and family structure, but probably also related to living and work patterns), and therefore is presumably much harder to change than behaviour that has to do with shopping routines or energy savings in the home. It is sometimes not so much what people believe (about the global or future consequences of local behaviour), what people have become (altruist, leftist) or what people wish to do (save money), but rather *who people are* (in terms of age, gender, income and education), which determines how they behave. This is an important point, although it is usually overlooked by the different theories on environmental behaviour. The policy implications of our results are that it is unlikely that 'soft tools' such as information campaigns or community activities will be able to influence transport behaviour significantly. In order to do this, 'harder' regulations like taxes or other types of systemic changes (e.g. improvement of public transportation systems, etc.) are necessary. And as we can see from our survey, a majority of people support this type of approach.

References

Ajzen I (1985) From Intentions to Actions: A Theory of Planned Behavior, in Kuhl J and Beckman J (eds) *Action-Control: From Cognition to Behavior*, Springer, Heidelberg, 11–39.

Ajzen I (1991) The Theory of Planned Behavior, *Organizational Behavior and Human Decision Processes* 50 179–211.

Ajzen I and Fishbein M (1980) *Understanding Attitudes and Predicting Social Behavior*, Prentice-Hall, Englewood Cliffs, NJ.

Cialdini R B, Reno R R and Kallgren C A (1990) A Focus Theory of Normative Conduct: Recycling the Concept of Norms to Reduce Littering in Public Places, *Journal of Personality and Social Psychology* 58(6) 1015–1526.

Dunlap R and van Liere K (1978) The 'New Environmental Paradigm': A Proposed Measuring Instrument and Preliminary Results, *Journal of Environmental Education* 9(4) 10–19.

Energistatistik (2011) *Data, tabeller, statistikker og kort*, Energistyrelsen, Copenhagen. (www.ens.dk/sites/ens.dk/files/info/tal-kort/statistik-noegletal/aarlig-energistatistik/Energistatistik%202011.pdf)

Fishbein M (1967) Attitude and the Prediction of Behaviour, in Fishbein M (ed.) *Readings in Attitude Theory and Measurement*, Wiley, New York.

Fishbein M (1968) An Investigation of Relationships Between Beliefs About an Object and the Attitude Towards that Object, *Human Relationships* 16 233–239.

Fishbein M and Ajzen I (1972) *Beliefs, Attitudes, Intentions and Behaviour: An Introduction to Theory and Research*, Addison-Wesley, Reading MA.

Fishbein M and Ajzen I (1974) Attitudes Towards Objects as Predictors of Single and Multiple Behavioural Criteria, *Psychological Review* 81(1) 29–74.

Jackson T (2005) *Motivating Sustainable Consumption: A Review of Evidence on Consumer Behavior and Behavioral Change* [A report to the Sustainable Development Research Network], Centre for Environmental Strategy, University of Surrey, UK.

Palmgreen P (1984) Uses and Gratifications: A Theoretical Perspective, in Bostrom R N (ed.) *Communication Yearbook 8*, Sage, Beverly Hills, CA, 61–72.

Regeringen (2011) *Energistrategi 2050 – fra kul, olie og gas til grøn energi* [Energy strategy 2050 – from coal, oil and gas to green energy], Klima- og Energiministeriet, Copenhagen.

Schwartz S (1977) Normative Influences on Altruism, *Advances in Experimental Social Psychology* 10 222–279.

Stern P C (2000) Towards a Coherent Theory of Environmentally Significant Behavior, *Journal of Social Issues* 56(3) 407–424.

Stern P C, Dietz T and Guagnano G A (1995) The New Ecological Paradigm in Social-Psychological Context, *Environment and Behavior* 27(6) 723–743.

Uzzell D, Muckle R, Jackson T, Ogden J, Barnett J, Gatersleben B, Hegarty P and Papathanasopoulou E (2006) *Choice Matters: Alternative Approaches to Encourage Sustainable Consumption and Production*, Report to Department of the Environment Food and Rural Affairs, University of Surrey, UK.

6 Energy renovation models in private households in Denmark

Lise Tjørring and Quentin Gausset

Introduction

In 2011, the Danish Ministry of Energy and Climate launched a new national energy strategy to contribute to the mitigation of climate change and global warming (Danish Ministry of Climate, Energy and Building 2011). This strategy stipulates that by 2020, 50 per cent of the country's electricity consumption should come from renewable sources and that the country should be fossil-free by 2050.

Reducing energy consumption in private households is an important part of this strategy: consumption at the household level constituted 28 per cent of the total national energy consumption in 2011. [Transport, the second biggest source of energy consumption, accounted for 26 per cent of the total (see Danish Energy Agency 2012, 20).] According to the National Register for Buildings and Habitations (BBR), Danish houses in a municipality like Sonderborg, one of the case studies analysed in this chapter, are an average of 65 years old and were built before any energy standards were implemented in the country. Hence, there is a great potential for reducing the energy consumption by targeting these older private households.

There are two main public actors involved in trying to reduce energy consumption at the household level: energy companies and municipalities. On the one hand, the Danish government compels Danish energy companies to reduce their clients' energy consumption by 10.7 Petajoule (PJ) annually in 2013–2014 and by 12.2 PJ annually in 2015–2020 (Energispareaftale 2012). Thus, energy companies have to convince their clients (including private households) to save on conventional energy by investing in green energies and/or by reducing their energy consumption.

On the other hand, even though the Danish government does not compel municipalities to develop local climate plans, 72 per cent of Danish municipalities have done so voluntarily (Hoff and Strobel 2013). Climate plans are developed because they can be used to brand and give a positive image to the municipalities and to the local politicians who develop them. They can also help municipalities realise substantial energy savings and create 'green jobs' in the municipality (Hoff and Strobel 2013).

Some Danish municipalities have developed pilot projects in collaboration with energy companies that are designed to reduce energy consumption by promoting home energy renovation. This chapter reviews four of the best-known and successful projects: ZEROhome in Sonderborg, ESCO-light in Middelfart, MyClimatePlan in Middelfart and Green Business Growth (GBG) in Kolding, Middelfart and Odense. All these projects are public–private partnerships between municipalities and energy companies intended to trigger new renovation projects in Danish households with the help of energy advisers who provide homeowners with energy reports on their houses and builders who receive training in energy savings and 'green' renovation.

All these projects meet the same challenges:

- What is the best way to approach people about the benefits of home renovation (information campaigns in the media, neighbourhood meetings, social networks, green ambassadors)?
- Which actor is the most successful in convincing people to renovate their homes – energy advisers, builders, municipal agents, neighbours?
- What are the best arguments to convince people to renovate their houses – economic savings and payback period? Comfort? Reduction of carbon dioxide (CO_2)? A mix of these?
- What is the best method to subsidise energy consultation and energy renovation?
- How can we evaluate whether the project has triggered additional and new renovations that were not already planned?
- How can an existing project continue to operate when its budget is exhausted?

In order to deepen our understanding of the different home renovation models and evaluate their strengths as well as their weaknesses, we describe and discuss below how these projects have addressed the challenges listed above as well as the difficulties they encounter during the renovation process. Our goal is to provide these four energy renovation models as inspiring examples of social technologies that create synergies between citizens (private households) and institutions (energy companies and municipalities) to reduce energy consumption at the local level – an important step in the journey to meet the climate challenge.

Method

The data presented in this chapter were collected between 2011–2013 by different methods. MyClimatePlan had already ended by the time the research for this chapter began; for data about this project we relied primarily on secondary literature and on interviews of the head of the project and two participants. We also participated in three meetings about a future low-energy village project that had been triggered by MyClimatePlan.

We studied ESCO-light by participating in a variety of meetings spread over the entire life of the project, including both information meetings for citizens and managerial meetings with energy companies and builders. We also monitored the production of three energy reports for specific households, conducted interviews with the project managers, three builders and two customers (or 'beneficiaries') and participated in two conferences at which the results achieved by Esco-light were presented and debated.

Green Business Growth was studied by participating in two energy fairs (including preparation and evaluation meetings), and by interviews with the managers of the project and two builders. Fieldwork in the ZEROhome project included participant observation and semi-structured interviews with ten families; first, during their meetings with the energy adviser of the project, and periodically for the next six months. We also attended several bi-weekly meetings of the ZEROhome project group.

Presentation of the four models

The ZEROhome model

ZEROhome began in 2010 with the goal to promote energy-friendly behaviour and energy renovations in private households in the municipality of Sonderborg in southern Denmark. It was part of ProjectZero, which is a public–private partnership organisation focused on creating a CO_2-neutral municipality by 2029. ProjectZero itself was established in 2007 by Sonderborg municipality, the private companies of South Energy (Danish energy company), DONG Energy (Danish Oil and Nature Gas, a Danish energy company), Danfoss (an international company producing components and solutions including renewable energy solutions) and by the Nordea Fund (established by the Nordea Bank). The overall focus of ProjectZero is: 1) to reduce energy consumption not only in private households, but also in private companies and public institutions, and 2) the conversion of energy sources to local renewable sources such as biomass, biogas, solar heat, wind power and geothermal energy in the areas of district heating and electricity production. Another objective of ProjectZero is to combine the development of CO_2-neutral energy production with economic growth that generates green jobs in the area.

ZEROhome offered free energy advice, and recruited private households through advertisements posted by ProjectZero in the local newspapers, by word of mouth and in other public campaigns. In addition, ProjectZero hosted a stand at the annual housing fair in the municipality, where visitors could sign up directly for free energy advice for their homes. ProjectZero also began cooperating with all local banks in the area. The banks arranged information evenings for their customers to encourage them to consider an energy renovation of their house. They also offered to help with loans and arranged free energy advice by ZEROhome for their customers.

When the members of private households signed up for free energy advice, they were asked to complete a form about the condition of their house, including its age, source of heating, the thickness of wall and loft insulation and the number of residents in the house. Houses that were constructed after 1996 were not chosen for renovation assistance because these houses had complied with the relatively high standard building regulations of that year and because there was more potential for positive energy results by focusing on reducing energy consumption in older houses.

After completing the form, homeowners waited for approximately one month for a visit from the energy adviser. The energy adviser began the visit by discussing with family members how they could reduce their energy consumption by changing habits, avoiding using electricity on stand-by and replacing old domestic appliances such as refrigerators and freezers with energy-saving models. The energy adviser then asked the family for a tour of the entire house to review the types of windows and toilets, the suitability of the roof for installation of solar panels, the setting on the heating source and the central heating pump, among others. He also measured the thickness of the insulation in the attic and estimated the insulation standard in the walls.

Based on his observations, the energy adviser then discussed the different options for energy improvement with the family and made a list in order of priority of the most economically profitable energy investments. Because every house is different, the energy adviser's recommended list of investments varied from house to house. However, some of the most common recommendations included replacing old windows with low-energy windows, converting from oil and gas to district heating and investing in additional insulation. After the visit, the energy adviser mailed the family a report that was customised to the specific house. The family was also given a list of the builders in the municipality who had completed an energy course; in the interest of impartiality, the energy adviser did not recommend a specific builder.

The ZEROhome project received a lot of favourable media attention, both on national and European levels. In 2012, ZEROhome was designated as a 'European role model in energy advice' by the European Union (EU) (ProjectZero 2013). Because of the project's potential to lower energy consumption in private households and create green jobs among builders, it was generally presented by the national media as a model to be followed by other municipalities. In the 3-year-period from 2010 to 2013, 1,109 home owners received energy advice from ZEROhome; 61 per cent of these households made energy renovations that totalled 103 million Danish Kroner (DKK), which at the current exchange rate equals 13.9 million Euros.

Since its funding period expired in June 2013, ZEROhome has been reconfigured. Instead of offering costly free energy advice, it has developed an education programme for builders who want to become energy advisers. To date, 80 building companies have completed the training programme.

MyClimatePlan and ESCO-light models

The municipality of Middelfart takes pride in being one of the first 'green growth' municipalities in Denmark. It has been spearheading the introduction of the ESCO ('Energy Service Company') concept in Denmark, which is a financing model by which a company conducting energy renovation in bigger buildings, e.g. offices and schools, can guarantee a certain level of energy savings. The payment of the renovation is directly financed by the energy savings realised. In this way, municipalities are able to renovate their municipal buildings without having to increase their municipal budget. The municipality continues to pay the same operating cost to heat its communal buildings as it did before the reno-vation; the savings realised from the energy renovation finances the cost of renovating the buildings over a period of two to fifteen years. At the end of this period, the municipality has gained the full benefit of the energy savings and can then reduce its operational costs.

Having had some success with the original ESCO model, the municipality then decided to help its citizens benefit from energy renovation. However, the model required some adjustments in order to apply it to home renovation. This model adapts well to bigger municipal buildings because their operational costs are large and relatively stable over time. However, it is much more difficult to apply the model to energy renovations to houses. Because houses are smaller than municipal buildings, it is more difficult to guarantee energy savings, and the energy consumption can be subject to wide variations.

Middelfart municipality then devised a new approach to trigger energy reno-vation in private buildings that was first called '*minklimaplan*' (MyClimatePlan) and later re-named 'ESCO-light' (although the model in practice is very differ-ent from the traditional ESCO model).

MyClimatePlan began in March 2008 and ended in January 2010. The munic-ipality offered free home energy evaluations to any group of a minimum of 10 citizens living in the same neighbourhood. On a given date, an energy adviser from the local energy company, two representatives from the municipality and two builders (one plumber and one carpenter/mason) visited the different houses to identify those with the highest potential for energy and monetary savings. These procedures are similar to those used in the ZEROhome project described above. The adviser then sent an energy report to each household, and the builders sent an offer covering the different points mentioned in the report. People were free to select which problems (if any) they wished to address, and were free to choose another builder.

However, they were also promised a 15 per cent cost reduction from the builder who had made the first offer, under the condition that the renovation be conducted at the same time as the other members of the neighbourhood group. This was justified by the fact that the builders could save money on transport when working for several families living in the same neighbourhood, and could save money when ordering the same kind of material in larger quantities. Renovating houses in the same neighbourhood, which were generally built during the same period, maximised the chance that the material requested in one house would be the same or similar to that requested in neighbouring houses.

A total of 89 houses benefitted from the initial offer and received an energy report. Most of them went further to address some of the problems mentioned. Some did it themselves, others relied on builders (often those who had visited their home). Moreover, some did it together with the other members of the group, while others waited a few months until certain circumstances in their personal lives allowed them to invest in energy renovation.

The ESCO-light project began in March 2011 in Middelfart as a continuation of MyClimatePlan. One of the major problems identified in MyClimatePlan was the large amount of human resources invested in energy consultation, which was paid for by the municipality and provided free of charge to citizens. To avoid this problem, the municipality, in collaboration with local energy companies, decided to train builders (and other people working in manual trades) in energy counselling. The municipality devised a three-day training for builders that focused on different aspects of energy renovation and on how to calculate precisely and with confidence the number of kilowatt-hour (kWh) saved for each type of renovation. After this training, builders were then able to deliver to their clients individual energy reports that described the potential energy savings that could be made, how much they would cost, and how long the payback period would be. The builders would also be available to help their clients to sell these savings to energy suppliers.

The municipality then organised a series of four meetings (advertised in local newspapers) to inform its residents about the new possibilities offered by ESCO-light. Individual households were then free to choose a builder from the list of those who had taken the ESCO-light training, who would then visit their houses and provide an energy report. Households could then decide whether they wanted to invest in all or in a restricted number of the recommendations made.

From the point of view of the end users, this project provided both free and qualified energy counselling as well as an additional subsidy to individuals who renovated their houses. The advantage for builders was that they increased their knowledge about energy renovation and gained an edge in a growing niche market. They also benefitted from increased visibility in the general building market: the municipality advertised the project in local media, and the municipality awarded diplomas to the builders for the training course that could be used in the builders' marketing of their businesses. Energy companies could also outsource to the builders some of the burden linked to generating energy savings in private households.

As for the municipality, this project was an important component of their CO_2 reduction goal. In addition, more renovation projects would create more jobs in the building industry and generate more tax revenues to the municipality. Thus, the project created a sustainable, win-win situation for all stakeholders.

Green Business Growth

'Green Business Growth', or GBG, is a public–private partnership that includes four municipalities (Middelfart, Kolding, Odense and Faaborg-Midtfyn), several builders and energy companies, teaching institutions and local banks (see www.groenerhvervsvaekst.dk). The project began in 2010 and was the initiative of the Middelfart municipality, which wanted to test a new approach based upon its experience with previous climate change mitigation projects. It received funds from the EU, the region of southern Denmark and participating municipalities, and is still running today. Its main goal is to create 300 jobs in the building industry by promoting energy renovations in private households as well as in public buildings, businesses and offices.

The activities developed by GBG are built on the experience of past similar projects and are eclectic. Like ESCO-light, GBG has organised several educational training sessions for builders, and promotes the builders who receive their training certificates. It also offers free energy counselling to individuals through a mix of independent energy counsellors subsidised by the project (like ZEROhome) and the builders trained by GBG (like ESCO-light).

GBG has also organised several energy fairs in participating municipalities, which give the trained builders the opportunity to present examples of their renovations to the public. Keynote speakers make presentations at the fairs on themes ranging from sustainable islands or villages to more technical issues such as solar energy.

Another successful activity organised by GBG has been evening schools on energy renovations that provide participants with tools to identify the potential for energy savings as well as techniques and know-how to renovate their house themselves. These evening schools have attracted citizens who are willing to pay for these classes to learn about home energy renovation in their homes.

GBG was awarded the prize of the best 'private–public partnership' in 2012 by the Danish Fund for Corporate Social Responsibility (CSR). It was also nominated as one of the five finalists in the RegioStars Award of the European Commission in the category of Sustainable Growth in Small and Medium Enterprises (SMEs).

The value of the energy renovation models: Similarities and differences

The four models presented above represent different ways of motivating private households to conduct energy renovation. All models have met their own targets in the sense that they have resulted in numerous energy renovations in private households. But these models differ in terms of the role of the energy adviser, the financing model, the project evaluation methods, the value of community vs. individual approaches and the strategy adopted to motivate private households. We now turn our attention to these five factors.

The role of the energy adviser

Energy advisers play an important role in reducing energy consumption in private households by providing home visits and personal advice about the possibility for energy renovating. Through face-to-face interaction, they relate directly to the people in their private households and thus are able to influence homeowners' choices enormously. They also become an informational instrument for the families because they offer expert knowledge on the subject (Mahapatra et al. 2011a).

As external actors who meet people directly in their homes, the builders' approach to the members of the households depends on qualities such as impartiality, credibility, trust, personality and competence. But what do these factors mean and what are their values?

An energy adviser can be a representative of the municipality, the energy company or an independent builder. Representatives from the municipality or energy company are usually considered impartial, while builders can easily be considered partial, since they have a vested interest in securing a renovation contract. Moreover, potential clients may feel that the builders as energy advisors lack an overview of the different possibilities that exist for house energy renovations. In this light, builders may be expected by potential clients to be more interested in recommending a renovation he can perform rather than a renovation that a builder specialised in another area can perform. People may feel that an impartial energy adviser will give them the neutral overview they need.

Literature on the role of the energy advisers also indicates that impartiality is considered more valuable than working for a profit motive because it gives homeowners a sense of trustworthiness (Rogers 2003; Mahapatra et al. 2011a). Trust in this context is to be understood not just as a state of mind, but as an inter-subjective process with a relational quality (Möllering 2001; Jimenez 2011). Trust is knowledge- and competence-based (Lewicki and Bunker 1996), which means that the energy adviser creates trust through the robust knowledge and expertise that he delivers. However, people will always interpret his knowledge and expertise according to their reality and experiences (Möllering 2001; Jimenez 2011). Conveying the right technical knowledge about the house is therefore not always convincing enough to the families, but requires an understanding of their particular way of living in the house. This aspect of the motivation of the private households is clarified later in this chapter.

Also, the personality of the energy adviser plays an important role. Being an energy adviser is considered a service trade, which means that their behaviour, emotions and attitudes affect service quality (Wilson and Frimpong 2004). The homeowners can be seen as customers who meet the energy adviser with pre-established expectations regarding service quality; if these expectations are not met, homeowners are more likely to feel that the service they received was insufficient (Schneider and White 2004). Besides hiring a builder who exhibits a pleasant demeanour, homeowners tend to want an energy advisor who has both good communication and technical skills. These are also the skills that the energy advisers themselves point out as important for fulfilling their role (Mahapatra *et al.* 2011b).

What is important to note is that although there will always be a suspicion that a builder will be biased when working as an energy adviser, his knowledge, experience and personality can create credibility, and help him convince his potential client that he is interested in investing in certain energy renovations.

Credibility, like impartiality, can generate trust. Many families choose to talk to a builder who has been recommended by neighbours and friends; in these cases, the families are predisposed to trust the builder from the very beginning of their business relationship. Certain builders also manage to create a trustworthy relationship with the homeowners because of their personality traits and convincing nature. This was the case in the ESCO-light project, where one builder performed half of the total energy advice and energy renovation in the project because he was extremely good at promoting himself. One of his strategies was to offer two bottles of wine to any family he visited as an energy adviser. This gesture, along with his personality, helped create a close and trustworthy relationship with the homeowners.

Impartiality and/or credibility are therefore important values in a good energy adviser. Impartiality refers to the energy adviser who is not biased by economic interests, while credibility refers to the energy adviser who, although representing a building company, nevertheless manages through his personality to be convincing. Both impartiality and credibility are based on trust that is achieved by conveying knowledge, information, competence and expertise.

Financing

Money is a powerful incentive in environmental management (Perman *et al.* 2003; Millard 2012). In the projects described above, the payback time and the money saved are the most important arguments used by energy advisers and builders to convince people to invest in energy renovation. Converting the number of kWh a family can save on an energy renovation into a sum of money in order to make the economic benefits as visible as possible makes a renovation project more understandable and attractive to people.

Most energy renovation projects are economically advantageous, but vary in payback time. For example, changing an old electric bulb with a low-energy bulb will usually pay back in one or two years. Most people can afford this purchase on the spot, while investing in a solar panel system may require a loan and take up to ten years to pay back.

However, banks require a guarantee that the money borrowed is invested reasonably and will be repaid in time. The problem is that energy consumption in private households varies a good deal, and energy savings are difficult to use as a loan guarantee. Consequently, until recently, most banks had no specific product to finance private energy renovation. Both ESCO-light and ZEROhome approached local banks to help overcome this problem. Since then, local banks have sent some of their employees for training on energy renovation and devised new products specifically adapted to finance energy renovation.

Subsidies can also help trigger new energy renovations. Because local energy companies are required by the state to realise consequent energy savings and are interested in buying the energy savings realised in private households, this constitutes a new type of subsidy that depends on the size of the renovation projects and can amount to between 500 DKK (67 Euros) for medium-sized investments and 5,000 DKK (672 Euros) for the biggest projects. Whilst this subsidy represents only 1 or 2 per cent of the total cost, it nevertheless generates a certain amount of interest among potential renovation clients.

Moreover, with time and increasing pressure on energy companies to save on energy, there is the hope that the price paid for each kWh saved (between 0.20 and 0.25 DKK, or 0.03 Euro, in 2012) will increase and become a real incentive for renovating. To give an idea of the impact that a higher price may have, ESCO-light decided to buy the first 100,000 kWh saved at a price of 1 DKK (0.13 Euro) per kWh in order to speed up the launching of the project. The first 100,000 kWh were saved within three weeks, even before all neighbourhoods in the municipality had been made aware of this possibility (which created frustration among those who were informed too late). Subsequent kWh were bought at the price of 0.24 DKK (0.03 Euro), but the pace of energy renovation was then much slower than when the subsidy was four times higher.

Few people know about the possibility of their selling their energy savings to energy companies – even fewer know how to do it. Public–private partnership projects can play an important role in informing citizens about this opportunity, and in bridging the gap between them and energy companies. The ESCO-light model provides the easiest process for people to sell their energy savings – in fact, this process is an important goal of the project. In this model, the builders, after receiving appropriate training, calculate the energy savings and work as administrative mediators between their clients and energy companies. The builders who have been trained in calculating energy savings have an advantage over their competitors who are unable to facilitate the same subsidy to clients.

The ESCO-light model has advantages for all actors. The energy company outsources the administrative cost of calculating energy savings and checking that they have been correctly realised to builders. Builders are able to propose a new subsidy to their client, which can help them gain more contracts. Private individuals can apply the subsidy to their energy renovation costs. And municipalities reduce CO_2 emissions and can document that they have created new green jobs.

In ZEROhome, it is the energy advisor (employed by the local energy company) who encourages people to sell their energy savings directly to the energy company and who offers to help with the application. Energy companies are making it increasingly easier for individuals to sell their energy savings, but this possibility is still largely ignored by the general population. This means that builders and energy advisers can still benefit from their position as middlemen as more people become aware of this possibility in the future.

Project evaluations

All projects need to be evaluated, but measuring the impact in terms of number of jobs created or tons of CO_2 saved is not an easy task (see Strobel *et al.* in Chapter 2 of this book). When evaluating such projects, 'additionality' is a key concept. What project leaders need to demonstrate in order to justify their budget and actions is not so much how much was achieved during the time frame of the project but, more importantly, how much was achieved that would not have been achieved without the project. In other words, how much did the project 'add' to the process when compared to normal practices? Additionality can best be measured when compared to a base-line measured prior to the renovation project, but this is rather difficult to establish. Instead, these projects often measure their success by recording how many renovation projects have been completed *after* the visit of one of the project's energy advisers, and how much money was spent and how many jobs have been created by the project.

For example, the ZEROhome project reports that its energy adviser has visited 1,109 families, of whom 61 per cent have made an energy renovation of their house for an average price of 153,000 DKK (20,567 Euros). The total price of energy investments for all these houses is 103 million DKK (13.85 million Euros). The ESCO-light project can document that its builders have realised energy renovations that led to a savings of more than one million kWh in a year.

However, this method of evaluating projects is problematic. First, it does not take all incentives into account. For example, much of the energy renovation claimed by ZEROhome consists of the installation of solar-panels that were generously subsidised by the state during the project period. These subsidies have been drastically reduced by the state since then, which led to a drop in energy renovation projects as measured by the project.

Second, people requesting a visit by an energy adviser are often people who have already decided to invest in energy renovations and who want advice on the best way to do it. Many of these people would probably renovate their house anyway, with or without the visit of an energy adviser from the project. For example, a telephone survey was conducted by our research team of the people recorded as having received the visit of a builder/energy adviser from ESCO-light and having subsequently conducted an energy renovation. A total of 80 per cent of survey respondents declared that they had not heard about ESCO-Light and would have invested in energy renovations anyway, whilst only 20 per cent declared that they contacted their construction worker specifically in order to benefit from ESCO-Light's conditions.

In May 2013, GBG claimed to have triggered energy renovations in 1,250 houses for a total of 90 million DKK (12.1 million Euros), saving between 1800 and 3600 tons of CO_2 and creating an estimated 150 jobs (COWI 2013). Although the method used to evaluate these numbers is not well-documented, GBG also used data provided by Statistics Denmark (the central ministerial authority on Danish statistics), and compared the business levels of the builders trained and involved in GBG with the business levels of other builders working in the same municipality. This compilation demonstrated that the business of GBG builders improved by 29 per cent on average between 2010 and 2012, at a time when the building sector was severely hit by the global financial crisis and was stagnating. This difference accounts for the direct creation of 90 new full-time jobs in that period which, although below the 150 jobs announced in the COWI report, is a significant achievement.

Of course, one can wonder whether the 29 per cent increase in business is a consequence of the builders' participation in GBG, or whether the participation of these builders in GBG was a consequence of their success prior to the GBG project. Certainly builders' business levels are not just linked to energy renovation. But the point we wish to make here is that evaluations require good base-lines.

Individual versus community approaches

Changes in environmental behaviour can be addressed either individually or collectively, and the approaches taken can lead to very different results (Gausset 2013). A focus on individual choices generally relies on transferring knowledge, raising awareness and using economic (dis)incentives (see e.g. Ajzen 1991; Godin and Kok 1995; Armitage and Conner 2001; Kollmuss and Agyeman 2002; Marteau et al. 2009). This approach is described as the 'ABC model' (Attitude, Behaviour and Choice, see Shove 2009). A focus on collective action, on the other hand, appeals to norms, values, social compliance and collaboration (Schwartz 1977; Dunlap and van Liere 1978; Cialdini et al. 1990; Stern et al. 1995; Hoffmann and High-Pippert 2010). While individual approaches resonate with egoistic motives to improve one's own livelihood and well-being, collective approaches appeal to people's morale and consciences, their will to do good not just for themselves but for others and their will to conform to social expectations.

Both ZEROhome and ESCO-Light addressed energy renovation at the level of households. They relied on relatively classic individual approaches based on increasing knowledge and awareness (through the visit of energy advisers) and economic incentives (in the form of subsidies or future energy savings). There is, however, an increasing recognition of the limits of these individual approaches, and of the need to address behaviour change through groups (Shove 2009; Hoffmann and High-Pippert 2010). *Community* is slowly emerging as a new trend in promoting energy-friendly behaviour, but very few programmes work with such an approach, as experience is still lacking in the area, and the success of the approach varies from case to case (Walker 2011). MyClimatePlan is a good example of such a collective approach.

By the simple fact that it only helps groups of a minimum of 10 households, MyClimatePlan triggered a social dynamic: neighbours talked to one another. According to our interviews, MyClimatePlan did succeed in reaching some 'environmental sceptics' who were convinced by their neighbours to join the group and invest in energy renovation. People can be drawn into a project not because of a particular interest in the specific project, but because of the influence of a network of friends or acquaintances. Recruitment into community energy programmes can be more successful when conducted through a network of personal contacts and neighbourly relations rather than by reading adverts placed in newspapers (Verba *et al.* 1995; Hoffmann and High-Pippert 2010; Mahapatra *et al.* 2011a; Tjørring 2013). Instead of being confined within the four walls of the individual household, a collective approach can promote the issue of energy renovation through social networks, where it can reach people who are normally immune to adverts in the traditional media.

It is also easier and less time-consuming to be part of a group, since the bulk of the administration is usually done by a few enthusiasts for the benefit of the group. It is also less risky to conduct energy renovation as a member of a group. Housing renovation often represents heavy investments and long and sometimes disruptive building processes in which many things can (and do) go wrong. Many frightening stories of incompetent builders circulate, e.g. of builders who sometimes go bankrupt in the middle of a project, which can be a major obstacle to energy renovation. Renovating one's house as part of a larger group that is using the same builder gives more power leverage and more security to the individual household. It also has the advantage of speeding up the renovations because it forces people to move at the same pace as others if they want to benefit from group reductions and do not want to be left to deal with their renovation project on their own. On the downside, however, the pressure to use the same builder to renovate 10 houses can generate some frustration when the builder chosen by the group does not enjoy the full confidence of all members of the group.

But community approaches are more complex than individual approaches, and can also fail. For example, the ZEROhome project also experimented with addressing communities. The energy adviser made contact with a village and arranged for several households to receive communal energy advising at only one house. All people met in the selected house and were taught energy renovation, using the host's house as an example. The plan was that the participants could serve afterwards as energy advisers for the rest of the village and would go from door-to-door to convince people to invest in energy renovations.

However, in practice, participants did not feel well-equipped to serve as energy advisers for other families; nor did they feel they had the time to do so. People in the village also felt it was more of a burden than an advantage to take part in the project. Another important aspect is that such projects rely heavily on a few local passionate participants who volunteer time and energy (Verba *et al.* 1995; Hoffmann and High-Pippert 2010). An important lesson to be learnt in this regard is that community approaches do not automatically equal success – they require hard work.

This was also the case in the MyClimatePlan project, where one or two locals ended up doing most of the work of spreading the word and motivating neighbours and friends to join the collective energy renovation project. Whilst community approaches can be an effective tool to reach environmental sceptics or people who are immune to individual approaches, they are also more complex: their success depends on the way they are designed and whether they take the local context into account.

Motivation of private households – the issue of 'comfort'

When communicating with the private households, the energy advisers usually stress two main motivational factors: money and comfort. The argument is that people in the long run can save money on an energy renovation and enjoy a more comfortable house. It is well-known that there are good economic incentives to investing in energy renovations, and the energy advisers tend to focus on this aspect when communicating with people. They tend to place all other incentives under the umbrella of 'comfort', including having a warmer house or the healthy effects of a new and more effective ventilation system.

Yet, our qualitative interviews with homeowners indicate that this very broad concept of comfort and people's perceptions of home have a strong influence on their decisions on energy renovations. A house is not just a shell protecting us from the cold outside, but a home in which our lives unfold; it is where we engage in activities and in our relationships (Ingold 2000). When buying a house, we do not just look at the technical quality of the walls, the windows and the kitchen. Rather, we imagine how our life is going to be expressed in the house, what we can do in the different rooms and in what way the house facilitates our social life.

An illustration of this is found in one of our cases, in which a family debated whether they should invest in cavity wall insulation (insulation of the gap inside the outer wall, which is often found in older houses) or a new front door. The energy adviser advised them that the wisest decision economically would be to choose cavity wall insulation because the payback time was very short and they would save a lot of money on their energy bill.

However, the family kept focusing on the need to change the front door because they constantly felt a draught. The family ended up choosing to replace the door instead of insulating the walls, and most energy advisers would tend to label this decision 'for comfort reasons'. However, complex perceptions of life and home are hidden behind this label. It was not just a matter of being affected by the constant draught from the door (in fact, the draught could be considered minimal because the door was in a hallway that people just passed through). It was also about the door being a central entrance point to the house that did not 'look good'. In other words, the door's lack of aesthetics did not match the family's idea of what a nice home should look like and what they felt good about showing the neighbours. This was a matter of constant visibility. When walking in and out of the door, the homeowners were constantly reminded of it: the door was automatically more visible in their minds than cavity wall insulation.

Another important aspect of understanding comfort is that a family is not a homogenous unit: it consists of different family members with different attitudes about their home and different practices within the home. Some rooms are used more than others and, depending on the individual, different values are given to different aspects of the house. For example, family members who spend a lot of time cooking tend to prioritise renovating the kitchen over others, while garden enthusiasts tend to value putting time, money and effort into the land surrounding the house.

There are interesting differences between how men and women use and prioritise the house. Many popular articles about the matter (such as Bolius 2013, among others) claim that men are more involved in maintenance, repair work and measuring and paying for utilities in the house, while women are more involved in interior design and shopping for the house. This classic division of labour is also reflected in our fieldwork findings: men are associated with the technical aspects of the house, while women are associated with 'creating the sense of home'.

For example, a lot of women resist installing energy-saving light bulbs in the home because they are very concerned about the quality of the light, or resist turning down the underfloor heating in the bathroom because it affects their perception of what a nice bathroom is. In general, energy advising projects tend to focus mainly on the technical aspects of the house. Most energy advisers are men, as are builders or engineers, which are male-dominated professions that focus on technical matters. As a consequence, the language spoken during an energy adviser's visit is directed largely at men and is expected by the families to be directed at men, for which reason the man is usually the person who meets the energy adviser in the home. Insight into the way women think and act in the house is usually lacking.

Comfort and perceptions of home are also closely tied to the different phases of life people go through. People tend to be more prone to investing in energy renovations when they are already planning to do something about the house. Wanting to change the house often happens along with important landmarks in the course of people's lifetimes, including marriage, divorce, moving to another house, having children or when children move away from home. These are significant moments that are often followed by a desire to change one's current or future home. For example, when marrying and moving into a new house, a couple often feels the urge to make the house *their home* by rebuilding rooms, changing the garden or putting in a new kitchen.

This knowledge about people's lives creates obvious opportunities to promote energy renovations that fit into people's ways of life. None of the energy advisers in any of the projects described above seem to include these considerations about the meaning of comfort and life in their work. However, the aforementioned communication skills that energy advisers wish to develop might refer precisely to this: the need to better understand the way people in private households live their lives and at what times they are particularly apt to make changes and invest in their homes. Such insights make it possible to talk the language of the home-owners and spur more energy renovations.

Conclusion

In the comparison of the different projects of energy renovation, five aspects appeared as important focal points for discussion, i.e. topics that all the energy renovation projects address in designing their projects. These topics are the role of the energy adviser, financing issues, project evaluation, individual vs. community approaches and motivations of the individual households. The projects differed from each other in the way they approached these different topics. There is, of course, no simple answer as to what works best, but it has been shown that impartiality and credibility are important values in an energy adviser, that economic incentives can trigger renovations, that projects need to be evaluated with sound base-lines and that community approaches have the great advantage of reaching sceptics and making energy renovations 'talked about'.

What is not made explicit in any of the energy renovation models, but nevertheless seems to hover beneath the surface, is the value of empathy, which is understood as the capacity to put oneself in another person's place. There seems to be a gap between what the energy advisers think people want and what people really want. Energy advisers tend to approach people's houses as mere technical constructions and focus on the financial benefits of energy renovation instead of focusing on peoples' houses as *homes*. The commonly used concept of comfort is used to cover this 'soft value'.

However, such labelling reduces more than it enhances the huge potential that lies in unfolding the concept of comfort and focusing on gaining insight into people's lives and perceptions of home. If we place more focus on the energy adviser's capacity for empathy, we place him or her in the midst of the homeowners' lives and not as an external expert on the house who merely views the house as a technical construct. This empathy makes it possible for the energy adviser to talk the language of the homeowners. It is also the strength we find in the community approaches, because neighbours generally have better insights into each other's lives and can talk directly to the needs of a person. Energy renovation projects would gain much by focusing more on the lives lived within the buildings to be renovated, and by talking more about *homes* rather than about houses.

There are, of course, various actors at play in the challenge of increasing the number of energy renovations in the private housing stock. On the one hand, there are the citizens who own the houses, and on the other hand are the energy companies, builders and political authorities, who have their own particular interest in motivating people to make energy renovations to their private houses. These actors play an important role as facilitators of the process. Citizens influence and are influenced by their surroundings, and the energy companies, builders and political authorities can and do actively engage in promoting energy renovations in private households.

However, the energy companies, builders and political authorities often focus on *influencing* citizens to make an energy renovation rather than *being influenced by* citizens and letting that be the starting point for promoting energy renovations. This would require focusing on understanding citizens' daily lives and promoting solutions that are in touch with homeowners' daily practices and their own understanding their home, so that making an energy renovation becomes an easier choice than not making an energy renovation.

Acknowledgements

We are grateful to all the employees at ZEROhome, MyClimatePlan, ESCO-Light and Green Business Growth for providing us with information about the projects and for facilitating our field work. We would also like to thank all project participants who welcomed us into their homes and shared their insights with us.

References

Ajzen I (1991) The Theory of Planned Behavior, *Organizational Behavior and Human Decision Processes* 50 179–211.

Armitage C and Conner M (2001) Efficacy of the Theory of Planned Behaviour: A Meta-Analytic Review, *British Journal of Social Psychology* 40 471–499.

Bolius   (2013)   (www.bolius.dk/alt-om/boliglaan-og-oekonomi/artikel/maendene-bestemmer-over-boliglaanet/) Accessed 22 May 2013.

Cialdini R, Reno R and Kallgren C (1990) A Focus Theory of Normative Conduct: Recycling the concept of norms to littering in public places, *Journal of Personality and Social Psychology* 58 749–758.

COWI (2013) *Grøn Erhvervsvækst Slutevaluering* [Green Business Growth Final Evaluation Report], Project Number A037714–003.

Danish Energy Agency (2012) (www.ens.dk/sites/ens.dk/files/info/tal-kort/statistik-noegletal/aarlig-energistatistik/energistatistik2012.pdf) Accessed 19 March 2014.

Danish Ministry of Climate, Energy and Building (2011) *Energistrategi 2050 – fra kul, olie og gas til grøn energi*, Klima-og Energiministeriet, Copenhagen.

Dunlap R and Van Liere K (1978) The New Environmental Paradigm: A Proposed Measuring Instrument and Preliminary Results, *Journal of Environmental Education* 9 10–19.

Energispareaftale (2012) (www.danskenergi.dk/Holdning/Energieffektivitet/Aftale.aspx) Accessed 22 January 2015.

Gausset Q (2013) Comparing Different Approaches to Addressing Environmental Behavioural Change: A Review of Ten Case Studies from Denmark, *Transdiciplinary Environmental Studies* 12 (1) 30–40.

Godin G and Kok G (1995) The Theory of Planned Behavior: A Review of Its Applications to Health-Related Behaviors, *American Journal of Health Promotion* 11 87–98.

Hoff J and Strobel B (2013) A Municipal 'Climate Revolution'? The Shaping of Municipal Climate Change Policies, *The Journal of Transdisciplinary Environmental Studies* 12(1) 3–14.

Hoffman S M and High-Pippert A (2010) From Private Lives to Collective Action: Recruitment and Participation Incentives for a Community Energy Program, *Energy Policy* 38 7567–7574.

Ingold T (2000) *The Perception of the Environment: Essays in Livelihood, Dwelling and Skill* Routledge, London.

Jimenez A C (2011) Trust in Anthropology, *Anthropological Theory* 11 177–196.

Kollmuss A and Agyeman J (2002) Mind the Gap: Why Do People Act Environmentally and What Are the Barriers to Pro-Environmental Behavior? *Environmental Education Research* 8(3) 239–260.

Lewicki R J and Bunker B B (1996) Developing and Maintaining Trust in Work Relationships, in Kramer R M and Tyler T R (eds) *Trust in Organizations*, Sage, Thousand Oaks, CA, 114–139.

Mahapatra K, Nair G and Gustavsson L (2011a) Energy Advice Service as Perceived by Swedish Homeowners, *International Journal of Consumer Studies* 35 104–111.

Mahapatra K, Nair G and Gustavsson L (2011b) Swedish Energy Advisers' Perceptions Regarding and Suggestions for Fulfilling Homeowner Expectations, *Energy Policy* 39 4264–4273.

Marteau T M, Ashcroft R E and Oliver A (2009) Using Financial Incentives to Achieve Healthy Behaviour, *BMJ* 338 983–985.

Millard M (2012) *Environmental Economics*, World Technologies, Delhi, India.

Möllering G (2001) The Nature of Trust: From Georg Simmel to a Theory of Expectation, Interpretation and Suspension, *Sociology* 35(2) 403–420.

Perman R M Y, McGilvray J and Common M (2003) *Natural Resources and Environmental Economics*, Pearson Education, Edinburgh, UK.

ProjectZero (2013) (www.projectzero.dk/da-DK/Artikler/2013/Marts/Regeringens-klima-n%C3%B8l-koster-arbejdspladser.aspx) Accessed 5 January 2015.

Rogers E M (2003) *Diffusion of Innovations*, The Free Press, New York.

Schneider B and White S (2004) *Service Quality: Research Perspectives*, Sage, Thousand Oaks, CA.

Schwartz S (1977) Normative Influences on Altruism, *Advances in Experimental Social Psychology* 10 222–279.

Shove E (2009) Beyond the ABC: Climate Change Policy and Theories of Social Change, *Environment and Planning* 42 1273–1285.

Stern P, Dietz T and Guagnano G (1995) The New Ecological Paradigm in Social-Psychological Context, *Environment and Behavior* 27(5) 723–743.

Tjørring L (2013) The Power of Practice and Community: A Case Study of Environmental Living in El Bolson, Argentina, *Transdiciplinary Environmental Studies* 12(1) 41–52.

Verba S, Schlozman K L and Brady H E (1995) *Voice and Equality: Civic Voluntarism in American Politics*, Harvard University Press, Cambridge MA.

Walker G (2011) The Role for Community in Carbon Governance, *Wiley Interdisciplinary Reviews Climate Change* 2(5) 777–782.

Wilson A and Frimpong J (2004) A Reconceptualisation of the Satisfaction-Service Performance Thesis, *Journal of Social Marketing* 18 471–481.

7 Climate ambassador programmes in municipalities

Encouraging climate change mitigation in public administrations and institutions

Michael Søgaard Jørgensen and
Stine Rahbek Pedersen

Introduction

This chapter discusses environmental and climate ambassador programmes that some Danish municipalities have instituted in order to strengthen environmental and climate change mitigation efforts in local public institutions and administrations. These programmes are part of local efforts to achieve national and local environmental and climate objectives through local energy-saving activities, investments in renewable energy technology and improved waste management, among others. An ambassador programme is typically organised around a steering committee, a central coordinator and ambassadors in various municipal departments and institutions who are responsible for initiating local environmental and climate change mitigation activities. The following section provides an overview of the distribution of tasks within public administration and services in Denmark as background for the analyses.

Public administration and services in Denmark

Denmark has three main administrative levels – state, region and municipality – and is organised into five regions and 98 municipalities. The Danish Constitution stipulates that some areas of public responsibility be allocated to local governments. The Danish Parliament, Folketinget, decides which specific responsibilities should be allocated to municipalities. Performance of these responsibilities by the municipalities is subject to state supervision.

The 1968 Local Government Act specifies that the affairs of a municipality be managed by the local council, which implies that management of and responsibility for the entire organisation of the municipality rest with the local council. The Act also devolves a number of powers to the local council, including the adoption of the annual budget and annual accounts. Every municipality as an administrative unit is normally divided into different areas, including technical, social service and healthcare and tax administrations (Ministry of Economic Affairs and the Interior 2014).

At the national level, Folketinget makes both overall decisions about environmental and energy policy and passes laws, while the ministries are responsible for the implementation. Major responsibilities at the regional level include hospital service, psychiatry and the National Health Service. The regions also have responsibilities in the areas of regional development, including soil pollution, and planning of quarrying of gravel and sand, and of regional public transport.

Municipalities handle many different areas of public service, including the institutions of child day-care, eldercare, public schools and libraries. Furthermore, they have responsibilities related to transport, the environment and utility services. This includes responsibility for the local road network, participation in regional transport companies, nature, environment and land use planning, the utility sector (which is partly-privatised), emergency services and local business services (Ministry of Economic Affairs and the Interior 2014). Municipal annual budgets are determined by local negotiations, the municipal tax payment, national economic redistribution among municipalities and negotiations between the national government and the national association of Danish municipalities, Local Government Denmark, about the level of local taxation and investments.

The state attends to general nature and environmental tasks, including establishing the rules for land use approvals and supervision of activities that pollute. Local governments approve and supervise local business activities and their environmental impacts, and prepare local planning for wastewater, waste and water supply. Furthermore, the municipalities are responsible for the protection of groundwater, nature and the environment. Municipalities traditionally undertook the delivery of utility services, e.g. water, heating and solid waste collection and disposal, which are primarily user-financed. In recent years, however, utility companies have been sold or established as independent companies. The supply of electricity and water and the handling of wastewater have been privatised by state statute (Ministry of Economic Affairs and the Interior 2014).

Each of the 98 municipalities is required to develop a 12-year municipal plan for land use, energy supply, employment and housing, among others. In the first half of the 4-year local election period, each municipal council must adopt a political strategy for municipal planning and decide whether and how the municipal plan will be revised (Danish Ministry of the Environment 2007). According to an amendment in 2000 of the 1992 Danish Planning Act, the municipal councils must also within the first half of the 4-year election period publish a report on their strategy for contributions to sustainable development, a so-called Local Agenda 21 strategy (Danish Ministry of the Environment 2007). The strategy should address the issues highlighted in the Agenda 21 document agreed upon at the 1992 Rio Summit's (United Nations Conference on Environment and Development 1992). The Local Agenda 21 strategy must include local political objectives for contributions to reduction of the environmental impacts of the municipality's activities, and of local citizens' and businesses' activities (Danish Ministry of the Environment 2007). Furthermore, the municipality must describe how they will involve citizens and businesses in environmental decisions and how they will ensure the integration of environmental, social and economic concerns into municipal decisions (Danish Society for Nature Conservation 2014).

What is an environmental and climate ambassador programme?

An environmental or climate ambassador programme is typically organised around a steering committee, a central coordinator and local ambassadors who are located in the various municipal departments and institutions and responsible for initiating activities within their respective departments and institutions. An ambassador on climate and/or the environment is mandated to bring environmental and climate issues forward to colleagues and users of the public institution (including citizens), and initiate activities that reduce negative impacts on the environment and climate.

The first municipal programme that used the term 'climate ambassador' was developed in the municipality of Hvidovre in 2008 and focused on initiating climate efforts in its public institutions and administration. The term 'ambassador' – with reference to the use of the word in the sphere of foreign affairs – connotes that the position serves the interests of the environment or climate concerns, just as a Danish ambassador posted in another country is supposed to serve the interests of Denmark. The ambassador term has also been used in relation to environmental efforts in the UK directed towards citizens in a specific project (Hall and Bassot 2009) and in a peer education programme intended to integrate sustainability issues into university curricula (Hopkinson *et al.* 2009). Another often-used term for a coordinating role in systematic internal environmental activities in public institutions is 'environmental coordinator' (Zutshi *et al.* 2008; Emilsson and Hjelm 2009).

An ambassador programme can be understood as a social technology by which civil servants of a municipality advocate for environmental and/or climate concerns and represent these interests, taking as a starting point the activities and conditions of the specific institution. At the same time, an ambassador should be able to create a commitment from colleagues and sometimes also from the users of the institution that helps to engage them in local efforts to reduce climate and/or environmental impacts.

Some of the most competent ambassadors are able to get results without the support of the central coordinator; for example, when an ambassador successfully motivates colleagues and users to adopt environmentally friendly practices and the local consumption of electricity, water and heat thereby is reduced, or when they successfully motivate colleagues and users to adopt environmentally friendly mobility practices such as cycling. Often the ambassadors get help from the central coordinator of the programme. The ambassador is supposed to convey the ideas for environmental and climate change mitigation projects to the central coordinator in a way that makes the coordinator understand the ambassador's workplace so as to jointly design efforts that suits the individual institution.

As social technology, ambassador programmes address the local institution as a socio-political community. The programme can imply changing some of the structures and mechanisms of the local government, including the development and implementation of action plans and changes in the mechanisms for the payment of energy and other resources and allocation of cost savings from resource savings.

Based on the experiences of environmental and climate ambassador programmes in the Danish municipalities of Furesø, Lyngby-Taarbæk, Frederiksberg and Hvidovre, this chapter discusses and analyses the roles and impacts of such programmes. This analysis also demonstrates that differences among these programmes are related to:

- Whether the focus of the ambassador programme is limited to climate impact or focuses on several sustainability fields such as climate, water and waste;
- How formalised the programme is;
- What role the managers in the local institutions have in the programme;
- What networking takes place among the ambassadors; and
- Whether and how the users of the institutions, e.g. schoolchildren and users of sport facilities, are involved in the climate mitigation activities.

Theoretical and methodological approaches

The analysis of ambassador programmes is inspired by theories about professionals as 'political reflective navigators' (Broberg and Hermund 2004), communicative action and structural transformation of the public sphere (Habermas 2002, 2004) and Oscar Negt's ideas about collective learning from everyday activities (as described in Weber *et al.* 1997).

Broberg's and Hermund's (2004) concept of the political reflective navigator was developed to characterise the work of consultants and coordinators within the field of the occupational health and safety when such actors pursue a health and safety agenda inside an organisation. These scholars recognised that such consultants and coordinators have to have different roles and switch between these roles during an occupational health and safety project. At the same time, the concept can be seen as a third alternative to the dichotomy between professional experts providing solutions and process consultants helping others to help themselves in solving their own problems. We have adapted Broberg's and Hermund's concept to the environmental field in order to cover the following four different skills, or competencies, that are necessary for people engaged in pursuing an environmental agenda within an organisation (Pedersen and Jørgensen 2012):

- *Ability to support the establishment of political programmes on the environment:* This is the ability to establish or support a process to integrate environmental aspects into decision making. Such a programme might compete with other political programmes, e.g. those concerning productivity, efficiency or quality.

- *Ability to navigate in organisations*: This is the ability to identify decision makers and other influential actors who can support the programme politically.
- *Ability to understand and mediate between different professions*: This is the ability to mediate between different actors and their professional knowledge, language and concepts.
- *Ability to move between different roles and mobilise different types of knowledge*: This involves the ability to understand the context of the organisation and which methods and type of knowledge will perform best in different phases and situations. It may be necessary to adopt both facilitation and expert roles.

A combination of Habermas's idealism and Negt's realism inform our understanding of ambassadors' and coordinators' activities and conditions within the municipal ambassador programmes. Habermas's ideal for societal development is the development of public spheres between state and citizens where dialogues *as communicative action* create common understanding within areas where participants recognise common obligations (Habermas 2002, 2004). By contrast, Negt does not see any public spheres associated with communicative action and highlights the need for bottom-up learning processes based on everyday experiences. Negt also stresses that only through collective learning from everyday experiences is it possible to imagine social changes, i.e. concrete problems need to be unfolded from everyday experience into an expression of basic social conflicts (Weber *et al.* 1997).

The empirical material for this chapter is different types of public documents and earlier analyses of the four environmental and climate ambassador programmes, and interviews and meetings with coordinators and ambassadors from the municipalities. An interview guide was developed for three-hour, semi-structured interviews with the coordinators. Subsequently, some ambassadors were invited to an inter-municipal workshop for Furesø and Lyngby-Taarbæk, where ambassadors exchanged experiences and discussed their work. Each group at the workshop appointed a chairperson to record the minutes of the discussions. Based on the interview, the workshop and available written materials, a case description and analysis was completed for each of the four programmes within their individual municipal contexts. A draft of our analysis was reviewed by each local coordinator.

Overview of the ambassador programmes

Table 7.1 provides an overall description of the four ambassador programmes with respect to the coordinators' positions in the organisation, the organisational anchoring of the programmes in the respective local administrations, the background and focus of the programmes and their important tools and activities.

Table 7.1 Overview of the four municipal ambassador programmes with respect to background and focus, organisational structures and elements

	Organisation of the four municipal ambassador schemes			
	Lyngby-Taarbæk	Frederiksberg	Hvidovre	Furesø
The background and the focus	Climate municipality – focus on municipal activities. Main focus on energy	Climate municipality – focus on municipal activities. Main focus on resource consumption	Climate municipality – focus on municipal activities. Main focus on energy	Climate municipality – focus on municipal activities and on the municipality as geographical area. Broad environmental focus
Coordinators' organisational positions	Three people: the Agenda 21 coordinator and two from Energy Group in Technical Division	Agenda 21 employee is project manager, based in the Environmental Department	Coordinator part of Environmental Department until 2010, supported by the Technical Department; after 2010 informal coordinator from Building Department.	Coordinator employed in Nature and Environmental Department
The anchoring of the programme in the municipal organisation	Management group. Participation from Technical Division, School and Sport Department, and a day-care manager	Coordination group. Participation from Environmental Department, Estate Office, and Children and Youth Department	Working group at the level of the municipal administration	Permanent management group. Participation from all administrative areas. Support from Building Service manager
Elements of the programme	Informal programme based on technical staff and local managers. Developed through 30-year focus on energy consumption. 50 local ambassadors. Smileys based on monthly consumption. Local visits from central technician. Workshop every three years. Municipal fund for energy upgrading. Awareness campaign	Formal programme, 120 climate ambassadors. Initial focus on day-care institutions (staff, children, parents). Resource consumption mapping. Dialogue about local action plan. Integration into educational plans	Informal programme, 90 climate ambassadors. Focus on buildings and user practices. Two technicians support the local institutions. Loans to local institutions for energy upgrading	Formal programme, 80 local environment and climate ambassadors, mostly managers. Small fund for environmental initiatives. Municipal funding for energy upgrading

Sources: Pedersen and Jørgensen 2012; Furesø Kommune 2014a; Frederiksberg Kommune 2013; Hvidovre Kommune 2013.

More details can be found in Pedersen and Jørgensen (2012) and the following section.

Political context and organisational structures of the ambassador programmes

This section describes the local political context and background of each of the four ambassador programmes. It also describes the organisational structures, important tools and mechanisms and the impacts of each of the four programmes. The descriptions and analyses of the programmes are based on Pedersen and Jørgensen (2012) and are combined with local reports as mentioned in each section.

The Furesø ambassador programme

The Furesø Municipality's environment and climate ambassador programme is anchored in the municipal Agenda 21 Action Plan 2009, which generally describes the concept and practice of ambassador programmes. It is also anchored in the municipal Climate Plan 2010–2012. The ambassadors have influenced the development of the municipal Environment and Climate Policy 2014 drawn up in 2013. They have participated in a workshop about the policy and they have contributed with a response that was included in the consultation documents together with a contribution from the local Agenda 21 Association.

Furesø's Steering Committee for their programme was established in 2010 and consists of the heads of the administrations of Culture and Recreation, Schools and Leisure and Eldercare. Steering Committee members have the overall responsibility for activities within their respective areas in the municipality. The Committee includes three additional members – the operations and construction manager, building service manager and the manager of the Nature and Environment Department (who is the chairman of the Committee). The coordinator of the programme cooperates with these three members on a day-to-day basis. The Steering Committee decided that the ambassador programme should focus on climate-friendly behaviour; if ambassadors wish to do more, they can create nature, environment and climate projects that make sense in the individual workplaces. The Steering Committee also decided that the heads of each institution – e.g. kindergarten, school or culture house – must take on the role of local environmental and climate ambassador. However, the local manager might appoint a local employee as the local ambassador.

Contact from the coordinator of the programme to the managers of the local institutions is passed through the steering committee. The coordinator involves committee members when there is need to support the programme. Steering committee members have also instructed the environmental and climate ambassador coordinator to make presentations at management meetings about the programme and its requirements and obligations.

Furesø's programme allows the ambassadors to set their own local targets for reduction of resource consumption and to decide upon environmental activities, which implies that the ambassadors have taken ownership of the programme. This impact of such a participatory approach is confirmed by Clematide (2009), who emphasises that learning in organisations should be based on methodological freedom. Freedom of action of the ambassadors within the focus areas is also found to promote the anchorage and resilience of this top-down ambassador programme, because the ambassadors can incorporate environmental and climate activities in a way that is meaningful to them in their daily tasks.

From its inception in 2010 until 2013, Furesø's ambassadors have implemented activities that have actively involved over 25,000 employees, citizens and users in nature, environment and climate activities. These activities include:

- Focus on how children, their parents and staff ride to and from schools and kindergartens;
- School children and staff record each time they remember to turn off excess consumption of electricity, water or heat;
- Local municipal employees develop their own innovative activities, such as installing an indoor propeller under the loft in a big living room in a nursery home so that the hot air inside the room near the loft is moved downwards to the residents and staff in the room;
- All home nurses, who visit parents with babies, have replaced their cars with electric or normal bikes;
- Organic food made from seasonal ingredients has been introduced in all the local public kitchens; and
- Ambassadors have developed day-care and school kitchen gardens in cooperation with an organic farmer. The school kitchen gardens were developed in connection with the introduction of organic food in the public kitchens.

Quantitatively, the ambassadors have helped to reduce electricity consumption in buildings by 7.4 per cent during 2010, 14.2 per cent during 2011 and 6.3 per cent during 2012. This was accomplished by changing habits and without new technical solutions. In total, the Furesø Municipality reduced the carbon dioxide (CO_2) emissions from the local public activities by 28 percent from 2008 to 2012 (Furesø Kommune 2013).

The Lyngby-Taarbæk ambassador programme

There is broad support for climate action in Lyngby-Taarbæk. The environmental and climate ambassador programme is based on local political and administrative leadership. For the past 15 years, the programme's coordination group has, on an annual basis, decided what type of environmental and climate activities will be implemented in the coming year. The coordination group consists of managers from schools, sports facilities and a day-care centre, as well as the head of the Energy Group from the Buildings Department in the Technical

Division. Decisions about new projects and central support for local energy investments that are important to the local technical service managers are reported to them by the central administration through local managers.

The Lyngby-Taarbæk's organisation of the programme can be described as informal, in that the local ambassadors are not formally appointed as ambassadors. The programme grew out of a focus on resource savings and especially energy savings in municipal buildings that a coordinator in the Technical Division has overseen since the 1980s. This 'early' focus on environmental and climate change projects was the impetus for the formation of a municipal Energy Group within the Technical Division (comprised of two employees and the coordinator) and the formation of the coordination group.

The management of the Technical Division has always insisted that participation in efforts to reduce resource consumption should be voluntary. As a result, the Energy Group has used technical improvements, a 'smiley' system (an assessment of the previous month's energy consumption compared with the expected consumption with a green, yellow or red smiley) and so-called energy checks (allocation to the local institution of all or part of the cost reduction from energy savings) to encourage managers and technical service managers and employees to take responsibility as ambassadors for climate-friendly behaviour. The model in Lyngby-Taarbæk requires long and sustained facilitation from the central administration. The result is, however, a culturally rooted and robust ambassador programme where the focus on energy has not been lost, even though the energy check was not allocated to the local institutions for three years.

Often the local technical service manager will contact the central Energy Group if a 'red' smiley, which indicates higher-than-expected energy consumption, is shown by the computer-based reporting system when the service manager makes the monthly online reporting of the energy consumption. Central regulation technology has been installed in Lyngby-Taarbæk's 37 largest buildings, which enables easier surveillance of resource consumption and assessment of the monthly consumption figures compared to the expected consumption in these local institutions. Furthermore, the Department of Estate and Energy in the Technical Division has service agreements on some equipment in municipal buildings, which implies that an external company follows the consumptions and contacts the Energy Group in case of deviating performance of the equipment.

Since 2008, the informal ambassador programme has played a role in Lyngby-Taarbæk Municipality's commitment to ongoing reduction of the energy consumption as a so-called 'Climate Municipality' as part of the programme organised by the non-governmental organisation called the Danish Society for Nature Conservation (DN). (All four municipalities discussed in the chapter are members of this national Climate Municipality programme.)

There is political focus on climate at the level of Lyngby-Taarbæk's city council. Every year the council grants economic resources to pay for energy initiatives that lower resource consumption in the municipal institutions. As part of the aforementioned agreement with DN, the Council has committed to reducing municipal CO_2 emissions by an average 2 per cent annually until 2025. It also supports a local energy-saving campaign that has been carried out twice in recent years, which uses the networks of local technical service managers and local managers. From 2007–2011, CO_2 emissions from municipal energy consumption in buildings and municipal functions such as street lighting were reduced by approximately 12 per cent (Lyngby-Taarbæk Kommune 2012). This reduction was caused by both investments in new equipment and changed user practices. The first energy-saving campaign recorded a 3.6 per cent reduction of energy consumption during the campaign period compared to the consumption levels for the same period in the previous year (Theilby 2010). These activities were coordinated by the local Agenda 21 coordinator, together with the Energy Group.

The Frederiksberg ambassador programme

In City of Frederiksberg, the environmental ambassador programme appears in the municipality's Plan of Action for Sustainable Development of 2008, which calls for measures to ensure climate-friendly behaviour. This commitment was further developed in a CO_2 Action Plan 2009–2012, which was adopted in 2010. The municipality's environmental ambassador programme is seen as one of a number of initiatives that will contribute to Frederiksberg's CO_2 reduction target of 3 per cent per year (City of Frederiksberg, personal communication, 20 May 2014).

The ambassador programme was approved by the municipal administration's Executive Board and by all the municipality's political committees. Its Steering Committee is comprised of managers from the Environmental Department and Property Department and is managed by the Nature and Environment Division. The project team is comprised of employees of the Environmental Department and Property Operations. The Information Technology (IT) Department has also had an important role: the head of the IT Department has organised a scheme that involves the installation of energy-saving power boards in all 750 work stations in the city hall, making it easier at the single work station to turn off the power of all lamps and computers simultaneously.

Frederiksberg's programme began with a focus on the day-care institutions and the schools. Later on, it was expanded; today, at least one person has been appointed as environmental ambassador in each municipal property and institution. The ambassadors perform several tasks, and there are different kinds of ambassadors. So-called *technical* ambassadors register the consumption of electricity, heat and water every month. They participate in skills development and share new knowledge and experience at network meetings. They cooperate with the Frederiksberg Energy Team about optimising the operation of their facilities. So-called *behavioural* ambassadors take responsibility for climate behaviour at each workplace, and work to include climate behaviour on the agenda of each workplace. Smaller institutions combine both roles into the job description of one ambassador.

During the period of 2007–2013 the municipal institutions and administrations in Frederiksberg have reduced their CO_2 emissions by 17.2 per cent. In

2013, the reduction was 3 per cent (Frederiksberg Kommune 2014a). This reduction has been possible despite an increase in the number of institutions and the
number of users of public buildings (Frederiksberg Kommune 2014a). Such
energy savings give each institution a specific financial incentive – they are
allowed to keep the energy costs they have saved unless the savings is due to
technical improvements. Some institutions have made visible results, including,
among others, a reduction of energy consumption by optimising the ventilation
system and increased recycling. By contrast, it is difficult to see the results of the
ambassador's activities in some other institutions in Frederiksberg (City of
Frederiksberg, personal communications, 20 May 2014).

The Hvidovre ambassador programme

The municipality's climate activities began in 2001 with development of annual
'green' accounts, which report on the environmental impacts and resource
consumption of local municipal activities, and 'green' budgets for each municipal institution developed by the central municipal administration. The
municipality's ambassador programme was launched in 2008 as a follow-up to the
approval of a municipal climate plan. At that time, the programme was rooted in
the Environmental Department, where it received considerable political attention. A working group for the programme operates at the management level of
the municipal administration.

When the programme's project manager resigned his position in 2010, the
Building Department chose to continue the programme because the Department
believed it might help the Department's efforts to create more local climate-
friendly behaviour and focus on energy and resource consumption. However,
since 2010, the programme has had no specific budget and no allocated hours.

The role of climate ambassadors in Hvidovre is legitimised by the municipality's climate agenda, which is set by the local city council. The council's
announcement that Hvidovre Municipality will reduce the municipal institutions' resource consumption has support from both within the municipal
administration and among citizens. For example, if a light is left on in a municipal building after 6 p.m., citizens sometimes call to inform the Technical
Department or the local police (Pedersen and Jørgensen 2012; Hvidovre
Kommune 2013).

The position of climate ambassador in public institutions and administration
in Hvidovre is voluntary. Therefore, the ambassadors constitute a very mixed
group of managers, technical services managers and staff. When the programme
was launched, all ambassadors were offered participation in a network that
provided training in the reading of electricity, heating and water meters and
understanding their institution's technical equipment. They were also offered the
opportunity to conduct a climate review of their institution, together with a
municipal technician, in order to identify possibilities for savings through
changes in user practices and technical improvements.

Hvidovre's Building Department has earned broad political support for their efforts to reduce resource consumption through technical changes and improvement of the envelopes of public municipal buildings. There is an annual budget for building refurbishment of around 1.5 million Euros, but the Building Department does not have enough staff to initiate projects every year for the full budget (Hvidovre Kommune 2013).

The coordinator of Hvidovre's programme has the impression that the activity level among the municipality's ambassadors has decreased in recent years because the Building Department is only able to support the technical aspects of resource savings. At this time, the Department does not give advice about changes in user practices that could reduce resource consumption. Not all institutions in Hvidovre have developed procedures for reading and reporting the levels of resource consumption, and the number of climate reviews of local institutions has declined due to a reduction of the number of central technical service managers from two to one (Hvidovre Kommune 2013). The coordinator suggests that the municipality could save more resources and costs if the Building Department focused fully on technical investments for resource savings and did not spend as much time coordinating the ambassador programme. However, local budgets for electricity and heating of each institution and the possibility for retaining the saved costs locally are also seen as a potential measure for resource savings.

The coordinator organises an annual meeting for the climate ambassadors where they can exchange experiences and receive information about central municipal initiatives. Despite the lack of systematic central support for the climate ambassadors, two groups of Hvidovre's climate ambassadors have organised their own network independent of the central administration. One network covers day-care institutions and has managers, employees and technical service managers as members. Experiences are exchanged in this *de facto* network in different ways. One climate ambassador developed a list with advice on how to save energy during the winter season. A second network for technical service managers for all types of municipal institutions also operates in Hvidovre.

Besides being a Climate Municipality, Hvidovre Municipality had for three years (until the end of 2013) an energy savings agreement with a national energy saving fund, the Centre for Energy Savings. (The fund was closed down in 2012.) According to the Climate Municipality agreement, Hvidovre should reduce its annual CO_2 emissions by 2 per cent per year; according to the agreement with Centre for Energy Savings, the electricity consumption should be reduced by 2 per cent per year. In 2012, Hvidovre was able to reduce municipal CO_2 emissions by 3.1 per cent and heat consumption by 4.6 per cent, whilst electricity consumption increased by 0.4 per cent (Hvidovre Kommune 2013).

The shaping and impact of environmental and climate ambassador programmes

Based on our analysis, we identified the following themes as important aspects of municipal environmental and climate ambassador programmes:

- Focus of the programme;
- Organisational structures of the programme;
- Internal networking among the ambassadors;
- Economic incentives in the programme;
- The roles of the programme coordinator; and
- The role of citizens in the programme.

These themes are discussed in the following sections.

Focus of the programmes

In Furesø and Frederiksberg, and until 2010 also in Hvidovre, the ambassador programmes are based on Agenda 21 work and cover areas such as energy, climate, waste and recycling, water and environmental learning. The focus in Lyngby-Taarbæk's programme is narrower – mostly like Hvidovre's present programme – and concentrates in large part on energy savings and renewable energy. As noted above, all four municipalities are part of the 'Climate Municipality' programme initiated by the DN, where municipalities commit themselves to reducing their CO_2 emissions by 2 per cent every year.

Organisational structures of the programmes

The four ambassador programmes are organised in four different ways with respect to who the ambassadors are and how the programme is anchored in the municipal administration. One aspect concerns the role of the local managers; another concerns the types of employees that are involved.

Furesø Municipality engages local managers as ambassadors, while Lyngby-Taarbæk engages both local technical staff and local managers as ambassadors. In the two other programmes, the ambassadors are local employees. Frederiksberg engages different types of local employees. Technical employees are supposed to focus on optimisation of the technical equipment and are seen as 'technical ambassadors', while employees with non-technical, more 'social' backgrounds, including pedagogues and teachers, are seen as general ambassadors. The ambassadors in Hvidovre Municipality are general ambassadors.

The advantage of Furesø's method of appointing local managers as environmental ambassadors is that the coordinator of the ambassador programme can seek and receive support from the central administration's management group relatively easily and also use this group as a communication channel when it is necessary to get a message out to the local institutions quickly or when there is a need for relatively quick decisions. Using central managers as a communication channel to local managers – and making local managers the ambassadors – ensures that everyone knows that there is strong management support for the programme, and that it is legitimate to spend time on environmental and climate activities.

However, central managers who have made unpopular decisions and are not well-regarded in their own organisations tend to transfer resistance to the programme when they communicate with local managers. There are also ambassadors who have so much opposition to top-down initiatives that they only engaged in the ambassador programme after several months or years (Pedersen and Jørgensen 2012).

The top-down initiatives in Hvidovre, Furesø and Frederiksberg were implemented quickly and produced rapid results. These programmes were developed from the top, and are seen as a centrally initiated response to many years of community expectations of a municipal commitment to environment and climate initiatives. This has helped these top-down programmes become a success.

All four programmes have central steering or coordination groups that are supposed to ensure both central and local focus on the programme and its activities. The committees have a broad representation from several – and in some cases from all – parts of the municipal administration. These committees and groups seem to occupy different levels of importance in the four programmes, with the least important role probably played in Hvidovre.

The roles of programme coordinators

In all four municipal administrations, continuous efforts are made to make the ambassadors visible in the municipal administration and at the city council level. In Hvidovre, Frederiksberg and Furesø, the position of programme coordinator calls for both internal and external competencies: it creates networks among ambassadors with common interests and between ambassadors and the central administrative and political management. In Lyngby-Taarbæk, it is not the ambassador programme that has led to the development of the competencies of the local ambassadors. Rather, the informal ambassador programme here is the result of central and local skills development that has occurred over a number of years. By forming alliances with the city council, the coordinator in Lyngby-Taarbæk has been granted the responsibility for an economic framework that encourages focus on energy savings, i.e. the use of so-called energy checks as a way of allocating some of the cost savings from reduced energy consumption back to the institution and allocating some of the savings for development of a central fund for investments in improvements.

Internal networking among the ambassadors

The daily workday does not necessarily allow the local ambassador time enough to construct a meaningful ambassador role. Time for planning activities, collecting information about the central administration's efforts and surveying one's own institution's resource consumption may be difficult to find.

Information from the four municipalities indicates that some ambassadors form networks and develop ideas during joint events within such networks. Joint seminars can give ambassadors a space with time for reflection, knowledge sharing, creative thinking and inspiration. The disadvantage of this kind of facilitation of the work of ambassadors is that it is also time-consuming and might discourage ambassadors who can devote only 3–5 hours to networking meetings every six months.

Such networks have been organised in Hvidovre and Furesø as so-called 'experience groups'. These groups can foster a culture in which ambassadors liberate themselves from the initiatives taken by the coordinators and develop their own ideas. This can anchor environmental and climate actions more deeply into the organisation: both the technical service managers in Furesø and Hvidovre have had some success with this tool.

In Furesø, the most innovative and creative experience groups are those that include managers from different types of local institutions and with different educational backgrounds, including technical service managers and administrative managers. Mutual learning about how the individual ambassador can implement his or her environmental and climate change agenda often occurs in these groups. This confirms the ideas of Clematide (2009), who suggests that methodological freedom and good cooperative relationships promote a good learning environment.

Joint events in Hvidovre and Furesø are also used to present the central administration's efforts to reduce resource consumption; these events are often where ambassadors become aware that they are not the only ones who are trying to reduce environmental impacts. The events are also one of the channels for ambassadors to influence the central administration at city hall.

Economic incentives in ambassador programmes

The four ambassador programmes make use of three different economic incentives that support the ambassadors' efforts:

- Allocation of the cost savings from an institution's energy savings back to the institution's own budgets;
- Creation of a central fund of cost savings derived from energy savings; and
- Prizes and rewards for local institutions.

As earlier mentioned, one of the incentives in Lyngby-Taarbæk for several years has been an increase in the budget of the local institution proportionate to the energy costs that the local institution has saved through lower energy consumption. For large institutions, the allocation back to the institution is 50 per cent of the savings, while the other 50 per cent is allocated to the central fund for energy investments. The allocations to the local institution in these instances are large enough to support the ambassadors' objectives, together with a smiley system and annual local visits from the central Energy Group.

In Hvidovre, the incentive in the climate ambassador programme is primarily economic. The expected resource consumption for each local institution is assessed; on that basis, a budget for resource consumption is allocated to each institution. The money saved can be retained by the individual institution. The development of this incentive model has required a lot of resources in order to calculate the expected resource consumption and the subsequent processing of the responses from the institutions to budget proposals. However, once the incentive model was instituted, it requires few resources to update local budgets when technical improvements that are supposed to reduce resource consumption have been made.

In Furesø, the financial incentive is symbolic, or at least less directly economic. Every year the two environmental and climate ambassadors who have reduced resource consumption the most are awarded prizes for their specific institutions of approximately 300 to 900 Euros respectively. The three ambassadors who have promoted the most effective and innovative environmental and climate activities are awarded around 700 Euros each. These prizes do not require a lot of economic resources, but they do require that the incentive structure be supported by intense formal and informal facilitation of the work of the ambassadors.

In Frederiksberg, a central climate change fund for new projects is created from the cost savings obtained from local energy savings. As in Furesø, the incentive does not drive the programme: it is a supplement of intensive formal and informal facilitation of the central coordinator.

The role of citizens

The four programmes all involve citizens either directly or indirectly in their activities. The Frederiksberg programme integrates specific environmental issues into the learning plans of day-care institutions and schools. In Furesø, the programme includes children in school-initiated projects such as lessons about renewable energy and local waste segregation into several different waste types (such as paper, plastic and metal) in order to enable recycling and thereby reduce the consumption of 'virgin' raw materials. The target group is the children, but indirectly also their parents. The development of a book collection on climate issues at the local library is also directed towards citizens. Ambassadors in libraries, cultural centres and at the swimming bath in Værløse in Furesø Municipality arrange climate events where citizens can learn to take responsibility for climate-friendly initiatives. Similarly, day-care centres and schools use bicycle campaigns to teach children to cycle and encourage parents to support and choose green transportation.

The Lyngby-Taarbæk programme does not include the citizens directly, but its ambassadors have in some cases included concerns about the practices of the users of local institutions. The library became aware of user practices in its newspaper reading room when planning the change of the light bulbs as part of its energy-saving activities. Furthermore, the technical service manager of a sports facility experienced the importance of dialogue with the users of the facility when it comes to automatic control of ventilation and light from both energy and users' perspectives. If the settings do not fit the practices of the users, they might try to bypass the systems and their settings. These examples show that citizen involvement in the programmes is based in part on the citizens' role as users of different types of public institutions (when integrating concerns about the users' social practices into an institution's saving activities), and is based in part on their role as citizens (when developing a climate book collection at the local library and when informing parents about environmental concerns and activities that become part of their children's education).

All four municipalities conduct other environmental activities directed towards citizens that are not directly related to their ambassador programmes. Furesø has initiated public energy advice sessions with external experts and sessions about the financing of energy-saving investments, both of which encourage citizens as homeowners to engage in energy-saving activities (Furesø Kommune 2014b). Frederiksberg has recently organised activities aimed at improving citizens' waste segregation and recycling (Frederiksberg Kommune 2014b). Lyngby-Taarbæk and Hvidovre have set up environmental councils comprising citizens, environmental organisations and businesses that establish a framework for dialogue among citizens, businesses and the administrative and the political management of the municipalities. The focus of these councils is on day-to-day issues and on dialogue about municipal planning; as a rule the councils do not have formal influence on municipal planning and decision making (Hvidovre Kommune 2014; Lyngby-Taarbæk Kommune 2014).

Discussion

This section discusses environmental and climate ambassador programmes from the theoretical perspectives of political reflective navigators and public spheres.

Ambassadors and coordinators as political reflective navigators

An ambassador is responsible for getting environmental and/or climate concerns on the local institution's 'agenda' which are directed to colleagues and in some cases also to other users of the institutions (for example, school children) in order to ensure more environmental- or climate-friendly practices. Local ambassadors in the four municipalities have acquired (or already possess from earlier practice) some of the competencies that enable them to act as political reflective navigators within environmental and climate activities of their local institution. To varying degrees, the ambassadors use the central coordinator of their programme as their navigator in relation to the central administration.

In Hvidovre, the ambassadors themselves instituted their own network, while in Furesø the coordinator set up groups of ambassadors to exchange experiences. The only ambassadors who meet all four criteria for acting as a political reflective navigator are the school managers, some managers in cultural centres and libraries, and notably, in the maintenance department in Furesø, which is probably the result of their experience with political navigation as managers in a political, administrative setting.

One of the major requirements for acting as a navigator – the ability to support the establishment of political programmes on the environment – seems to be a competence that requires prior knowledge about navigation in a political organisation. Ambassadors in Furesø, who are managers of local institutions, are, as mentioned, more likely to have prior navigation experience than for example, the technical service managers and service employees who are ambassadors in Lyngby-Taarbæk or Hvidovre. These technical professionals are simply not accustomed to dialogue with the central administration about budgets, annual plans and broader municipal issues.

The coordinators of the programmes in Furesø and Frederiksberg give local navigational support a high priority. By contrast, the central ambassador coordinators in Lyngby-Taarbæk see themselves as technical experts, not as navigational and facilitation experts. However, the ambassadors in this programme see the present joint meeting every three years as insufficient for the timely exchange of experiences and information about the installation and use of energy-saving equipment (Theilby 2010). As a result, they have requested more focus on and support for networking among the local ambassadors.

In some cases, the ambassadors have used the coordinator to develop interest in an initiative in the central administration. The coordinator of the Frederiksberg programme became aware of substantial energy losses in the building that houses a day-care centre from a dialogue with the local manager. The coordinator communicated this information to the municipal estate office to make them aware of the problem. This case demonstrates that the coordinator sometimes has skills related to the second criteria for acting as a political reflective navigator: the ability to navigate in complex organisations and identify decision makers and other influential stakeholders.

In Furesø, the ambassadors also use their experience groups to discuss and develop their project ideas and initiatives together. The coordinator sometimes serves as facilitator in relation to the central administration and to find out whether a project idea seems feasible. An example: the central coordinator had a dialogue with the waste department staff, the building service manager, the chief engineer of the building service department and the environmental and climate ambassadors across all experience groups in order to promote the idea of some environmental and climate ambassadors for a waste segregation scheme in local institutions. Ambassadors of four schools wanted in particular to begin segregating solid waste at the schools. The coordinator made an appointment with the head of building services and waste departments about a cardboard and paper recycling system that involved schoolchildren, teachers and technical service managers. This programme was subsequently extended to all schools in the municipality. This case indicates that the coordinator needs skills related to the third and fourth criteria for being a political reflective navigator: the ability to understand and mediate between different professional languages and the ability to change between different roles and mobilise different types of knowledge.

The results from the four case studies are both similar and different from the experiences of an environmental management programme conducted in an Australian state, which is the administrative level below the country's federal level (Zutshi *et al.* 2008). As in the Danish cases, the importance of the environmental coordinators' knowledge and skills, and the difficulty in accessing resources were made clear. However, the lack of support from top management and resistance from employees in the Australian case proved to be major obstacles to the programme, which is certainly not the case in the four Danish case studies analysed here.

Ambassador programmes as public spheres

An ambassador programme can be analysed from the perspective of the public sphere, as understood by Habermas (2002), who talks about the public sphere as a space between the state and the citizens. We analyse the ambassador programmes as a sphere between and among the local municipal political and administrative management, its employees and citizens. Our analysis demonstrates that an ambassador programme can be seen as a sphere where ambassadors meet and discuss their challenges, share solutions, develop a broader understanding of their own experiences, are inspired by other environmental initiatives and receive navigational, funding or other professional support from the coordinator.

Although the ambassador programme is created by the municipal administration as a publicly legitimate sphere, only the experience groups where ambassadors use the sphere to influence the municipal political agenda and create their own reasons for engagement and ideas for activities can be seen as having the same functions as Habermas's public sphere.

The framework provided in the Furesø programme has developed the ability of its local ambassadors to frame the sustainability agenda from their own professional perspectives as an alternative to the central coordinator's more science- and expert-based agenda. This experience confirms Negt's idea that only through collective learning from everyday experiences is it possible to imagine social changes (Weber *et al.* 1997). These ambassadors' ideas might also be inspired by their roles as active citizens. In that case, the ambassador programme can also be seen as a kind of workplace activism, where social movements in civil society influence the orientations and attitudes of employees because the employees also are part of 'the larger society and culture' (Ball 2007).

When the coordinator of an ambassador programme allows and enables its ambassadors to frame their own environmental activities, the programme can be seen as an attempt by the ambassadors to avoid the coordinator's more expert-based and perhaps also his or her more discipline-based approach to environmental aspects. There is always the possibility that a coordinator's ideas and skills might overshadow the ambassadors' experiences as professionals and as citizens (Weber *et al.* 1997).

Similarly, Fischer (2000) highlights (with a reference to Foucault) the disciplinary power of experts as different from experience-based knowledge and warns of the risk that experts are not able to accommodate experience-based arguments because such experiences may cross over several disciplinary boundaries. In a study of employee participation in environmental activities in private and public workplaces, Forman and Jørgensen (2001) stressed the importance of negotiations about the role of the employees, environmental managers and coordinators, and about the focus of the environmental activities, i.e. whether the work environment (also called occupational health and safety) at a given workplace is allowed to be part of the focus of an environmental initiative.

None of the ambassador programmes analysed here are anchored in a formalised environmental management system. This is, however, the case of another Danish ambassador programme in City of Copenhagen. This programme is anchored in an environmental management system based on the international standard ISO14001. This management system is an important driver of local environmental efforts due to the joint certification of all institutions within each administrative area and the related obligation to develop and implement action plans. The management system is anchored in the joint decision making organisational structure in administrations that covers strategy, environment and work environment. Despite this anchoring and the action plans, the central coordinator still has an important role in some institutions – together with the local management and the health and safety representative – in identifying environmental aspects of their type of activities (like eldercare or childcare) and developing environmental initiatives which the local management and employee representatives find relevant to the core activities of the institution (The City of Copenhagen, personal communications, 28 June 2013 and 20 May 2014).

Emilsson and Hjelm (2009) analysed environmental management systems in three Swedish municipalities. After some years of operation, the focus of these systems evolved towards a broader understanding of environment, and was developed into management systems with a broader sustainability focus (Emilsson and Hjelm 2009), similar to the focus of the ambassador programmes in Furesø and Frederiksberg. Just as in the four Danish ambassador programmes, the mature Swedish environmental management systems and the later sustainability management programmes focused on all municipal departments and had a central coordinator.

Conclusion

This analysis has identified the following important aspects of municipal environmental ambassador programmes:

- The possibilities for networking among and initiatives from the local ambassadors;
- The central coordinator's ability to support the local ambassador with knowledge of mapping and reducing environmental impacts;
- The central coordinator's ability to facilitate local ambassadors' needs in relation to the central administration and support the ambassadors in initiating activities they find meaningful to their daily tasks and experiences; and

- The economic mechanisms related to the allocation of cost savings from local resource savings to investment in ambassador programme initiatives.

The more the central coordinator can facilitate and support the ambassador programme internally and externally, the more capacity building takes place. Incentives should be structured in a way that helps anchor ambassador programmes in the short- and long-term in both the municipal administration and in its institutions.

Some programmes are based on systematic registrations and action plans for the institutions involved, while others are based more on single ideas for initiatives. The activities are always directed towards the local institutions' employees and their practices, but also involve citizens in some cases, for example by:

- Developing their knowledge about environmental aspects;
- Facilitating more sustainable citizen practices like parents walking or biking to the day-care centre or school with their children; or
- Encouraging more sustainable user practices in local municipal institutions, for example, among children in schools and users of sport facilities.

The organisational structures of the ambassador programmes and the experiences of the single ambassador are critical to whether and how ambassadors are able to act as political reflective navigators. The experiences related here indicate that an ambassador who either is incapable of acting as a political reflective navigator or does not have the time might nevertheless be able to realise environmental and climate initiatives if the central coordinator of the programme manages to complement the ambassador's skills. It is therefore critical to the success of a programme that its central coordinator is able to act as a political reflective navigator.

References

Ball A (2007) Environmental Accounting as Workplace Activism, *Critical Perspectives on Accounting* 18 759–778.

Broberg O and Hermund I (2004) The OHS Consultant as a 'Political Reflective Navigator' in Technological Change Processes, *International Journal of Industrial Ergonomics* 33 315–326.

Clematide B (2009) Ledelse af læring [Management of learning], in Helth P (ed.) *Lederskabelse – det personlige lederskab* [Making managers: Personal leadership], Samfundslitteratur, Frederiksberg.

Danish Ministry of the Environment (2007) *Spatial Planning in Denmark* (http://naturstyrelsen.dk/media/nst/Attachments/Planning_260907_NY6.pdf) Accessed 25 January 2015.

Danish Society for Nature Conservation (2014) *Det danske plansystem* [The Danish Planning System] (www.dn.dk/Default.aspx?ID=7319) Accessed 21 November 2014.

Emilsson S and Hjelm O (2009) Towards Sustainability Management Systems in Three Swedish Local Authorities, *Local Environment* 14(8) 721–732.

128 *Jørgensen and Pedersen*

Fischer F (2000) *Citizens, Experts, and the Environment*, Duke University Press, Durham, NC.

Forman M and Jørgensen M S (2001) The Social Shaping of the Participation of Employees in Environmental Work Within Enterprises: Experiences from a Danish Context, *Technology Analysis and Strategic Management* 3(1) 71–90.

Frederiksberg Kommune (2013) *Frederiksberg Kommune Grønne regnskab 2012* [City of Frederiksberg Green Account] (www.frederiksberg.dk/~/media/Forside/Om-kommunen/groenne-regnskab/Grønt%20regnskab%20for%20Frederiksberg%20Kommune%202012.ashx) Accessed 21 November 2014.

Frederiksberg Kommune (2014a) *Frederiksberg Kommune Grønne regnskab 2013* [City of Frederiksberg Green Account] (www.frederiksberg.dk/~/media/Forside/Om-kommunen/groenne-regnskab/Grønt%20regnskab%20Frederiksberg%20Kommune%202013.aspx) Accessed 10 January 2015.

Frederiksberg Kommune (2014b) *Genbrug Frederiksberg* [Recycling Frederiksberg] (http://genbrug.frederiksberg.dk/) Accessed 21 November 2014.

Furesø Kommune (2014a) *Furesø Kommune Grønt Regnskab 2013* [Furesø Municipality Green Account 2013] (www.stien.furesoe.dk/sitecore/content/Forside/Kommunen/Oekonomi/Regnskaber/~/media/7950109895334BCC90D7C0F9150F14A1.aspx) Accessed 21 November 2014.

Furesø Kommune (2014b) *Velkommen til 'Energien i boligen'* [Welcome to 'The Energy in the Home'] (www.furesoe.dk/energieniboligen) Accessed 21 November 2014.

Habermas J (2002) *Borgerlig offentlighet* [The Structural Transformation of the Public Sphere] (2nd edn, Norwegian version), Gyldendal, Oslo.

Habermas J (2004) *Teorien om den kommunikative handlen* [The Theory of Communicative Action], Aalborg Universitetsforlag, Aalborg.

Hall M and Bassot B (2009) Becoming Eco-Responsible, Active Citizens Through Participation in the Eco Ambassadors Project: A Reflective Analysis, *Journal of Applied Research in Higher Education* 1(1) 4–11.

Hopkinson P, Sharp L, Miles S L and Boyes L C (2009) From Harvard to Bradford: Experiences of Running a Peer Education for Sustainable Development Project, *Planet* 22 34–38.

Hvidovre Kommune (2013) *Hvidovre Kommune Grønt Regnskab 2012* [Hvidovre Municipality Green Account 2012] (www.hvidovre.dk/dokumenter/Kommunalbestyrelsen/2013/130924/BilagKB130924_pkt.14.01.pdf) Accessed 21 November 2014.

Hvidovre Kommune (2014) *Det Grønne Råd* [The Green Council] (www.hvidovre.dk/Politik/dagsordener-og-referater-fra-udvalg/andre-udvalg/det-groenne-raad.aspx) Accessed 21 November 2014.

Lyngby-Taarbæk Kommune (2012) *Lyngby-Taarbæk Kommune Grønt Regnskab 2011* [Lyngby-Taarbæk Municipality Green Account 2011] (www.ltk.dk/sites/default/files/uploads/public/user_uploads/Erhverv/groent_regnskab_samlet.pdf) Accessed 16 April 2015.

Lyngby-Taarbæk Kommune (2014) *Grønt råd* [Green Council] (www.ltk.dk/groent-raad) Accessed 21 November 2014.

Pedersen S R and Jørgensen M S (2012) *Ambassadørordninger på miljø – og klimaområdet – en analyse af erfaringer fra fire kommuner* [Ambassador Programmes Within Environment and Climate: An Analysis of Experiences from Four Municipalities], Furesø Municipality and DTU Management Engineering (www.furesoe.dk/~/media/2CB425DDED7947A7B3628A4E4B4B26F3.aspx) Accessed 21 November 2014.

Ministry for Economic Affairs and the Interior Municipalities and Regions (2014) *Tasks and Financing June 2014* (http://english.oim.dk/media/670682/municipalities_and_regions_-_tasks_and_financing__june_2014.pdf) Accessed 21 November 2014.

Theilby T (2010) *Fremtidigt perspektiv for kommunal energiledelse i institutioner* [Future Perspective on Municipal Energy Management in Institutions], Unpublished Bachelor thesis, DTU Management Engineering.

United Nations Conference on Environment and Development (1992) *Agenda 21*, United Nations Conference on Environment and Development Rio de Janeiro, Brazil 3 to 14 June 1992 (http://sustainabledevelopment.un.org/content/documents/Agenda21.pdf) Accessed 9 January 2015.

Weber K, Nielsen B S and Olesen H S (eds) (1997) *Modet til fremtiden* [The Courage for the Future], Roskilde Universitetsforlag, Roskilde, Denmark.

Zutshi A, Sohal A S and Adams C (2008) Environmental Management System Adoption by Government Departments/Agencies, *International Journal of Public Sector Management* 21(5) 525–539.

8 A local energy transition success story

Stefanie Baasch

Introduction

This chapter looks at an example of a decentralised energy transition process on the local level. The crucial question for our analysis of the process conducted in Wolfhagen, one of Germany's most successful renewable energy communities, focuses on the factors that have contributed to the town's energy transition process on both individual and societal levels and the effects of framework conditions. The chapter begins with a brief overview of Germany's recent energy policies on the federal and *Länder* (regional) level before looking at the specific outcomes of the local case study. The analysis focuses on Wolfhagen's key stakeholders and their underlying motivations, the interplay between local politics and framework conditions and the impact of the participation of citizens on local energy policies. The study was conducted with an incremental multi-methodological approach, which included a document analysis, a participative network analysis and semi-structured interviews. The document analysis focuses on the records of proceedings (town council and committees, in particular), articles in the communal gazette about the town's energy transition process, magazine articles and local information leaflets distributed by the municipal service company and energy agency, among others. The network analysis was conducted with local key stakeholders in the energy transition process to collect information about energy stakeholders' networks. The semi-structured interviews explored stakeholders' underlying motivations and their roles and networking activities in the transition process. These methodological steps should allow conclusions about the drivers and barriers of the process and about the development of local energy governance.

Germany's 'Energiewende' policies

Germany's turnaround in energy policy ('*Energiewende*') is now supported by a broad public and political majority. Still, the details of how to achieve the goals of (more) sustainable energy production and consumption remain controversial. In general, the country's abandonment of nuclear power production after the 2011 nuclear catastrophe in Fukushima, Japan, certainly influenced Germany's attitude towards increasing the use of renewable energy. Extended production of renewable energy in Germany is now widely accepted as an important step towards establishing a comprehensive energy transition process and eventually, a more sustainable society (German Advisory Council on Global Change [WBGU] 2011).

The term *Energiewende*, which can be translated as *a turnaround in energy politics* or *energy transition* process, is not clearly defined in public or political debate. Instead, it is an umbrella term for a variety of actions that may contribute to more sustainable consumption and production patterns, including a reduction of carbon footprints, the abandonment of nuclear power, more efficient energy use and the expansion of renewable energy production.

Two major decisions at Germany's national level helped define this *Energiewende*. First, in 2011, the German parliament decided to phase out the use of nuclear power by the end of 2022. Second, it stipulated that the amount of renewable energy for the country's power supply should increase to 80 per cent by 2050. Before this parliamentary decision, Germany's power mix included 22 per cent nuclear power. Figure 8.1 illustrates the percentages of the use of energy sources in the year 2010.

Renewable energy in 2010 was generated in large part by wind power and biomass plants, as Figure 8.2 demonstrates.

Germany's nationwide renewable energy production at that time indicates that farmers, private stakeholders, investment funds, banks and project planners had the highest amount of renewable generation capacity (Klaus Novy Institute

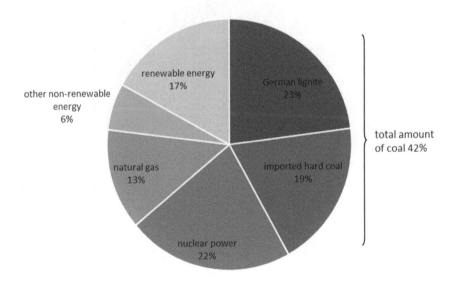

Figure 8.1 Germany's power mix 2010

Source: Agentur für Erneuerbare Energien [Agency for Renewable Energy] 2011.

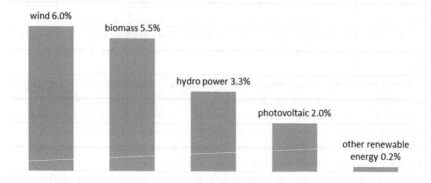

Figure 8.2 Types of renewables in the national power mix 2010

Source: Agentur für Erneuerbare Energien [Agency for Renewable Energy] 2011.

[KNI] 2011). Figure 8.3 indicates that by the end of 2012, the energy transition process – especially the deactivation of nuclear power plants – had led to significant changes in Germany's power mix. Nuclear power production dropped by 6 per cent, while the amount of coal and renewable energy increased.

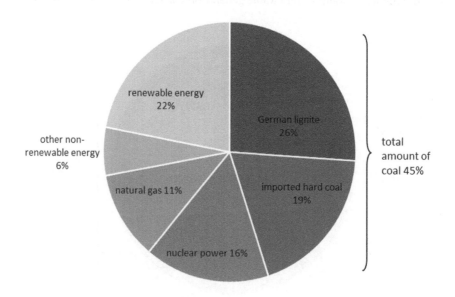

Figure 8.3 Germany's power mix 2012

Source: BDEW – Bundesverband der Energie – und Wasserwirtschaft e.V [German Association of Energy and Water Industries] 2013.

Figure 8.3 also shows us that the amount of renewable energy in Germany's power mix increased by 5 per cent from 2010 to 2012.

Figure 8.4 demonstrates that there was a significant increase of photovoltaic energy, which more than doubled in the two years. However, the other renewable energy sources (except hydropower) could also increase their share.

Due to Germany's political structure as a federal state, there is no national master plan that defines in detail how to achieve the expansion of renewable energy. By contrast, the energy transition process is a relatively fragmented multi-scale process that includes a variety of interests and stakeholders on federal and regional levels. Today, there are two significant and partially conflicting trends in the expansion of renewable energy production: the centralised or decentralised production of renewable energies.

Centralised production of renewable energy is most prominently connected with major industrial offshore wind power plants operated by 'big energy players': RWE, E.ON, Energie Baden-Württemberg [EnBW], and Vattenfall. These companies are applying a good deal of political pressure to extend and renovate the high-voltage grid across Germany in order to transport wind power from offshore wind farms on the northern coast to the consumption centres in the south.

On local and regional levels, whilst municipal service companies and other regional energy supply companies (e.g. energy cooperatives) are crucial stakeholders in energy transition processes (Guy *et al.* 1996; George *et al.* 2009; Berlo and Wagner 2011), their renewable energy generation capacity is still limited (Brocke 2012).

Decentralised production of renewable energy focuses on the regional and local levels, and is characterised by a wide variety of both public and private stakeholders. It is also characterised by a diverse mix regarding energy production

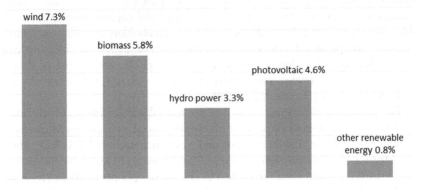

Figure 8.4 Types of renewables in the national power mix 2012

Source: BDEW – Bundesverband der Energie – und Wasserwirtschaft e.V [German Association of Energy and Water Industries] 2013.

itself, including onshore wind power, biomass, photovoltaic and early-stage experimental developments such as wood gasification.

From a local perspective, renewable energy production is often seen as a promising economic option. Many regional energy suppliers (both public and private) have focused recently on the expansion of renewable energy production (Diermann 2011), mainly in the fields of biomass and onshore wind turbines (Klaus Novy Institute [KNI] 2011). Municipalities benefit from renewable energy production because the trade tax flows into municipal budgets. Direct income to municipalities can also be created when a municipal company is producing energy, which is one of the few money-making options available to municipalities. In times of demographic change, ageing and decreasing population in rural areas and a decrease in trade taxes, municipalities sorely need to find new financial resources in order to sustain their infrastructure.

The German energy transition process did not begin immediately after the Fukushima event – it has a history of more than thirty years, and began with niche initiatives at the local level. The history of decentralised renewable energy production shows us a number of new regional and local energy producer groups that have been established since the end of the 1980s by different stakeholders (e.g. energy cooperatives, citizen wind parks and foundations initiated by citizens). Since then, these stakeholders have been cooperating or competing with public and private service companies in various ways. In general, the production of renewable energy is becoming more important for regional and municipal service companies and private regional energy suppliers (Sauthoff and Schön 2010). This trend of decentralised energy production is increasing because German energy and environmental politics offer a prioritised integration of renewable energy into the grid (Staab 2011; Brocke 2012).

Energy transition on the regional scale could have a positive impact on sustainable regional development by generating regional value and jobs (Hirschl et al. 2010), and also could contribute to strengthening structurally weak (rural) regions. Public acceptance of decisions about locations for renewable energy production is seen as a crucial aspect for the successful implementation of renewable energy strategies that influence political stakeholders and also consumers, investors and project developers (Wüstenhagen et al. 2007). In Germany, case studies illustrate the close connection between public acceptance of decentralised renewable energy production and perceived regional economic and ecological benefits (Hirschl et al. 2010).

The town of Wolfhagen is located in the federal state of Hesse, which before 2011 had produced up to 70 per cent of its energy needs (Hessisches Ministerium für Umwelt, Energie, Landwirtschaft und Verbraucherschutz [HMUELV: Hesse Ministry for the Environment, Energy, Agriculture and Consumer Protection] 2012). In the last ten years, about half of the energy (47 per cent) in Hesse was produced by nuclear power plants, although in some years, including 2009, temporary shutdowns of nuclear power plants led to strong deviations in the energy production mix. The energy transition process had significant implications regarding the federal power mix when regional nuclear power plants were taken off the grid and shut down in August 2011. The impacts of this shutdown become visible (Figure 8.5) when the power mixes in 2010 and in 2011 are compared. The total amount of energy produced in Hesse decreased from 30,168 m.kwh in 2010 to 19,229 m.kwh in 2011. In 2012, there was no nuclear power production in Hesse at all and the total energy production diminished to 16,169 m.kwh (Hessisches Statistisches Landesamt [Hessian Statistical Office] 2014).

The total amount of renewable energy in Hesse's power production accounted for 6.9 per cent in 2008, 16.23 per cent in 2009 (due to a temporary shutdown of the nuclear power plant Biblis, which led to a higher amount of renewable energy) and 10.6 per cent in 2010 (Agentur für Erneuerbare Energien [Agency for Renewable Energy] 2012). Figure 8.6 below shows the diversity of renewable energy sources in Hesse in 2011.

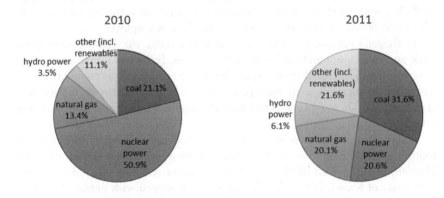

Figure 8.5 Hesse's power mix 2010 and 2011

Source: Hessisches Statistisches Landesamt [Hessian Statistical Office] 2013a.

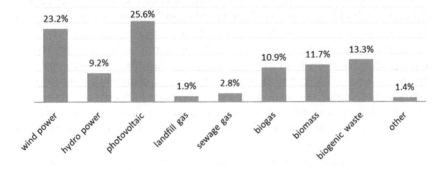

Figure 8.6 Types of renewables in Hesse's power mix 2011

Source: Hessisches Statistisches Landesamt [Hessian Statistical Office] 2013b.

When the renewable energy production in all federal states in Germany is compared, Hesse was ranked in the lower third in 2012 (Agentur für Erneuerbare Energien [Agency for Renewable Energy] 2012). This demonstrates that on a federal scale Hesse can hardly be defined as a region in the forefront of renewable energy, at least so far. For these reasons, it comes as a surprise that Hesse is home to one of the most innovative energy transition communities in the country.

The case study

Wolfhagen is a small town located 30 kilometres west of Kassel, Germany. Similar to other rural towns in Germany, the town area is subdivided into a core area and a number of rural villages (eleven in this case). Out of the total of 13,840 inhabitants, about 7,620 live in the town centre. The town's population is expected to decline by approximately 6 per cent by 2020. A large percentage of Wolfhagen's employed have to commute to work in Kassel or to Baunatal, where a Volkswagen automobile factory is the biggest employer.

Wolfhagen's economy is diverse: retail trade, crafts, car dealers, fragmented trade and traditional and medium-sized industries. Innovative small enterprises have sprung up in recent years, especially in the energy sector: energy technology, wood gasification, a thermal power station and an energy-saving window glass business. These types of companies are expected to increase in the coming years.

Studies of prospective economic sectors in Wolfhagen designate the sectors of tourism, education and renewable energies as the most promising (Industrie und Handelskammer Kassel [IHK: Chamber of Industry and Commerce Kassel] and University of Kassel, 2010). Wolfhagen is well-equipped with public facilities – kindergartens, schools, trade schools, a hospital, a retirement home and a senior citizen centre, a rural district office and a police station. Nevertheless, the community faces a number of challenges, including demographic changes and ageing population, a decrease of jobs and rising vacancy rates in both commercial and residential buildings in the historic town centre. Such issues are common in many communities in Germany, especially in rural areas. At first glance, then, Wolfhagen seems to be a typical small German town, with the same characteristics and the same challenges as other towns across the country.

However, when we take a closer look, Wolfhagen reveals some very specific developments regarding local energy policies, including the 2008 municipal decision to become a 100 per cent renewable energy community by meeting the town's entire energy demands with locally generated renewable energy from 2015. In addition, a number of projects and initiatives have been implemented in recent years to reduce the local carbon footprint, foster energy efficiency and reduce energy consumption.

Wolfhagen's municipal service company, Stadtwerke Wolfhagen GmbH, is responsible for the local water supply (which is still publicly owned in Germany), and also provides gas and electricity to private and trade customers. Since the liberalisation of the German energy market in 1998, customers are now free to choose their energy supply company. Also since then, energy is provided by numerous private or municipal suppliers that operate on different levels, from international to local. This means that local municipal service companies are competing with a variety of other companies, including 'big players' like E.ON (which is a stock exchange-listed company), low-cost internet operators and national renewable energy suppliers (e.g. Greenpeace Energy and Lichtblick).

Windows of opportunity: Framework conditions influencing the local energy transition process

Some important contextual factors have supported the development of Wolfhagen's energy transition process, including legal developments, contractual relationships and technical development in the field of renewable energy production.

Since 1991, the national law on feed-in tariffs ('*Stromeinspeisungsgesetz*') modulated the access of renewable energies to the energy grid. At that time, renewable energy could barely be produced at a reasonable price. In the year 2000, the German Renewable Energy Act (*Erneuerbare-Energien-Gesetz (EEG)*) came into force and has triggered a tremendous development of renewable energies in Germany. Because the Act grants a fixed feed-in tariff for every kilowatt-hour generated from renewable energy facilities, investments in renewable power plants to date are a very secure investment vehicle. These guaranteed payments support small and medium-sized enterprises in particular by offering a high rate of planning security with a fixed feed-in tariff for twenty years.

In 1998, another Renewable Energy Act (*Energiewirtschaftsgesetz* [EnWg]) liberalised the electricity market. Energy customers could now choose their energy utility regardless of the location of their residence. This led to increased competition for municipal service companies and a number of municipal service companies being privatised or at least partly-privatised (e.g. in Berlin, Essen and Düsseldorf), whilst other municipal service companies faced budgetary and staff savings.

These national legal developments had a critical impact on the local energy transition process in Wolfhagen. The liberalisation of the electricity market forced the municipality to decide how they wanted to operate their municipal services in the future. In 2002, the former municipal utility was transformed into a completely municipal-owned service company with limited liability (*Gesellschaft mit beschränkter Haftung GmbH*) in order to gain more flexibility regarding the company's management.

Technical developments and the rising degree of effectiveness in the generation of renewable energy in recent years have made investments in power plants more attractive and financially feasible for municipalities. This made it a worthwhile for Wolfhagen to produce renewable energy to meet its local energy requirements. In 2015, Wolfhagen plans to produce its energy needs with locally produced renewable energy. Another important influence of the decision to invest in municipal energy production is the increased electricity costs that are burdening municipality budgets. Instead of spending more and more money to fulfil the municipality's energy requirements, the local energy production could create income for the community.

The energy transition process in Wolfhagen

The following timetable provides an overview of the milestones of Wolfhagen's local energy transition process:

Phase 1: 1991–2003

Innovative energy-efficient redevelopment began and building systems were installed. In 1991 and 1994, innovative energy efficiency systems for recycling waste heat (energy absorbers) were installed as part of the redevelopment of two municipal open air swimming pools. In 1992, Wolfhagen's first photovoltaic installation was constructed on the roof of a public building (*Haus des Gastes*). In 2002, the municipal service company moved into their new administrative building, which was constructed as a passive or ultra-low energy building. In the same year, the municipal service company began a free energy consultancy programme for its customers in order to encourage energy efficiency.

Phase 2: 2003–2005

The municipal energy transition process begins. In 2003, the town council decided to 're-municipalise' the energy grid, i.e. to move it back to the public sector. In 2005, the power grid's licensing agreement between Wolfhagen and the private energy supply company E.ON expired. Often, such contracts are renewed as a matter of course. Wolfhagen then decided to hand over the right of use to the municipal service company, which was one of the first cases in Germany in which a community discontinued a power grid contract with a big energy supplier like E.ON. After years of quarrelling about the value of the grid and the level of repurchase, Wolfhagen succeeded in taking over their local energy grids through an out-of-court-settlement with E.ON. This was an important step in the entire energy transition process.

The operation of power grids is not only linked to economic benefits (job creation, regional value creation), it is also an important symbolic step that demonstrates the municipality's will to take responsibility for the energy transition process. Nowadays, re-municipalisation of power grids, district heating and gas supplies has become a mainstream practice for communities and is widely supported and even forced by citizens.

The privatisation trend of the late 1980s and 1990s often did not meet the municipalities' financial expectations, which led to the opposite trend of re-communalisation, which places privatised public services back into the hands of municipalities. It appears, then, that citizens have become more and more sceptical of the benefits of privatisation processes and prefer an extension of public services operated by public authorities and public companies. For example, in a referendum about the re-municipalisation of energy grids in Hamburg in September 2013, 50.9 per cent of the voters supported full re-municipalisation of the energy grid. This is remarkable because Hamburg's two biggest political parties, the conservatives (CDU) and social democrats (SPD), were strictly opposed to the idea of re-municipalisation, which, the parties argued, ran the risk of high and unforeseeable costs.

Phase 3: 2006 –2012

Long-term targets were designed and citizen participation encouraged. In 2006, the screening of former United States (US) Vice President Al Gore's film *An Inconvenient Truth* and public dialogues on climate change issues were organised by the manager of Wolfhagen's municipal service company and the owner of the local cinema. These events were the stimulus for the foundation of the town's climate initiative. In that same year, re-municipalisation of the energy grids was finalised and the operation of the grids was handed over to the municipal service company.

In 2007, the local climate initiative (*Klimaoffensive Wolfhagen*) was founded and the municipal service company began to deliver 100 per cent renewable energy from water power plants to all their customers. Currently, the energy requirements are covered by hydropower bought in Austria. In 2008, the manager of the municipal service company organised an information tour with local politicians from all parties to the Windpark Druiberg (near the district of Dardesheim in Saxony-Anhalt) to convince them of the benefits of locally produced wind power.

Only four weeks later, the town council agreed to take further steps in the municipal energy transition process and asked the municipal service company to develop appropriate concepts for the process. The town then conducted participation processes with municipal administrators and stakeholders from different fields of action, including forestry and nature protection non-governmental organisations (NGOs), and commissioned studies about potential sites for wind power plants. This process and the results of the studies were communicated to the public via the internet and press releases. In addition, the municipal service company organised guided tours for interested citizens to nearby wind parks. In 2008, the town council decided to cover its energy requirements with 100 per cent locally produced renewable energy by 2015 and also decided to participate in the national prize competition called 'Energy Efficient Town' (*Energieeffiziente Stadt*, Federal Ministry of Education and Research).

In 2010, Wolfhagen was designated as one of five German 'Energy Efficient' cities (along with Delitzsch, Essen, Magdeburg and Stuttgart) by the Federal Ministry of Education and Research in Germany (BMBF). The award included project funding to implement more innovative strategies and services for energy efficiency. In Wolfhagen, projects that benefitted from this additional funding included energy-efficient building and redevelopment, renewable energy production and distribution, smart metering and consumer information, public relations and educational opportunities.

Phase 4: 2012–ongoing

A municipal/citizen energy partnership was solidified. In 2012, the local citizens' energy cooperative, *BürgerEnergieGenossenschaft Wolfhagen* (BEG) was founded by 265 people and had a share capital of 1.47 million Euros (BEG 2012). The cooperative pursued two main targets from the beginning. The first, which is similar to many other energy cooperatives in Germany, consisted of providing investment capital for renewable energy power plants. The second target was, by contrast, quite unique and much more far-reaching, because it included a 25 per cent share of the municipal service company. Today the citizens' energy cooperative is represented by two members on the managing board of the municipal service company (Baasch *et al.* 2015). Fifteen months after its founding, the cooperative had 626 members and a share capital of nearly 2.5 million Euros (BEG 2013).

According to the municipal target set in 2008, Wolfhagen should cover its entire energy demand by 2015 with locally produced energy from wind power, biomass and photovoltaic. The major part of this energy should be produced by the citizen-owned wind park. The location of this wind park has led to conflicts in Wolfhagen. Whilst the majority of political stakeholders support the project, a local protest group opposes the location for nature conservation reasons ('no wind power plants in the woods'). Although a lot of effort was expended through a mediation process, this conflict was still unresolved. But the opponents were not able to stop the construction of the wind park and in 2014 the wind turbines were built and put into operation.

However, whilst this issue is quite complex, it has little influence on the process as a whole because it is restricted to a conflict about location. In general, local wind power opponents do not reject the target of Wolfhagen's becoming a community, which satisfies its entire energy needs with renewable energy. It is quite improbable that the wind power critics could compete against its supporters. The wide local support for the energy transition process, the successful start of the citizen's energy cooperative and non-partisan political agreement seem to be more powerful than the numerically disadvantaged wind power opponents.

The energy transition in Wolfhagen is a step-by-step process. Each step enables further developments such as the re-municipalisation of the energy grid, or the facilitation of the feed-in of decentralised-produced renewable energy that led to the expansion of renewable power plants. We come now to a discussion of who the stakeholders are in Wolfhagen's energy transition process.

'Who is who' in the energy transition process

To identify the stakeholders in Wolfhagen's energy transition process and identify their networking activities, a Participatory Network Analysis (PNA) was conducted in 2011 with a member of the local energy agency who had been working in the field for many years. The PNA results were then presented to key stakeholders, whose comments have been integrated in the diagram in Figure 8.7 below, which illustrates the major stakeholders of Wolfhagen's energy transition process.

Figure 8.7 explained

At the centre of the diagram in Figure 8.7 are the four stakeholders identified in our interviews as the initiators of the transition process. The manager of the municipal service company plays a leading role among the identified stakeholders. In all the interviews we conducted, he was named the most important process initiator.

The head of the municipal department of building inspection, the energy agency Energie 2000 e.V. and a local politician who is simultaneously the manager of Energie 2000 e.V. were also identified as important process initiators. Energie 2000 e.V. advises communities and community facilities, associations, private citizens and companies on energy saving and the use of renewable energy devices. These consultations follow the product-independent model, i.e. they not guided by selling interests, but emphasise finding equally ecological and economic practical solutions for an individual case. They also offer training for operators and users of energy devices, prepare technical and economical calculations and implement public relations activities for renewable energy and energy savings.

From 2000 to 2003, Energie 2000 e.V. supported and supervised the local Agenda 21 process in the administrative district of Kassel. (Local Agenda 21 processes were initiated in the aftermath of the Rio Summit in 1992 to foster sustainable development on the local level.) The agency also cooperates with other regional and trans-regional advice centres to offer citizen-friendly and demand-oriented information.

The 2007 local climate initiative, shown *at the bottom of the diagram* on the left, is seen by many stakeholders as an important step in the energy transition process. Interestingly, many of the 37 NGO foundation members were already actively involved or employed in local politics (as members of the town council), a state-owned enterprise (the manager of the municipal service company) and civil society (representatives of the Protestant Church). This is quite unusual because NGOs tend to emerge from alternative grassroots movements and are rarely initiated by local decision makers and members of administrative bodies. Because of the conflict about the location for the wind power plants, this initiative split up into two other NGOs: the pro-wind power citizen's group and their opponents from the local protest group.

Since 2012, the pro-wind citizen's group has merged with the citizens' energy cooperative. Political stakeholders in the field of the local energy profile, including Wolfhagen's mayor, the leader of the supporting parliamentary parties (social-democrats, conservatives, liberals and a local citizen's party that cooperates with the liberal party) and the town council are also identified as supporters of the tran-

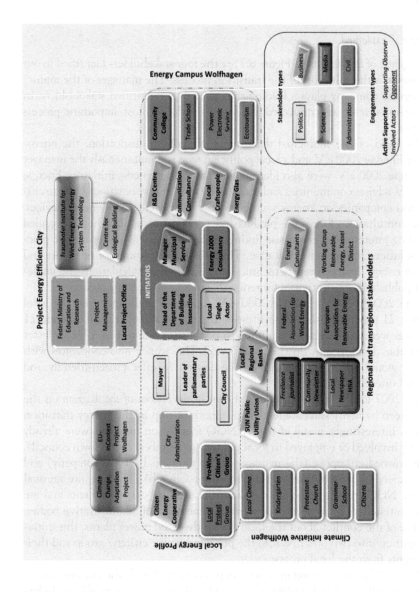

Figure 8.7 Wolfhagen's Energy Transition Stakeholders Network

sition process. In the business sector, local and regional banks have supported the transition process by the granting of credits. The citizens' energy cooperative BEG also supports the process financially with their cooperative shares and their participation in the managing board of the municipal service company.

On the *right-hand side of the diagram*, a number of economic and educational stakeholders in the field of the energy campus are shown. The 'energy campus' is an area under development that is located on a former site of the German Armed Forces, which vacated the barracks in 2008. At this location, the company Energy Glass started its production of energy-saving window glass in 2008. Further small businesses in the field of innovative energy production (wood gasification) and energy efficiency products are planned or currently under construction at the site. Additionally, a trade school is located on the campus. The top of the former tank hangar is now completely covered with an innovative transparent photovoltaic rooftop.

At *the upper left of the diagram* in Figure 8.7, we see two scientific projects that have been classified as supporters. One of them is the European InContext project (2010–2013) under which this study was conducted. The other project, 'Participation, Acceptance and Regional Governance', based at the University of Kassel, was part of the regional climate change adaptation project network KLIMZUG-Northern Hesse (2008–2012), which focused on energy issues in the context of adaptation to climate change. Both projects were mentioned in interviews as contributing to the increase of environmental / energy awareness and also as expanding local knowledge about social and scientific aspects of energy transitions, e.g. potential barriers and drivers. The box in the upper middle of Figure 8.7 shows the project partners of the 100 per cent Energy Efficiency project. This project, funded by the Federal Ministry of Education and Research, focuses on implementing energy-efficient measures from inter- and trans-disciplinary perspectives.

At *the bottom of the diagram*, we find various stakeholders from the media and the business sector, NGOs and public administration that are supporting the transition process actively or at least take a favourable view of the process. These stakeholders operate on regional or trans-regional levels.

Why do things differently? Key stakeholders and their reasons for change

Looking at the history of the transition process and the stakeholder groups involved does not provide a sufficient explanation of why this process was initiated and has been sustained. In general, social-ecological transition processes result from decisions that stakeholders make for various reasons. As mentioned above, the energy transition process began very early in Wolfhagen compared to similar communities. Interviews were conducted with key stakeholders in order to identify the underlying motivations that drove them to change their mainstream practices. Three of the interviewees were identified as initiating stakeholders in the transition process (see PNA): one interviewee is a member of the citizens' energy cooperative and also a local decision maker in one of Wolfhagen's village district councils. All interviewees have been involved in the local climate initiative.

One of the key stakeholders reported that he was deeply shocked by the international oil crisis in the 1970s. This event convinced him of the vulnerability of non-renewable resources while he was still in school. He was also influenced by the beginning of the environmental pollution discourse at the time. Regarding his motivation for initiating the energy transition process in Wolfhagen, he refers to intergenerational justice, which is harmed by the current non-sustainable usage of resources and environmental pollution. These experiences and his awareness and ethical values influenced his choice of studies and his professional career as an engineer: he decided to work on technical solutions for more efficient energy use and more sustainable production of energy. From his point of view, a lot of technical solutions already exist that create more sustainable energy production and consumption, but a lack of knowledge, political resistance and the power of the large energy suppliers, who are still producing largely non-renewable energy, are hampering this development.

Two other key stakeholders described their motivation for implementing more energy sustainability as the result of a learning process that motivated them more because of budgetary concerns and the need for energy saving than by environmental considerations. Climate change issues became a more important factor in their decision making and environmental / climate change mitigation implementation processes came only later. Both interviewees said that their environmental / climate concerns were strongly triggered by the local climate change discourse, which more or less began with the screening of former US Vice President Al Gore's *An Inconvenient Truth*.

A slightly different learning process was reported by the fourth interviewee, who was also the only one of those interviewed who does not have a technical/engineering professional background – she holds a law degree. As a member of the local council, this woman has been involved in political decision making processes about the proposed site for the wind power plants. She is also directly affected by the proposed wind turbines because her house is located close to the proposed installation area. This double role forced her into an intensive consideration of her views. In the end, she decided that opposing the installation of the wind turbines would follow the so called 'St. Florian's principle' of shifting responsibility. In her view, local responsibility for the effects of climate change also includes bearing some negative or unintentional factors such as the impacts of wind turbines on the landscape. This interviewee cites local responsibility and global justice as her main motivations.

These interviews demonstrate that motivation for supporting or even initiating such an energy transition process can be diverse and can also have different starting points. It seems that perceptions of justice play an important motivational role. This matches findings in environmental justice psychology where justice is seen as a main driver for environmental behaviour (e.g. Montada and Kals 2000; Müller *et al.* 2008; Baasch 2012).

From an energy niche to new local governance formations

The energy transition process in Wolfhagen began about twenty years ago with individual symbolic actions, including the energy-efficient redevelopment of public buildings. From the beginning, municipal actors played a crucial role in the process. The liberalisation of the energy market put pressure on political stakeholders to decide whether they wanted to follow the mainstream or find other local solutions.

Simultaneously, the national law on feed-in-tariffs offered a window of opportunity that made investments in renewable energy production an acceptable if not a seductive option for both public and citizen investors. These framework conditions, plus the intrinsic motivation of key stakeholders to foster sustainable energy practices and/or reduce energy costs, can be seen as crucial drivers. Another important factor for the success of transition processes is the presence of local knowledge. The manager of the Wolfhagen's municipal service company is not only a highly motivated stakeholder, he is also an expert on renewable energy. Therefore, local political stakeholders relied on his expertise.

A particular driver for Wolfhagen's local energy transition process is the exceptional cooperation of local politicians. From a very early stage, inter-party cooperation and agreements concerning the re-municipalisation of the energy grid, the agreement to focus on renewable energy production and the fostering of energy efficiency involved political stakeholders from all political parties represented on the town council. This is even more remarkable because some political stakeholders, especially from the local conservative party, were acting in direct contrast to the regional and national energy policies of their own party.

Stakeholders referred in interviews to various motivational aspects and learning processes to explain their engagement in the energy transition process, including the values of global and intergenerational justice concerns. However, many stakeholders also identified their localised concern about future local development as a strong driver.

Public involvement in Wolfhagen's energy transition process began early and included intensive public relations activities. For example, in 15 articles beginning in 2010 in the communal gazette (*Stadtanzeiger Wolfhagen*), council members from the different parties jointly informed the public about the planned transition process and upcoming projects. These political leaders stressed to the public that the energy transition process was an important future project that was not tied to party politics but to an overall sustainability target.

Since 2006, the number of people involved in the energy transition process has increased continuously. The first important step for participating local citizens was the founding of the local climate initiative, which has led to the raising of awareness about the effects of climate change and local responsibility. Since 2012, the citizen's energy cooperation has played an important part in the transition process. First, their investments make the further expansion of renewable power plants possible. Second, the direct participation of citizens strengthens local acceptance of renewable energy. And third, citizen representatives on the managing board of the municipal service company can be seen as a new governance formation, which comprises aspects of direct democracy and power sharing.

In general, this participative process has positive impacts on social sustainability by strengthening local identity and environmental justice and by motivating citizens to take action on the local level. Public involvement in Wolfhagen goes beyond the scope of public relations by offering local citizens the opportunity to be an active part of the energy transition process. This includes direct influence on the public utility companies' decisions and direct access to information (as members of the managing board), but it also means that the members of the cooperative are taking direct responsibility for the local climate footprint. Depending on the number of citizens who take part in the cooperative venture in the future, this kind of involvement could also contribute to more direct democracy in the business decisions of the local municipal service company. The future will show if this development leads to more public engagement in other fields of action as well.

The future prospects are promising. Funded by the Federal Ministry of Education and Research, the inter- and trans-disciplinary pilot project 'Wolfhagen – 100% Energy-efficient Town' (duration: 2012–2017) is now working on developing and implementing more energy-efficient solutions in the community. The local project office of Energieoffensive Wolfhagen works as the interface between scientific, technical and communal project partners and citizens. This office also organises public lectures, exhibitions and a variety of participatory events with different target groups (e.g. kindergartens, schools, house owners and senior citizens) and is a main contact partner for all energy matters in the community.

Conclusion

Why has the energy transition process in Wolfhagen been so successful? Was it because of the key actors or because of national legislation that supported the expansion of renewable energy production? The answer is: *It's in the mix.* The particular mix in Wolfhagen includes *motivation + knowledge + windows of opportunity (legal, financial) + local political support + participation.* What's more, 'real' participation in this case includes civil actors and participatory decision making aided by supportive networks and the establishment of innovative energy businesses. This does not necessarily mean that every energy transition process needs all of these ingredients to be successful, but it does demonstrate that a transition process needs much more than just technical developments and some financial incentives.

To summarise: individual aspects like *motivation and knowledge* are critically important at the beginning of a transition process. Another important factor is the initial actors' specific knowledge, which in Wolfhagen's case helped identify options for change, fostered the acceptance of a trustworthy spokesperson for the process and helped to convince decision makers of its feasibility and its beneficial impacts on the community. It is important to note that individual environmental concerns can work as both drivers and barriers in the renewable energy transition debate. Whilst they can influence actors to change production and consumption patterns, they can also hinder the process, e.g. if actors are concerned about the impacts of renewable production sites on natural habitats.

The *group and community level* is important for sustaining and disseminating information about the transition process. This case study demonstrates that even diverse individual motivations can be integrated into a common energy objective. In Wolfhagen, the energy transition process was accompanied by extensive participatory actions, which actively involved citizens in the process and led to a change in the distribution of power concerning the local energy policies.

Structural factors can offer windows of opportunity, e.g. by making investments in renewable energy production more attractive and by reducing financial risks such as via the feed-in-tariff. In addition, infrastructural features can facilitate the implementation of the transition process: the fact that the Wolfhagen municipality was operating the local utility company at the beginning of the process facilitated its development tremendously. By contrast, legal and financial provisions can also work as barriers, e.g. by causing price increases for renewable energy through subsidy reduction and cutbacks of the feed-in-tariff.

The energy transition process also impacts the everyday life of civil society actors. A variety of programmes and incentives initiated by the local utility company, the citizen's energy cooperative, the project office of Energieoffensive Wolfhagen and by scientific programmes continue to promote energy-saving behaviour and energy efficiency on diverse levels.

The *participatory approach* in Wolfhagen's local energy transition process has transformed the relationship between citizens, institutions (the local utility company in particular) and local authorities. The most visible effect of the participatory approach is the power shift that occurred when the citizen's energy cooperative became a new local stakeholder directly involved in political decisions on energy.

Acknowledgements

The research leading to these results has received funding from the European Union FP7 ENV.2010.4.2.3 – 1 grant agreement n° 265191.

References

Agentur für Erneuerbare Energien (2011) *Der Strommix in Deutschland 2010* [Energy Mix Germany 2010] (www.dtc-energie.de/downloads/) Accessed 17 November 2014.

Agentur für Erneuerbare Energien (2012) *Renews Spezial Bundesländervergleich Erneuerbare Energien 2012* [Renews Special: Comparison of Renewable Energies among the German States] (www.unendlich-viel-energie.de/media/file/169.61_Renews_Spezial_Bundeslaendervergleich_Endfassung_online.pdf) Accessed 17 November 2014.

Baasch S (2012) Gerechtigkeit als Aspekt von Klimawandel-Governance [Justice in Climate Change Adaptation Governance], *Umweltpsychologie* 16(2) 86–103.

Baasch S, Schaub M, Linne K, Schomburg N and Neuroth T (2015) Akteure und Netzwerke der kommunalen Energiewende Wolfhagens, in Wagner H-J (ed.) *Wettbewerb 'Energieeffiziente Stadt' Band 6: Akteure und Netzwerke* [National prize competition 'Energy Efficient Town' Volume 6: Actors and networks], LIT Verlag, Berlin (forthcoming December 2015).

BDEW Bundesverband der Energie – und Wasserwirtschaft e.V. (2013) *Brutto-Stromerzeugung 2012 in Deutschland* [Gross electricity production in Germany 2012] (www.bdew.de/internet.nsf/id/17DF3FA36BF264EBC1257B0A003EE8B8/$file/Foliensatz_Energie-Info-EE-und-das-EEG2013_31.01.2013.pdf) Accessed 17 November 2014.

BEG – BürgerEnergieGenossenschaft Wolfhagen (2012) *Quartalsinformation Stand 06.09.2012* [Quarterly Report 06.09.2012] (www.beg-wolfhagen.de/attachments/article/102/2012-09-06%20BEG-Quartalsinformation%20Mitglieder%201.7.%20bis%205.9.12.pdf) Accessed 17 November 2014.

BEG – BürgerEnergieGenossenschaft Wolfhagen (2013) *Mitgliederinformation Oktober 2013* [Members Report October 2013] (www.beg-wolfhagen.de/attachments/article/102/BEG-Mitgliederinformation%20Juli%202013.pdf) Accessed 17 November 2014.

Berlo K and Wagner O (2011) Zukunftsperspektiven kommunaler Energiewirtschaft [Future Perspectives on the Municipal Energy Sector], *Raumplanung* 158/159 236–242.

Brocke T (2012) *Wertschöpfungs- und Koordinationsstrukturen der dezentralen Stromerzeugung. Eine akteur- und institutionenzentrierte Analyse anhand ausgewählter Fallbeispiele* [Value Creation and Coordination Structures in Decentralised Energy Production: An Actor and Institutional Analysis Based on Selected Examples], Kommunal-und Schulverlag, Wiesbaden.

Diermann R (2011) Kommune hält Kurs [Municipalities stay on course], *Erneuerbare Energien* 3/2011 22–25.

George W, Bonow M, Hoppenbrock C and Moser P (2009) Regionale Energieversorgung. Chance für eine zukunftsfähige Ziel- und Ressourcensteuerung in der Energiewirtschaft [Regional Energy Supply: A Chance for a Future-Compliant Control of Objectives and Resources in the Energy Sector], *Standort – Zeitschrift für angewandte Geographie* 33 13–21.

German Advisory Council on Global Change [WBGU] (2011) *World in Transition A Social Contract for Sustainability* (www.wbgu.de/fileadmin/templates/dateien/veroeffentlichungen/hauptgutachten/jg2011/wbgu_jg2011_en.pdf) Accessed 17 November 2014.

Guy S, Graham S and Marvin S (1996) Privatized Utilities and Regional Governance: The New Regional Managers? *Regional Studies* 30(8) 773–739.

Hessisches Ministerium für Umwelt, Energie, Landwirtschaft und Verbraucherschutz [HMUELV] (2012) *Energiebericht 2010 der Hessischen Landesregierung* [State Government of Hesse: Energy Report 2010] (www.energieland.hessen.de/infomaterial/Energiebericht%202010.pdf) Accessed 17 November 2014.

Hessisches Statistisches Landesamt (2013a) *Bruttostromerzeugung der Kraftwerke der allgemeinen Versorgung, der Industriekraftwerke und der sonstigen Marktteilnehmer nach Energieträgern und Nettostromverbrauch nach Abnehmergruppen 2000 bis 2011* [Gross Energy Production: Public Power Plants, Industrial Power Plants and Others Divided in Energy Sources, Electricity Consumption and Consumers 2000 to 2011] (www.statistik-hessen.de/themenauswahl/industrie-bau-handwerk-energie/

landesdaten/energieversorgung/bruttostromerzeugung-nach-energietraegern-und-nettostromverbrauch-nach-abnehmergruppen/index.html) Accessed 17 November 2014.

Hessisches Statistisches Landesamt (2013b) *Stromerzeugung aus erneuerbaren Energien* [Electricity Generation from Renewable Energies] (www.statistik-hessen.de/themenauswahl/industrie-bau-handwerk-energie/landesdaten/energieversorgung/stromerzeugung-aus-erneuerbaren-energietraegern/index.html) Accessed 17 November 2014.

Hessisches Statistisches Landesamt (2014) *Hessische Energiebilanz 2011 und CO₂ Bilanz 2011* [Hesse's Energy Balance 2011 and Carbon Footprint 2011] (www.statistik-hessen.de/static/publikationen/E/EIV6_j11_pdf.zip) Accessed 6 January 2014.

Hirschl B, Aretz A, Prahl A, Böther T, Heinbach K, Pick D and Funcke S (2010) *Kommunale Wertschöpfung durch Erneuerbare Energien* [Municipal Value Creation Through Renewable Energies], Schriftenreihe des IÖW 196/10, Berlin.

Industrie und Handelskammer Kassel [IHK] and Universität Kassel (2010) *Stadtbericht Wolfhagen* [Municipal Report Wolfhagen] (www.ihk-kassel.de/solva_docs/stadtbericht_wolfhagen_final_2010_01_04.pdf) Accessed 17 November 2014.

Klaus Novy Institute [KNI] (2011) *Marktakteure Erneuerbare Energien-Anlagen in der Stromerzeugung* [Market Participants in Renewable Energy Production] (www.kni.de/media/pdf/Marktakteure_Erneuerbare_Energie_Anlagen_in_der_Stromerzeugung_2011.pdf) Accessed 17 November 2014.

Montada L and Kals E (2000) Political Implications of Psychological Research on Ecological Justice and Proenvironmental Behaviour, *Journal of Applied Social Psychology* 35(2) 168–176.

Müller M, Kals E and Maes J (2008) Fairness, Self-Interest, and Cooperation in a Real-Life Conflict, *Journal of Applied Social Psychology* 38(3) 684–704.

Sauthoff M and Schön O (2010) EVU/EDU Neue, zukunftsfähige Geschäftsmodelle für Stadtwerke [Future-compliant Business Concepts for Municipal Services], *Energiewirtschaftliche Tagesfragen* 60(12) 58–62.

Staab J (2011) *Erneuerbare Energien in Kommunen. Energiegenossenschaften gründen, führen und beraten* [Renewable Energies in Municipalities: Founding, Managing and Consulting Energy Cooperatives], Gabler-Verlag, Wiesbaden.

Wüstenhagen R, Wolsink M and Bürer M J (2007) Social Acceptance of Renewable Energy Innovation: An Introduction to the Concept, *Energy Policy* 35 2683–2691.

9 Incorporating climate change mitigation programmes in local administration

The case of the CCP programmes in Australia and New Zealand

Jens Hoff

Introduction

During the last decade, most of the discussion on climate change has focused on questions about the effects of climate change on our natural environment and global negotiations, and agreements concerning greenhouse gas reductions. Less attention has been paid to the efforts to establish effective climate change administrations at national and local levels.[1] This is surprising because it is common knowledge, at least among public administration scholars, that integration of new policy areas in the thinking and routines of public administration is necessary if long-term action and change is to be achieved.

This chapter deals with the challenge of incorporating climate change politics into local public administrations. More precisely, the research questions this chapter addresses are:

1   How were concrete climate change policy programmes introduced and spread in specific local public administrations?
2   To what extent have such programmes become a well-established component of local public administration and part of the services that the administration routinely delivers?

The data used to illustrate the institutional challenge of climate politics at the local level concern the Communities/Cities for Climate Protection Programmes (CCP programmes) in New Zealand (NZ) and Australia. These two identical, voluntary programmes targeted local councils that committed to reducing their own and their communities' CO_2 emissions by following a quantifiable approach marked by the achievement of milestones. The programmes were joined by approximately 50 per cent of the local governments in both countries, which represented approximately 85 per cent of their countries' population. The Australian programme began in 1997, and the New Zealand programme in 2004. Both programmes were terminated in 2009.

There are three reasons why these two cases were chosen for study. First, the programmes were encompassing and long-lasting, and thereby provide good material for studying institutional effects. Second, the local level is the level at which most of the delivery of climate change policies (i.e. CO_2 reductions in councils' own operations and initiatives targeting citizens and businesses) took place. Third, because of 1) and 2), the CCP programmes constitute a 'critical case': if the institutional incorporation and anchoring of climate change thinking and action in these cases is limited and slow, this will probably also be true for most other local public administrations of a similar type (Flyvbjerg 2001).

The theoretical framework used to study this institutional challenge is 'new institutionalism' (March and Olsen 1989, 1995). This framework is normally seen as containing three different approaches (Hall 1996; Campbell 2004): *rational choice institutionalism, organisational* (or sociological) *institutionalism* and *historical institutionalism* (Skocpol 1985; Powell and DiMaggio 1991; Thelen and Steinmo 1992). While our analysis is most heavily indebted to organisational institutionalism, we do not spend time discussing the vices or virtues of the different approaches. Instead, accepting Campbell's (2004) criticism of the problems that all three approaches have in trying to explain change, we are more concerned here with understanding and explaining *institutional change*, and thus the development of adequate theoretical tools in order to do this.

The CCP programmes

The 'Cities for Climate Protection' and 'Communities for Climate Protection programmes in Australia and New Zealand were part of an international campaign by 'ICLEI – Local Governments for Sustainability' to address the challenge of climate change.[2] The point of departure for these programmes was that local action on climate change is important, and because local government is the level of government closest to citizens and communities, it is in a unique position to drive and sustain local action in this field.[3]

The voluntary CCP programmes[4] were intended to empower councils to reduce greenhouse gas emissions in their own municipal operations and in their communities. They were also intended to provide a strategic framework for the achievements of these reductions. Furthermore, the programmes assisted councils in identifying measures to reduce CO_2 emissions by saving energy and promoting sustainable energy, increasing sustainable transport, enhancing urban design, reducing emissions from landfills and supporting adoption of low-carbon technology.

The councils began the CCP process by following a quantifiable approach marked by the achievement of the following milestones:

- Milestone 1: Conduct a CO_2 emissions inventory, analysis and forecast;
- Milestone 2: Set emissions-reduction goals;
- Milestone 3: Develop a local action plan to achieve sustainable emissions reductions;

- Milestone 4: Implement the climate action plan and quantify the benefits of policies and actions;
- Milestone 5: Monitor progress towards the reduction goals and begin the process of re-inventory and review of the plan.

In Australia, the CCP programme was implemented in a collaboration between local governments, ICLEI Oceania and the Australian Government's Department of Environment, Water, Heritage and the Arts. In New Zealand, the CCP programme was a New Zealand Government initiative delivered by ICLEI Oceania and supported by Local Government New Zealand.

A distinction was made in both CCP programmes between emission reductions in a council's own operations and reductions in households and businesses located within the council's boundaries. The first type of reductions/operations is called 'corporate' while the second type is characterised as 'community'. This distinction will be maintained in the text below.

The CCP programmes focused on the larger, urban councils, at least in the beginning, and began with a focus on corporate actions. This choice was made in order to establish credibility for the programme before it turned its attention to community actions. (However, by the last few years of the programme in Australia, the majority of reported CO_2 reductions actually came from the community.) The focus on larger urban councils was also due to the fact that agriculture was exempted from the programme in New Zealand, and that only part of the Australian programme came to focus on agriculture (e.g. in Victoria). Furthermore, an extension of the programme to agricultural councils was actively discouraged, at least in New Zealand, by the funder.

It also appears that the early focus on corporate emissions was because such reductions were the easiest to achieve and also within the control and mandate of the councils:

> I think that was the easier thing to do. They [the councils] certainly did both their corporate and their community emissions. I think … the corporate are easier because it's easy to draw a boundary and say: 'This is what our corporate emissions are'.[5]

The data

Three types of data have been collected:

1   A survey covering all the local councils in Australia and New Zealand that participated in the CCP programmes was carried out in Spring 2010. The response rate was 29 per cent in both countries. However, even though the response rate was modest, the data are seen to be representative for the councils that were involved. Thus, in terms of the milestones reached in the programme, it is possible to compare the actual figures with the figures in our survey (see Table 9.1 below). Even though there are some disparities, the

tendencies in the two sets of data are quite similar. We have therefore chosen not to weigh the data, and see the reliability of the survey data as quite high.[6] However, it should be noted that the councils that participated in the programme are bigger both in terms of population and budgets than the average Australian or New Zealand council. For example, whilst the average Australian council in our survey has around 98,000 inhabitants, the real average is only 38,400 inhabitants. It should also be noted that in general, it was council officers who returned the questionnaires. Because the perceptions of officers, managers and elected officials are known to vary, what we have is a view from a certain group of staff. An assumption about this group is that they are often looking for operational and functional support while other stakeholders within councils (managers, politicians) might put a greater emphasis on political or framework developments. Furthermore, many of the council officers are younger, turn over often and might have had little involvement in the CCP itself. This might explain the relative high number of 'don't knows' concerning the question about the benefits of CCP. All data shown in tables below are from this survey unless otherwise indicated.

2   A series of semi-structured interviews was conducted with mayors, energy managers or climate change resource staff in local councils, civil servants from relevant ministries or crown entities and representatives from businesses and NGOs working in the area of climate change mitigation. All 21 interviews were fully transcribed. All citations used in this article are from these interviews unless otherwise indicated.

3   We reviewed official plans, reports and documents from ministries, local councils and organisations dealing with the question of climate change, and documents and information from the websites of these organisations and global networks dealing with the challenges of climate change.

The milestones completed by the councils provide us with a first overview of the data. What we see (Table 9.1) is that well over half (55.8 per cent) of all involved councils completed milestone 5. This amounted to councils systematically monitoring progress towards their reduction goals and beginning the process of re-inventory and review of their original climate change action plan. Approximately 67 per cent of all councils completed milestone 4 (implementation of a climate action plan) or 5, whilst approximately 21 per cent either did not complete any milestone or only milestone 1, which amounted to conducting an inventory of the council's greenhouse gas emissions.

It is noteworthy that there is a huge difference between the milestones completed by the Australian and the New Zealand councils respectively. While almost 75 per cent of the Australian councils reached milestone 4 or 5, this is the case for only approximately 12 per cent of the New Zealand councils. In New Zealand, as many as 59 per cent of the councils either did not complete any milestone (14.7 per cent) or only completed milestone 1 (44.1 per cent). This huge discrepancy is due to the fact that the programme started much earlier in

Table 9.1 Milestones completed in the CCP programme

Milestone completed	Australia %	N	New Zealand %	N	Total %	CI 95*	Survey %	CI 95*
None	8.8	(21)	14.7	(5)	9.4	(5.9–12.9)	2.5	(0.0–5.9)
1	7.5	(18)	44.1	(15)	12.0	(8.2–15.8)	8.6	(2.5–14.7)
2	3.8	(9)	0.3	(1)	0.7	(0.0–1.7)	4.9	(0.2–9.6)
3	5.4	(13)	23.5	(8)	7.7	(4.5–10.9)	8.6	(2.5–14.7)
4	11.2	(27)	11.8	(4)	11.3	(7.6–15.0)	9.9	(3.4–16.4)
5	63.3	(152)	0.3	(1)	55.8	(49.9–61.7)	65.4	(55.0–75.8)
Total N =		240		34		274		81

Notes: N = absolute numbers. *CI 95 = 95% confidence interval.

Australia than in New Zealand. Most of the Australian councils that reached milestone 4 or 5 began the programme in the late 1990s, while none of the New Zealand councils began their programme before 2004. This difference demonstrates that there is a considerable amount of work involved in completing the different milestones, and that a process of organisational learning is necessary in order for councils to progress to the last milestones.

An analysis of the differences between large and small councils in both countries in terms of milestones reached shows that organisational capacity seems to be critical to achieving the last milestones. Thus, 88 per cent of large councils (over 91,000 inhabitants) completed milestone 4 or 5, whilst this was only the case for 54 per cent of the smaller councils (less than 40,000 inhabitants).[7] We shall return to the question of size below.

When we look at the difference between the results of our survey and the results reported by ICLEI (the two last columns of Table 9.1), we see that councils that completed milestones 4 and 5 are somewhat over-represented in our survey (75.3 per cent against the real figure of 67.2 per cent), and that councils at the 'low end' (no milestone or milestone 1 completed) are somewhat under-represented (11.1 per cent against the real figure of 21.4 per cent). As noted above, since the difference between the two distributions is not statistically significant, we have chosen not to weigh the data in the analysis below.

Theoretical framework

In institutional theory, institutions are comprised of sets of formal and informal rules, monitoring and enforcement mechanisms and systems of meaning that define the context within which actors (people, businesses, organisations) interact (Campbell 2004, 178). Scott (2001) characterises these three basic dimensions of institutions as: *the regulative pillar*, which consists of legal, constitutional and other rules that constrain and regularise behaviour, *the normative pillar*, which involves principles that prescribe the goals of behaviour and the appropriate way to pursue them and the *cultural-cognitive pillar*, which entails the culturally shaped, taken-for-granted assumptions about reality and the frames through which it is perceived, understood and given meaning.

We apply this institutional perspective here to the introduction and incorporation of the CCP programmes in local administrations in Australia and New Zealand. We discuss changes in local administrations in terms of changes in three basic dimensions:

1   the regulative framework, including organisational set-up;
2   the norms guiding action in the field of the environment;
3   the frames through which reality in this area is understood.

Traditionally, institutional theory has not been very good at specifying how institutional change takes place in reality. Change has been discussed under such headings as 'punctuated equilibrium', 'punctuated evolution' or 'critical junctures' (March and Olsen 1989; North 1990; Powell 1991; Baumgartner and Jones 1993; Pierson 2000). However, whilst such concepts can be used to explain why major revolutionary changes occur, this approach often tends to focus on the key events that begin episodes of change, but stops short of analysing the ensuing process when actors try to figure out what consequences these changes might have for their institutions.

Campbell (2004, 47) is one of the first to launch this critique, and suggests that in order to be more precise in our understanding of institutional change, we must first, specify the important institutional dimensions we want to track, and second, identify the appropriate time frame over which we examine the institutional dimensions selected.

The institutional dimensions to track have already been selected above (regulative framework, norms and frames), and the time frame is the duration of the CCP programmes from when they began until they were analysed by the author, i.e. from 1997 to 2010. We then address the question of the mechanisms of change, or the processes that account for the causal relationships among variables.

Campbell proposes a number of concepts to deal with the mechanisms of change that we find very helpful. The first is the concept of *bricolage* (Levi-Strauss 1966, 16ff; Campbell 2004, 69), which is used to define a situation where actors create new institutional solutions by *re-combining already existing institutional elements*. Campbell distinguishes between two types of bricolage: substantive and symbolic.

Substantive bricolage is institutional change undertaken to achieve various substantive goals. This can be such matters as reducing transaction costs, improving product quality and managing labour relations problems. Substantive bricolage follows a logic of instrumentality (March and Olsen 1989).

Symbolic bricolage involves the re-combination of symbolic principles and practices. This thinking is connected with the logic of appropriateness emphasised in particular by March and Olsen (1989). Thus, the solutions that actors devise must be acceptable and legitimate within the broad social environment.

Moreover, for new institutions to take hold, they must be framed with combinations of existing cultural symbols that are consistent with the dominant normative and cognitive institutions.

Both substantive and symbolic elements may be involved in bricolage, but the point is that through bricolage, institutions evolve in a path-dependent way. This is because the range of actor's choices for innovation are more or less fixed by the set of institutional principles and practices at their disposal. However, even though the concept of bricolage is used to characterise evolutionary change, it does so in contrast to many analyses of evolutionary change, and directs our attention to the creative process through which actors make decisions about how to re-combine the institutional elements at their disposal. The bricoleurs, or the creative actors, who are responsible for re-combining institutional elements in innovative ways, are also called 'entrepreneurs' (Schumpeter 1934/1983), or in political-administrative settings 'policy entrepreneurs' (Kingdon 2011, 179ff).

Campbell emphasises that in order to understand why entrepreneurs make one bricolage rather than another, it is important to understand their social relationships and entrepreneurial skills. For example, if entrepreneurs have extensive ties to people beyond their immediate social, organisational and institutional locations, they are more likely to have a broad repertoire with which to work. They are also more likely to receive ideas about how to re-combine the elements in their repertoire. All of these relationships and skills increase the possibilities for creative and revolutionary thinking, innovation and bricolage (Campbell 2004, 74–75). It is also important to recognise that whilst the social, organisational and institutional location of entrepreneurs affects their capacity for creative innovation, they face institutional and resource constraints that affect their capacity to make their innovations stick. We will see examples of this in the analysis below.

A second concept Campbell uses to describe mechanisms of change is the concept of *diffusion* (Campbell 2004, 77). This concept refers to the spread of institutional principles or practices with little modification through a population of actors. The concept is used especially by organisational institutionalists, who argue that diffusion leads to isomorphic or homogenous outcomes in populations of organisations (Mizruchi and Fein 1999). Meyer and colleagues (1997) fit this profile when they argue that the development of a global scientific discourse that sees the world as an ecosystem led many national governments to establish environmental ministries in the late twentieth century.

However, a problem with Meyer and colleagues' argument, which they share with other organisational institutionalists (i.e. DiMaggio 1983; Mizruchi and Fein 1999), is that they assume that diffusion results in homogeneous or isomorphic outcomes, where all organisations in a field gradually adopt identical practices and converge with respect to their form and function. Thus, Meyer *et al.* omit any discussion of the national-level political processes that were responsible for the enactment of this global discourse, and apparently assume that environmental ministries are all the same.

However, case studies that are more fine-tuned and nuanced have shown that this is seldom the case (Dobbin 1992; Majoribanks 2000). More often, what happens when institutional principles and practices travel from one site to another is that recipients implement or enact them in different ways, and to a greater or lesser extent. New ideas are combined with existing institutional practices in a way that is very similar to bricolage. The difference is that *translation* involves the combination of new, externally produced elements received through diffusion as well as old locally produced elements inherited from the past (Campbell 2004, 80). In our case, where a new programme is introduced that seeks to be integrated into different local institutions at the same administrative level, the understanding of diffusion as a process of translation seems particularly promising.

In their continuing analysis of the process of translation, institutionalists have been looking for factors that can either constrain or enable the process of translation (Soysal 1994; Lounsbury 2001). Studies have shown that when organisations are exposed to new principles and practices through diffusion, they are more likely to translate them into practice substantively rather than just symbolically, if leaders (managers) inside the organisation are sympathetic and ideologically committed to the new practice. Substantive translation is also more likely if the organisation itself has the financial, administrative and other implementation capacities necessary to support the new practice (Hironaka and Schofer 2002; Zald *et al.* 2002). Campbell concludes his discussion on this matter by stating that the degree to which diffusing ideas and practices are translated into local practice depends on local institutional contexts, power struggles, leadership support and implementation capacities (Campbell 2004, 82).

In order to adequately deal with changes in the normative and the cultural-cognitive pillar (defined above), we also need to deal theoretically with the role of ideas in institutional change. We have found it useful to work with Campbell's concepts of '*programs*' and '*frames*' (Campbell 2004, 93ff). *Programs* are defined as cognitive concepts and theories that enable and facilitate decision making and institutional change by specifying for decision makers how to solve specific problems.

Programs include, inter alia, policy prescriptions and corporate strategies, depending on whether one is looking at the public or private sector. From the description of the CCP programmes above, it is very clear that these do indeed constitute programs in Campbell's sense, because they embody a milestone approach, which is a clear policy prescription.

Frames are defined as normative concepts in the foreground of decision making debates. They enable elites to legitimise their programmes and institutional change to their constituents and occasionally to each other.[8] A good example of a frame is the concept of 'green growth', which conveys the idea that sustainable development is compatible with economic growth.

Programs and frames can be used actively by decision makers to design the changes they want to see. In doing so, they most often depend on policy entrepreneurs, who can formulate a situation as a problem and provide a vision of how the problem can be solved. Policy entrepreneurs are normally good at formulating such visions in clear terms that are simple enough for decision makers to understand. Visions or solutions normally appear clear and simple if they resonate with (dominant) paradigms and public sentiments. Campbell (2004, 177–8) proposes the hypothesis that problems are more likely to be perceived as requiring institutional changes if there are policy entrepreneurs on hand who can articulate and frame them as such in clear and simple terms.

In our analysis below, we begin by looking at how climate change in Australia and New Zealand came to be seen as a problem that needed a solution, and how and why policy entrepreneurs 'imported' a solution that appeared both clear and simple to national and local decision makers, was considered legitimate and was therefore implemented by many local councils.

Having demonstrated how the CCP programme was introduced into Australia and New Zealand through a process of diffusion and translation, we then analyse the regulative, normative and cultural-cognitive impacts of the programme. This enables us to evaluate the breadth and depth of the institutional change brought about by the programme and also point to some unresolved problems.

Diffusion and translation: The introduction of the CCP programme to Australia and New Zealand

This section explains why a policy window for action on climate change opened in Australia in 1997, and how the CCP programme was imported from the US and later re-exported to New Zealand in a process of diffusion and translation.

According to Australian election studies (see Australian Election Studies 1990–2007; Pietsch and McAllister 2010), the environment was the most important non-economic election issue in Australia in 1990. The issue remained one of the most important election issues in the period between 1990 and 2007.

Towards the middle of the 1990s, the issue of climate change became prominent, as virtually every city and town across the continent began to struggle with droughts. Thus, public sentiments laid the foundation for political action in the field, which led to Australia's first national attempt to reduce greenhouse gas emissions – the voluntary Greenhouse Challenge Program – which was launched in 1995. Following this initiative, Australia contributed to the development of, and signed but did not ratify the Kyoto Protocol. Later in 1998, the Australian Greenhouse Office released the National Greenhouse Strategy, which recognised that climate change was of global significance, and that Australia had an international obligation to address the problem. In 2000, the Australian Senate's Environment, Communications, Information Technology and the Arts References Committee conducted an inquiry that produced a report called 'The Heat is On: Australia's Greenhouse Future', which sparked an intense political debate on climate change.

Our policy entrepreneur is at work in this political environment, and actively imported the CCP programme from the US. According to this person, who was central in the later implementation of the programme in both Australia and New Zealand, the process began like this:

ICLEI began in 1992 as an outcome of the Rio Earth Summit. ... Early on there was also an interest in climate change, and the Americans began a pilot project, which looked at how to work on climate change in local governments; did some work and came up with a programme called CCP. So they designed the five milestones and very broadly speaking did the initial work on that. ... So I went there (in 1996) and saw the program and thought: 'Oh, we could make this work in Australia'. Talked to the Australian Local Government Association. They agreed; they were happy to be a partner to it. I came back and spoke to Federal Government and then in June 1997, a couple of months later, we got the money and then later that year the Prime Minister announced a five-year program, which is what we did.[9]

However, importing such a programme causes an active translation to take place which transforms it substantially: 'We really worked hard on measurement and on recognition; those were the two big changes that we made to the existing program'.[10] So while the programme imported from the US was quite loose, especially regarding the later milestones (4 and 5), our bricoleur was instrumental in turning it into a well-defined and significant methodology. He was also aware that recognition was very important in terms of having the programme accepted and spread among local governments. As he put it:

Before any local government was recruited, we would insist on having a council discussion in the town hall, and we would stand up, and we would discuss with them the climate change, the program and all that. ... And you know, we still have got Mayors to this day who say 'We remember when you came to the council and talked about climate change'.[11]

This process of translating the programme, and having it accepted and incorporated into local government was probably successful also because ICLEI Oceania, the provider of the programme in both Australia and New Zealand, were adept at aligning the purpose of the programme with the purposes of the local governments. Again, our observer:

We talked about how this could be a big co-benefit for all of the policies and programmes that are in place. That they would save money, which they have. So we always recognised that councils would do a programme like this for a multiple number of reasons: not just to reduce CO_2 but to save money; because the next door council was doing it, because the state government was giving out grants to do it, because the national government was going to Kyoto in six months, etc.[12]

Another important reason for local governments to implement the CCP programme could have been pressure from national government. However, while there are legal requirements for local governments in both New Zealand and Australia to perform resource management, land planning and greenhouse gas accounting (see Hoff 2010, 17ff), partnerships and grants have been the preferred way of dealing with climate change at the local level. Realising that local government is the administrative level with the closest links to communities, they were imagined to be the actors best-suited to raise local awareness about climate change. In addition, because local governments emit pollution themselves, the bigger urban areas in particular were seen as good places to begin the programme. Asked about this relationship, a principal official from the Ministry of Environment said:

> Certainly, it was viewed as a partnership. The Ministry had certain things that it wanted to achieve, and that it wanted to have in a local government programme. Therefore, the ICLEI perspective: that they were the provider and had the intellectual property and the proven methodology [was a good solution— JH].[13]

This solution was also supported by the local government associations in the two countries (Australian Local Government Association [ALGA] and Local Government New Zealand [LGNZ]), who in different ways engaged in the programmes.[14]

Whilst importing the CCP programme to Australia and implementing it there required a process of substantial translation, the re-export of the programme to New Zealand seems to be closer to a process of diffusion. As one observer said, 'In a lot of respects (implementing the CCP programme) was taking a proven methodology and just sort of applying it to the New Zealand context'.[15]

In the following sections, we take a closer look at how the second step of translation of the CCP programme has worked. First, we look at how its regulatory framework (or methodology) has been implemented (translated) in local governments, and the organisational changes made in order to accommodate this new policy field. Second, we look at the shaping of organisational norms that were necessary to implement the CCP programme. Third, we look at the possible co-existence or collision between taken-for-granted cognitive frames in local government and the frames used in the climate change policy field.

Institutional change I: Regulatory framework and organisational set-up

In this section, we discuss the implementation of the CCP methodology in local governments, and how this implementation was addressed organisationally. Eventual changes in the legal (national) framework are not discussed: they were not part of our study.

To investigate how the translation process worked in both countries, we first look at the role that the size of the relevant local governments played in the programmes. Campbell (2004) suggests that the size of a given local government affects the success of a substantive translation of the programme. Since larger councils tend to command more financial and administrative resources than smaller ones, it is assumed that we are likely to see a more thorough implementation of the CCP programme in the larger councils.

Second, we look at the role that energy managers/climate change officers played in the translation process. We investigate whether the existence of such managers, who are likely to be sympathetic towards, and ideologically committed to climate change mitigation, leads to a more thorough and encompassing implementation of the programme in local governments, compared to councils that do not have such managers.

Regulatory framework

If we look at the content of specific climate change action plans (corporate and/or community) of councils, we find first, that 47 per cent of the councils report having such a plan. A total of 36 per cent report that they have a cross-departmental plan, while 17 per cent report having no climate change action plan at all. There is no difference between large and small councils in this respect: 50 per cent of small councils report having a specific plan, while the same is true for 49 per cent of the large councils.

All the councils that have an action plan have set reduction targets for their corporate emissions; many have also set reduction targets for their community emissions.[16] These reduction targets vary widely from very ambitious goals such as carbon neutrality for both sectors in 2012 to less ambitious goals such as a 10 per cent reduction for both sectors in 2010 or 2012 (base year 1999).

Some of the larger councils in our survey are among the most ambitious. The city of Brisbane aims at carbon neutrality for both sectors in 2026, while Christchurch aims for a corporate sector that is powered by 80 per cent renewable energy by 2025 and a community sector that is powered by 30 per cent renewable energy by 2025.[17]

Another characteristic of the action plans is that they generally cover a number of different areas. A total of 90 per cent of the councils include energy conservation in their plans, 80 per cent include waste reduction, 72 per cent include renewable energy, 68 per cent include sustainable transport and 57 per cent more sustainable living. A total of 31 per cent of the municipalities mention 'other areas', including biodiversity and water pollution. In addition, some councils have now integrated adaptation measures into their climate change action plan, and some action plans encompass areas such as governance, research and communication with citizens.

It is quite clear that large councils target more areas in their action plans than smaller councils (see Table 9.2). Whilst only 29 per cent of small councils target more than four areas in their corporate action plan, this is true for 63 per cent of large councils. In this sense, the corporate action plans of big councils are more ambitious than those of smaller councils.

When asking councils about which of the areas have the highest priority in their actions plans, *energy conservation* is the highest priority by far. A total of 71 per cent of councils give this area as the highest priority, whilst waste reduction

Table 9.2 Differences between large and small councils in terms of areas included in council's climate change action plans (percentages)

Council size	0–4 areas included	More than 4 areas included
Small councils (5–40,000 inhabitants)	71	**29**
Medium-sized councils (40,001–91,000 inhabitants)	61	39
Large councils (91,001–900,000 inhabitants)	38	**63**
N =	43	36

Notes: Gamma = 0.454, $p<0.01$.

is the highest priority for 10 per cent of the councils and 7 per cent of councils say their highest priority is renewable energy.

If we look at what sectors of their local communities councils targeted within the CCP programmes, almost half of all councils (47 per cent) do not have any community targets at all. In those councils that have set targets, *households* and *businesses* are the most common community sector targets, each targeted by almost half (48 and 43 per cent respectively) of the councils. A total of 28 per cent of active councils say that they (also) have other sector targets, whereas 15 per cent cite *youth* (i.e. schools) as a special target.

Table 9.3 shows that among small councils, as many as 67 per cent do not have community sector targets, whereas this is only the case for 28 per cent of the large councils. Also, as many as 72 per cent of the large councils have one or more community sector targets, whereas this is only the case for 33 per cent of the small ones. A likely explanation for this difference is that the larger councils, because they are in command of more resources than small councils, are able to involve more sectors of the community in climate change actions.

Table 9.3 Differences between large and small councils in terms of community sectors included in council's climate change action plans (percentages)

Council size	No sectors included	One or more sectors included
Small councils (5–40,000 inhabitants)	67	**33**
Medium-sized councils (40,001–91,000 inhabitants)	52	48
Large councils (91,001–900,000 inhabitants)	28	**72**
Average percentage	47	53
N =	37	42

Notes: Gamma = 0.509, $p<0.005$.

Organisational set-up

It is interesting to note that participation in the CCP programmes seems to have had profound effects on council organisation. A total of 45 per cent of the councils say that participation in the CCP programme has led to organisational changes in council administration.

Three types of organisational changes seem to be typical:

1 The creation of a position as Climate Change Officer or Energy Manager – a position that oversees climate change action/energy management across departmental sectors. A total of 63 per cent of councils now have such a position. Interestingly, there is no difference between large and small councils in terms of creating such position.

2 Creation of a new unit reflecting the importance of the environment, sustainability and climate change. A total of 21 per cent of councils say that they now have a department responsible for climate change action (33 per cent of the larger councils, but only 8 per cent of the smaller ones).

3 Incorporation of council climate change plans into long-term strategic plans. A total of 83 per cent of councils made this change: 94 per cent of the large councils and 73 per cent of the small ones.

If we look at the relationship between having a climate change officer/energy manager in the organisation and various aspects of implementation of climate change mitigation plans, we see, first (Table 9.4), that the presence of such a person seems to have been beneficial to the fostering of changes that adapt the organisation to such plans. A total of 54 per cent of councils that employ a climate change officer have seen such changes, whilst this is only the case for 30 per cent of councils without such a person.[18]

There is another area where the presence of a climate change officer/energy manager might make a difference, namely whether the council's action plan on climate change or other measures to make CO_2 reductions has been incorporated into the council's strategic plans. Our results find some indication that this is the

Table 9.4 Correlation between having a climate change officer / energy manager and organisational changes in council administration (percentages)

	Participation in CCP has led to organisational changes	*Participation in CCP has not led to organisational changes*
Climate change officer/ energy manager present	54	46
No climate change officer/ energy manager	30	70
N =	36	44

Notes: Gamma = 0.465, $p<0.05$.

case. A total of 88 per cent of councils with a climate change officer have done this, whilst this is only the case for 75 per cent of councils without such a person. However, this finding is not statistically significant at the desired level.

Organisational change II: The shaping of new organisational norms

The CCP programme was a policy prescription for how to tackle the problem of climate change at the local level. As such, on the surface it was a clear and simple programme that relates to milestones and measurable numbers. According to Campbell (2004), this is a prerequisite for convincing decision makers to adopt a programme.

However, even though the simplicity of the programme was a necessary prerequisite, it was not sufficient. We have already discussed above how our policy entrepreneur, and later his staff worked hard to convince local decision makers to take on the programme and realign it with existing council priorities. However, in order to genuinely embed the programme in local councils, it seemed necessary to work on their organisational culture. In line with this thinking, our policy entrepreneur talks about the programme as a 'culture change program'.[19]

The most important culture change needed in order to embed the programme in local councils, i.e. to convince them to accept and embrace the programme, was related to their taking on *project ownership*. Several of our interviewees stressed that the CCP programme allowed for exactly that, as its character as a coherent programme, and especially its milestone approach, gave councils a strong focus that allowed them to take on a leadership role in the local community.[20] One of our interviewees expressed it like this: 'I think a critical element is owning the programme … so what I used to say over and over is WE, we need to say "WE". When we say "WE", we mean "US" – local government'.[21]

Such ownership also seems easier to take on if others are doing the same thing. Our policy entrepreneur and his staff were aware that creating a network among participants would be very beneficial to programme acceptance, and went on to do just this. That the effort had a noticeable effect is clear from one of our interviewees:

> Sharing the experience, I think that was what the CCP did really well. It brought councils together to highlight what was going on. It brought us together to get the peer pressure on because that was a huge influence. … Our Mayor came back here totally fired up and motivated about it. He felt confident because all the other Mayors were taking it seriously.[22]

That the culture change has sunk in, and that climate change policy is now accepted as a political and administrative field on a par with other fields is confirmed by our survey data. A majority of councils (51 per cent) say that *the major benefit of the CCP programme is that it has led to the formulation of a coherent action programme on climate change*. A total of 16 per cent of councils refer to other things such as 'raising the awareness about climate change' and 'getting the issue on the agenda' and 'providing leadership and support'. Whilst a total of 12 per cent said 'it has led to fundamental changes in the way we conduct operations in one or more areas', another 12 per cent said 'it has led to a sharing of best practices with other councils'.

One example of such small but fundamental change is that financial systems in some councils are now geared to capture emissions data.[23] We also have many examples of the sharing of best practices: councils in Tasmania are now working together to develop and implement coordinated and consistent community-based actions on climate change.

Organisational change III: Co-existence or collision between cognitive frames?

Frames are normative concepts that are at the centre of decision making debates. According to Campbell (2004), they are used to legitimise programmes and foster their acceptance in the institutions in question.

In order to deal with this question, we asked councils which criteria they used when prioritising areas in their climate change action plan(s). We found a very clear indication that *financial savings* is the main criterion for prioritising areas. A total of 39 per cent of councils say that this is their main criterion (see Table 9.5), whilst 16 per cent of the councils say that their main criterion for prioritising is the existing budget, which means that action plan measures are negotiated mainly within an economic frame of reference.

These survey totals mean that well over half of the councils use economic reasoning as the main rationale for priorities in their action plan. However, we also see that 25 per cent of councils said that they use 'other criteria' for prioritising. When taking a closer look at these other criteria, we find that they are first and foremost connected with *impact on emissions*, meaning that reduction of greenhouse gas emissions per dollar spent is used as the main criterion for prioritisation. The criterion 'low hanging fruit' might also be associated with this criterion, where 'low hanging fruit' is taken to mean benefits that can be reaped without major investments.

Table 9.5 The council's main criterion for prioritising areas in the climate change action plan (percentages)

Financial savings	39
Other criteria	25
Existing budget	16
Low-hanging fruit	12
Existing technical expertise	4
Strongly supported by the community	4
N = 73	Sum = 100

Note: Respondents were only allowed to select one criterion.

As a rough estimate, we can say that for two-thirds of the councils, the potential for financial savings and their local economy plays a major role in how they
set priorities in their climate change action plans. The remaining one-quarter to
one-third of councils use an understanding of impact on emissions as their main
criterion when prioritising their interventions.

In order to probe deeper into the question of the importance of councils budgets as a dominant frame for legitimising action in the field versus other possible
frames, we asked how councils have financed activities related to climate change
mitigation activities, as well as what has happened to the financial savings from
councils' actions. If we take a look first at how councils have financed emission
reduction activities, we see that these have been financed overwhelmingly
within existing departmental budgets, from extra (temporary) funding and/or via
grants from other levels of government (Table 9.6).

Private sector partnerships and channelling savings from earlier rounds of
emission reductions into new activities are methods used by only 18 per cent of
councils.

Analysing further the question of what happens to financial savings from
councils' actions on climate change, 69 per cent of councils responded that
because such savings are integrated into the councils' general budgets, they are
not directly visible. However, 18 per cent of councils ring-fence some of these
savings so they can be used for further actions on climate change, and 6 per cent
of councils ring-fence all such savings. It is interesting to note that whereas more
large than small councils finance their activities related to climate change action
via savings generated by CO_2 reductions (27 per cent versus 4 per cent), there is
no statistical significant difference between large and small councils on the question of ring-fencing savings.

According to our interviews, ring-fencing some or all of such savings (eventually in a fund of some sorts) seems to be a very effective method of generating
funds for investments in future energy-conservation activities. It is therefore
surprising that this method is not more widely used to create resources as well as
to support further emissions-reduction measures. However, a possible explanation for this is probably the dominance of an economic frame of reference in
local councils when setting priorities concerning climate change action, or more
specifically the predominance of a focus on (short-term) financial savings.

Table 9.6 Methods for financing activities related to CO_2 reductions (percentages)

Within existing departmental budgets	83
Grants from other levels of government	72
Extra budget funding	40
Private sector partnerships	18
Savings generated by CO_2 reductions	18
Other methods	6
N = 78	

Conclusion

This chapter has discussed how a specific programme for climate change mitigation, the CCP programme, was imported from the US to Australia and New Zealand through a process of translation and diffusion. We also discussed how organisational norms were developed in order to embed the programmes in local councils politically as well as administratively, and how the programme was politically accepted by realigning it with an existing political agenda of financial constraint.

The data used to shed light on these questions are the results of a survey of all the local councils in Australia and New Zealand that participated in the CCP programme and a series of 21 semi-structured interviews with mayors, energy managers or climate change resource staff in local councils. Data were also collected from civil servants from relevant ministries, representatives from businesses and non-governmental organisations (NGOs) working in the area of climate change mitigation and official plans, reports and documents from ministries, local councils and organisations dealing with the question of climate change. All data were collected in 2010–11.

The theoretical framework used to understand these processes of institutional change was an institutionalist framework devised by Campbell (2004) in particular. This framework suggests that substantive translation is more likely if the implementing organisation has the financial, administrative and other implementation capacities to support the new practice, and if there are policy entrepreneurs on hand who can articulate and frame the policy problem in clear and simple terms.

In the first part of the analysis, we looked at these questions, and found support for both of Campbell's assumptions. We found that more large councils than small completed the CCP programme's milestone 4 or 5, large councils target more areas in their action plans than smaller councils and large councils are more likely to have set reduction targets for their communities and to have involved more sectors of their community than smaller councils. We also found that councils that appointed a climate change officer/energy manager were more likely to have initiated organisational changes in order to accommodate the CCP programme than councils without such a person. Also, according to our interviews, the presence of such staff members was an important factor for institutional capacity building concerning climate change mitigation, as well as for placing the issue firmly on the agenda of political and administrative decision makers in local councils.

Organisational norms that were developed in order to embed the program in local councils related to project ownership and network creation. Project ownership necessitated the creation of a strong sense of the project as belonging to the councils (not ICLEI or the government) in order for implementation to take place. This was a successful exercise for large councils in particular: they quickly outgrew the programme and went on to pursue their own climate change mitigation plans (Hoff 2010). Establishing networks in order to share experiences with other councils was necessary in order to create enthusiasm and support for the programme among both politicians and highly placed civil servants. Networking proved to be essential, particularly for the smaller councils, in order to gain access to the available pool of knowledge in the area of climate change mitigation.

According to Campbell, in order for a programme like CCP to be accepted politically and administratively, it is essential that it does not collide with the dominant cognitive frame(s) in the organisation(s) under consideration. In the case of the CCP programme, such acceptance was secured by its alignment with the dominant frame of financial savings/fiscal restraint.

The focus of this chapter has been the challenge of incorporating climate change policies in local public administration. For this reason, it has only superficially dealt with the question of the role the national and international context has played in the success or failure of the CPP programme. Such context is the point of departure in the official (ICLEI) reports that summarised the results of the CCP programmes, which stressed the reduction of greenhouse gas emissions and the financial savings that occurred on a national scale as a result of the programmes.

While the contribution of the CCP programmes towards these aims is significant and admirable, less attention is paid to the many other tangible and less tangible results that this chapter has discussed in detail. The official reports also do not consider whether barriers existed that hindered the translation of the programmes in local councils, and whether such barriers prevented optimal implementation of the programme. Campbell (2004, 172ff) conceptualises such barriers as something that might constrain the 'fit' with the regulative, normative and cultural-cognitive pillars of an organisation, resulting in a sub-optimal translation of the programme.

We encountered such barriers in our interviews. In one way or another, the barriers discussed with interviewees all related to the wider context of local councils; all of them constrained the fit between the different pillars in the local councils. The first barrier is related to the fact that local councils are dependent on national politics: national policies might change, which can jeopardise local plans and priorities. This is exactly what happened to the CCP programmes in both Australia and New Zealand: shifts in governments in both countries led to the termination of the programmes in 2009, and to cutbacks in funding for climate change action.

The second barrier is related to the fact that climate change action cuts across all other sectors in local councils. This makes such action difficult to coordinate, which is also the reason why a majority of councils created the positions of energy managers or climate change officers, and some have established new units to deal with the policy field. Whether these innovations have solved the coordination problems is not entirely clear.

The third barrier is that while short-term financial savings is the dominant frame for climate change mitigation measures in local councils, reaping major benefits in terms of reduction in energy consumption requires considerable investment. Local councils do not at present seem to have any clear-cut strategies for accumulating funds to make such investments.

Our conclusion is that incorporating climate change policies into local councils in Australia and New Zealand has been a success in the sense that a substantive and symbolic translation of the CCP programme took place. However, factors basically beyond the control of local administrations constrained the programme's success by contributing to a lack of fit among the different pillars of local administrations.

Notes

1   There is a limited amount of international academic literature dealing with implementation or development of climate change policy in local government. Authors who have dealt with the governance of climate change at various administrative levels are Bulkeley and Betsill (2005), Bulkeley and Kern (2006), Lemos and Agrawal (2006), Urwina and Jordan (2008). In our literature search, we found two articles that deal directly with the Communities/Cities for Climate Protection Programs (CCP programmes) that are the focus of this chapter: Zahran *et al.* (2008) and Gore (2010).

2   ICLEI was founded in 1990 as the 'International Council for Local Environmental Initiatives'. It is now called 'ICLEI – Local Governments for Sustainability', and is an international association of local governments and national and regional local government organisations that have made a commitment to sustainable development. More than 1,000 cities, towns, counties and their associations in 68 countries are now members of ICLEI (http://en.wikipedia.org/wiki/ICLEI; accessed 12 July 2010).

3   Local government units have a number of different names in Australia and in New Zealand. In Australia, the official name for a unit of local government is a Local Government Area (LGA), whilst the local governing body itself is generally known as a council. Although almost all LGAs have the same administrative functions, their names are quite different. Thus, urban or suburban LGAs are normally called 'cities' and have a city council, whilst rural LGAs covering a larger area are usually called a 'shire'. In addition, names such as municipality, district council, town and borough occur regularly. There are a total of 564 LGAs in Australia. In New Zealand, the word 'council' is consistently used to designate local government units. Here the distinction is between district (rural) and city (urban) councils on the one hand, and regional councils on the other. The first type of councils are called 'territorial councils' and have certain functions, while the regional councils, as the second tier of government, have other functions and normally cover a number of city and district councils. There are 12 regional councils, 16 city councils and 57 district councils in New Zealand. In order not to confuse the reader, the term 'council' is used consistently here to denominate a Local Government Area, including its political and administrative bodies. See http://en.wikipedia.org/wiki/Local_government_in_ Australia and www.lgnz.co.nz/home/nzs-local-government/local-government-basics/ Accessed 12 July 2010.

4   See Australian Government Department of the Environment, Water, Heritage and the Arts (2008) *Cities for Climate Protection Australia. Local Government Action on Climate Change: Measures Evaluation Report 2008*, p. 4.

5   Interview with officials in the Ministry of Environment, New Zealand, 28 April 2010.

6   In Table 9.1, the confidence intervals of the two distributions are shown (CI = 95). If the intervals are overlapping – which they are – we are able to say with 95 per cent certainty that the two distributions are not statistically different. This is a stronger test than just testing the difference in the average of the two distributions via a simple t-test.

7   This result is statistically significant at the 0.01 level (gamma = 0.479). Table not shown here.

8   When talking about frames, Campbell clearly draws on the definition of frames and framing in the literature on public opinion and political communication. See, e.g. Bennett and Entman (2001).

9   Interview with former director of ICLEI Oceania, 4 March 2010, Melbourne.

10   Interview with former director of ICLEI Oceania, 4 March 2010, Melbourne.

11   Interview with former director of ICLEI Oceania, 4 March 2010, Melbourne.

12   Interview with former director of ICLEI Oceania, 4 March 2010, Melbourne.

13   Interview with two employees at the Ministry for Environment, New Zealand, 28 April 2010.

14   Other obvious reasons for local councils to implement the programme could be their climate change vulnerability or if 'green attitudes' are dominant among its population and politicians. Zahran *et al.* (2008) have tested both of these assumptions on US data. They found that CCP-committed localities were quantitatively different from non-committed localities on both climate change risk and political attitudes. Thus, CCP campaign participation was found to increase significantly with the number of people killed by extreme weather events, projected temperature change and coastal proximity. In addition, the odds of CCP campaign involvement increases with the amount of citizens who vote Democrat and recycle. Such causality is also likely in both Australia and New Zealand, but unfortunately, we do not have the data to test it.

15   Interview with former director of ICLEI Oceania, 4 March 2010, Melbourne.

16   A fundamental difficulty with establishing reduction targets for communities is reported by the Hobart City Council in Australia. 'The council no longer has a community target, as it does not control these emissions. [We] can only seek to influence these, and do not have resources or access to data to measure emissions in this sector. [The council] is now working ... with other councils to develop and implement coordinated and consistent community based actions' [open question in survey].

17   Whether Christchurch's ambitious goals have been maintained after the devastating earthquake in February 2011 is not known.

18   Here we have to be aware that the organisational changes reported might pertain to the establishment of the position of climate change officer. There might be a tautological element in this correlation. However, due to the formulation of the question on changes we consider this unlikely.

19   Interview with former director of ICLEI Oceania, 4 March 2010, Melbourne.

20   'The CCP programme has given us a strong foundation. ... It focused us in on the five-step process that they have around starting to measure your emissions and set targets and reducing them and so on'. Interview with Climate Change Advisor, Wellington, 8 February 2010.

21   Interview with central official from ICLEI, 4 March 2010.

22   Interview with Sustainability Advisor, Christchurch, New Zealand, 24 March 2010.

23   This is the case in the city of Campbelltown, Australia.

References

Australian Election Studies (1990–2007) (http://assda.anu.edu.au/aestrends.pdf) Accessed 25 September 2010.

Baumgartner F R and Jones B D (1993) *Agenda and Instability in American Politics*, University of Chicago Press, Chicago, IL.

Bennett W L and Entman R M (eds) (2001) *Mediated Politics: Communication in the Future of Democracy*, Cambridge University Press, Cambridge UK.

Bulkeley H and Betsill M (2005) Rethinking Sustainable Cities: Multilevel Governance and the 'Urban' Politics of Climate Change, *Environmental Politics* 14 42–63.

Bulkeley H and Kern K (2006) Local Government and the Governing of Climate Change in Germany and the UK, *Urban Studies* 43 2237–2259.

Campbell J L (2004) *Institutional Change and Globalization*, Princeton University Press, Princeton, NJ

DiMaggio P J (1983) The Iron Cage Revisited: Institutional Isomorphism and Collective Rationality in Organizational Fields, *American Sociological Review* 48 147–160.

Dobbin F (1992) The Origins of Private Social Insurance: Public Policy and Fringe Benefits in America, *American Journal of Sociology* 97 1416–1450.

Flyvbjerg B (2001) *Making Social Science Matter: Why Social Inquiry Fails and How It Can Succeed Again*, Cambridge University Press, Cambridge, UK.

Gore C D (2010) The Limits and Opportunities of Networks: Municipalities and Canadian Climate Change Policy, *Review of Policy Research* 27 27–46 [Policy Studies Organization (http://works.bepress.com/cdgore/11) Accessed 26 October 2012].

Hall P (1996) Political Science and the Three Institutionalisms, *Political Studies* 44 936–957.

Hironaka A and Schofer E (2002) Decoupling in the Environmental Arena: The Case of Environmental Impact Statements, in Hoffman A J and Ventresca M J (eds) *Organizations, Policy and the Natural Environment: Institutional and Strategic Perspectives*, Stanford University Press, Stanford, CA.

Hoff J (2010) *Local Climate Protection Programmes in Australia and New Zealand – results, dilemmas and relevance for future actions*, CIDEA Project report no 1 Det Samfundsvidenskabelige Fakultets Reprocenter University of Copenhagen, Denmark.

Kingdon J W (2011) *Agendas, Alternatives, and Public Policies*, Longman, Boston, MA.

Lemos M C and Agrawal A (2006) Environmental Governance, *Annual Review of Environmental Resources* 31 297–325.

Levi-Strauss C (1966) *The Savage Mind*, University of Chicago Press, Chicago, IL.

Lounsbury M (2001) Institutional Sources of Practice Variation: Staffing College and University Recycling Programs, *Administrative Science Quarterly* 46 29–56.

March J and Olsen J P (1989) *Rediscovering Institutions: The Organizational Basis of Politics*, Free Press, New York

March J G and Olsen J P (1995) *Democratic Governance*, The Free Press, New York.

Marjoribanks T (2000) *News Corporation, Technology and the Workplace: Global Strategies, Local Change*, Cambridge University Press, New York.

Meyer J W, Frank J D, Hironaka A, Schofer E and Tuma N B (1997) The Structuring of a World Environmental Regime 1970–1990, *International Organization* 51 623–651.

Mizruchi M S and Fein L C (1999) The Social Construction of Organizational Knowledge: A Study of the Uses of Coercive, Mimetic, and Normative Isomorphism, *Administrative Science Quarterly* 44 653–683.

North D C (1990) *Institutions, Institutional Change and Economic Performance*, Cambridge University Press, New York.

Pierson P (2000) Increasing Returns, Path Dependency, and the Study of Politics, *American Political Science Review* 94(2) 251–267.

Pietsch J and McAllister I (2010) 'A Diabolic Challenge': Public Opinion and Climate Change Policy in Australia, *Environmental Politics* 19(2) 217–236.

Powell W W (1991) Expanding the Scope of Institutional Analysis, in Powell W W and DiMaggio P J (eds) *The New Institutionalism in Organizational Analysis*, University of Chicago Press, Chicago 183–203.

Powell W W and DiMaggio P J (eds) (1991) *The New Institutionalism in Organizational Analysis*, University of Chicago Press, Chicago, IL.

Schumpeter J A (1934/1983) *The Theory of Economic Development*, Transaction, New Brunswick, NJ.

Scott W R (2001) *Institutions and Organization*, Sage, Thousand Oaks, CA.

Skocpol T (1985) Bringing the State Back In: Strategies of Analysis in Current Research, in Evans P, Rueschemeyer D and Skocpol T (eds) *Bringing the State Back In*, Cambridge University Press, New York, 3–44.

Soysal Y (1994) *Limits of Citizenship*, University of Chicago Press, Chicago, IL.

Thelen K and Steinmo S (1992) Historical Institutionalism in Comparative Politics in Thelen K and Steinmo K (eds) *Structuring Politics: Historical Institutionalism in Comparative Analysis*, Cambridge University Press, New York, 1–32.

Urwina K and Jordan A (2008) Does Public Policy Support or Undermine Climate Change Adaptation? Exploring Policy Interplay Across Different Scales of Governance, *Global Environmental Governance* 18 180–191.

Zahran S, Brody S D, Vedlitz A and Miller C (2008) Vulnerability and Capacity: Explaining Local Commitment to Climate-Change Policy, *Environment and Planning C: Government and Policy* 26 544–562.

Zald M N, Morrill C and Rao H (2002) *How Do Social Movements Penetrate Organizations? Environmental Impact and Organizational Response*, Paper presented at the conference on Organization and Social Movement Theory University of Michigan, Ann Arbor, MI.

10 'A change of just a few degrees'

The possibilities and challenges of local American climate mitigation

Ebba Lisberg Jensen

Introduction

> America is a giant hologram, in the sense that information concerning the whole is contained in each of its elements.
>
> (Baudrillard 1986, 29)

In his well-known book, *America*, which was published in 1986, French philosopher Jean Baudrillard boldly (some would say recklessly) set out to capture the spirit of the United States (US) from the perspective of a European intellectual. The impossibility of describing America, with its enormous variety of landscapes, cultures, regions, political, even ideological divides and economic circumstances in one book, is all too evident. However, the impressionist quality of *America* has its uses. Baudrillard does not discuss sustainability issues or climate change in any great detail. But he unapologetically expresses scepticism about the ultra-modern American way of life, one that creates so much comfort and yet displays such systemic fragility: '... decentralization, air-conditioning, soft technologies. Paradise. But a very slight modification, a change of just a few degrees [in temperature], would suffice to make it seem like hell' (Baudrillard 1986, 46).

Baudrillard is right: The world is warming up. An increase of only a few degrees will affect weather patterns, agricultural production, fresh-water supplies, sea levels and ice covers. The Intergovernmental Panel of Climate Change (IPCC) suggests that it is possible to halt the warming at two degrees Celsius with technological and behavioural changes (IPCC Press Release 2014). But even so, the changes must be quite radical and will alter life-styles that have been taken for granted until now. It can be argued that no other country epitomises the issue of the consequences of climate change on life-style than the United States (US).

The idea of the dramatic consequences of a slightly raised global temperature is relevant to the purposes of this chapter. Understanding climate change mitigation, climate consciousness-raising and climate work in the local American context can be inspired by Baudrillard's macro view of the US in all its complexity. The consequences of the choices the US has made in the past – favouring the car over mass transportation, designing urban areas based on the car and an over-whelming dependence on fossil fuels – can be seen in the country's current local climate change mitigation efforts.

Today, climate change is one of the most urgent sustainability issues in most countries throughout the world. In the US, it is one of the most contested and provocative issues of contemporary public debate. Why this is so is obvious to any serious observer of US society and culture: extraction and use of fossil fuels are central to the American economy, how society is structured and how indi-vidual citizens conduct their daily lives. This chapter makes no claim to comprehensive coverage of the sociology of the agency and political debate in the issue of climate mitigation in the US. But it aims to provide some human ecological perspectives on the seemingly intractable obstacles to the country's support of effective local and national climate change mitigation measures.

In September 2014, less than three months before I began to write this chap-ter, demonstration marches for climate change mitigation were organised all over the world to put pressure on the world's political leaders at the United Nations (UN) Climate Summit. Around 311,000 participants were reported to have marched in New York City (Foderaro 2014). Still, many of the US informants interviewed for this chapter are very frustrated about the slow pace of climate work in their counties and municipalities. The goal of the national government's emission reduction program announced by President Obama in 2009 – to reduce greenhouse gas emissions by 14 per cent by 2020 as compared to 2005 levels – does not appear to be attainable in that time frame (Morrow *et al.* 2010). What are the informants' reflections on this? How and where is climate work underway in local and regional contexts? What are the most problematic obstacles? And how is the debate being met, and responded to, by groups of stakeholders other than climate activists?

A philosopher might think that everything is his, or hers, to make philosophy about. This generalist approach is applicable also for a human ecologist, who, from a very different angle, cannot help but try to get a glimpse of the totality. Human ecology is a discipline rooted in the civilisational and environmentalist critique of modern, industrialised society. It grew out of the 1972 Club of Rome, where scientists concluded that the state of affairs of climate change was precar-ious. In their report of the conference, 'The Limits to Growth' (Meadows *et al.* 1972), researchers stated that if economic growth was not halted or altered, the survival of humankind would be under serious threat. The report argued that the quality of life, or even survival, of all ecosystems was under siege from industrial-ist exploitation. Its authors used early computer modelling to account for the time it would take for resources to run out, or for the time it would take before the needs of a growing population could no longer be met with the productive methods known to humanity.

The report marks a new role of science in modern society: instead of provid-ing knowledge and information for increased productivity, 'Limits' turned the capacities of science back on modernity itself, and began to look at the logic of the socio-economic system from a neo-Malthusian perspective. It became part of the canon in the 'U-turn of modernity' (see Hornborg 1994), i.e. the rational scientific outlook on the world and the refined methods to assess results within the research community that turns its observational capacities back on itself.

Human ecology as a trans-disciplinary field of inquiry grew out of this U-turn. It deals with the analysis of relations – and interrelatedness – between and among nature, society and the existential dimensions of the self (see Steiner 1993). Nature in this case is comprised of the material basis, i.e. geophysical circumstances, ecosystems and natural resources. Society is comprised of all the structures organised by humans; it is where people interact and where natural resources are transformed and reproduced to be made available and useful to humans. The corner of the self in the human ecological triangle is the perspective of the individual, as relates to society and nature respectively. To a human ecologist, any of these corners can be deployed as a vantage point for analysing the interaction with the other dimensions. Hornborg (2001) calls for a *recontextualisation* of knowledge about human–nature relations, arguing that it is the local, specific context where alternatives to the ailments of modern society (i.e. environmental problems) can be found.

Torcello, on the other hand, argues that the strength of modern science is its inbuilt capacity to critically and systematically evaluate and test issues such as global warming (Torcello 2011). I highlight this tension to show that sustainability issues can be approached from two different epistemological angles. It is possible that contemporary, and compact, consensus about the fact that global warming is actually occurring, as formulated by the Intergovernmental Panel of Climate Change (IPCC), has made the U-turn of modernity, and modern reasoning, complete. The IPCC does not provide a local, contextualised perspective – rather the opposite – but still its results are globally pervasive and its forecast of the local effect of climate change if it is not mitigated is disastrous. The focus of this chapter, however, is how work is conducted locally in a given social structure on such a global issue.

Method

This chapter is the result of a visit to the city of Rochester, a city of 210,000 residents located in the State of New York, in December 2014. The empirical material consists of semi-structured interviews with six Americans engaged in climate issues on the local level. Two of the informants were local/regional officials. One was a professional environmentalist working in an academic setting. Two were academics with professional interests in climate issues who are also climate activists, and one was a retired conservationist and climate activist. Informants were asked to describe their engagement, professional or otherwise, in climate work. They were also asked what local and global climate issues they felt were the most urgent and how they worked with them. All informants were asked what they thought was the most problematic local obstacle and finally, to describe what reactions they had encountered in their engagement.

All these informants generously shared their personal experiences and their views on the issue in general with the foreign researcher. They also reflected on their own roles and possibilities, as well as their views about the obstacles and political structures that make climate mitigation in the US so problematic and inflammatory. The interviews lasted about 40 minutes each. Because I took notes during all interviews and transcribed them on computer immediately afterwards, citations may not be verbatim. This, together with the fact that the climate issue in the US is marked by so much political, religious and personal tension and even the use of attack language, led to the decision to present the quotes anonymously. Informants are identified by numbers.

Transcription of notes was followed by coding, or categorisation. Some themes came up repeatedly during interviews, themes that formed the basis for the reasoning I apply to the issue in this chapter. Obviously, there is a possibility that the small sample of six subjects engaged in climate work may be nothing but anecdotal. But I claim that the anecdotal, subjective and the narrative in this case represents if not the whole truth, then at least six truthful outlooks that are possibly pieces of the hologram. I present them because they make sense in their own right. It is my intention to understand these outlooks from a human ecological standpoint, looking at the connections between natural resources, society at large and finally, the self – the individual's role – and the possibilities of this triangulation.

Local and regional climate policy

The environmental issue of climate change is firmly established among Europeans. Wilson (2006) demonstrated that for people in the European Union (EU) climate change (according to a Eurobarometer study) is one of the four environmental problems they worry about the most. Local and municipal work to mitigate climate change has long been an established political and administrative field in Europe, even if actual adaptation in physical planning seems to be lagging behind (Wilson 2006), and actual outcomes, despite ambitious plans, sometimes can be 'fairly modest' (Granberg and Elander 2007).

One factor influencing the modest outcomes is the time-span over which climate change occurs. Wilson (2006) emphasises that a big obstacle to efficiency is that municipal planning is often performed within a shorter time-span – around five years. Whilst the effects of climate change, such as extreme weather, are already occurring, more profound consequences of climate change can only be seen farther off into the future – ten, twenty and fifty years. Another obstacle for American as well as European municipalities is that the effect of local mitigation on global climate change is unclear: global climate change may not affect local climate in a way that is easily connected to local mitigation policies (Betsill 2010).

Climate issues *are* complex: they challenge the basis of fossil-fuelled society, of which the US is one of the world's most predominant examples, and it may not always be evident what can be gained from mitigation. Rabe (2006) stated that a bottom-up perspective is pivotal for successful climate work, especially when enhancing collaboration between regions and states. Local officials, according to Betsill (2010, 394–395), may feel 'distant from the problem'.

Municipal climate work has been going on in many American cities since the early 2000s (Pitt 2010) with varying results. Betsill (2010, 402) states that whilst municipal mitigation efforts have been seen to produce economic and energy savings, these efforts generally do not extend beyond business-as-usual. Coordination between municipalities is also one of the key factors for success, and a challenge for many cities, as well as a lack of institutional barriers, or lack of administrative capacity (Betsill 2010). According to Pitt (2010), one central success factor for climate mitigation in American municipalities is regional collaboration, which seems to be a challenge even on the most local level. One of the informants in this study said she has trouble with how her society is organised:

> We have something called the Home Rule: Every town makes its own [physical planning rules]. There is no regional planning over shopping, schools, housing, etc. We are ruining our farmland, but nobody cares.
>
> (Informant 1)

For example, there can be car-accessible-only shopping centres that straddle the boundaries of two cities or towns, which contributes to the difficulties of forming mitigation policies between and among local entities. There seems to be less of a perceived need in the US for a centralised understanding, let alone a consensus, about climate change. Several researchers (Rabe, 2006; Lutsey and Sperling, 2008; Pitt, 2010; Betsill, 2010) discuss how tensions over the issues of local/municipal autonomy, regional planning and cooperation and federal legislation do not facilitate climate mitigation in the US. Lutsey and Sperling suggest decentralisation and a bottom-up approach:

Benefits of a more decentralised regulatory action include (1) allowing more experimentation by more policy makers, (2) local tailoring of specific actions to fit more aptly the environmental preferences of constituents of various states and locales, (3) testing the political response of innovative regulatory and policy actions and (4) gaining the benefit of local expertise and experience in enforcing programs and policies (Lutsey and Sperling 2008, 674).

It might be a political challenge in the US to allow local initiatives to flourish in order to foster greater creativity in climate mitigation. One of these grassroots strategies is the climate work being done at universities (Knuth et al. 2007). When seen in a proactive light, US universities could be seen as having the capacity to impact climate change that rivals that of smaller cities. Certainly the mitigation work currently conducted in academia is of great importance, not only when it comes to greenhouse gas emissions as such, but even more when it comes to producing and distributing knowledge to the public. Pitt (2010) concludes that a close cooperation with non-governmental organisations (NGOs) and private actors is a success factor in local climate mitigation. There is a need for alternative engagement, where small groups, NGOs, even religious

Figure 10.1 A section of the car park at Rochester Institute of Technology

Note: October 2013. The location of the campus and poor public transportation make it almost a
    necessity for students, staff and faculty to use their cars to commute. American universities
    sometimes have carbon emissions levels that equal those of small cities, and therefore
    climate work conducted there is of extra importance (Knuth *et al.* 2007).

Source: Ebba Lisberg Jensen.

and local action groups 'own' the issue, carry it forward and promote it. This is
called 'consciousness raising' (a term used by Informant 3), which is intended to
eventually make the issue both more political and at the same time more of a
personal engagement among individuals.

Private, local and informal political initiatives are a tradition in US local
policy making. In 1835, the French author Alexis de Tocqueville, who certainly
conducted a more thorough analysis of American society than Baudrillard,
reacted to the diversity of ruling structures and systems in the local communities
that he visited. He was simultaneously impressed with and sceptical about this
aggregation of local, spontaneous power:

> The difficulties which attend the consolidation of its independence rather
> augment than diminish with the increasing enlightenment of the people. A
> highly civilized society spurns the attempt of a local independence, is
> disgusted by its numerous blunders, and is apt to despair of success before the
> experiment is completed.
>
> (de Tocqueville 1835/2002, 77)

In short: The more knowledge local people have, and the more they want their knowledge to influence local governing, the more complicated it is to rule them. Local initiatives are good in principle, but are not so easy to build policy around. This tension between centralisation and locality seems to be problematic in contemporary climate mitigation efforts.

Working with climate locally, regionally and nationally

A political initiative to mitigate climate change was initiated in 2009 by the New York State Department of Environmental Conservation, which launched a project called 'Climate Smart Communities' in order to encourage communities to begin local climate work. According to one informant, climate work has lately become central for American environmentalism (Informant 1). Another stated that 'the number one political agenda is climate change now' (Informant 5). The City of Rochester joined Climate Smart Communities, and a more local initiative supports it in a joint venture between local communities called Cool Rochester:

> For too long, global warming has seemed like something that we have no power to stop. Cool Rochester's work is powerful evidence to the contrary. It is now clearer than ever that we have the power to lead the nation and the world to show the nation and the world how individuals and businesses can reduce their carbon emissions, and save money, without waiting for the government to act, starting right now.
> (Cool Rochester CO_2 Reduction Plan for Municipalities, 2014)

The march for climate change mitigation in New York City in September 2014 worked as a wake-up call for climate activists in Rochester, and translated into a commitment of communities beginning to influence climate change politics:

> Three buses went to NYC for the climate march. There is now a six-member board of people who have not been on [any] boards before [later commented upon as a strategy to avoid old conflicting interests between groups]. The plan is to educate their community to influence politicians to take action. The population should be highly aware of the situation and challenges.
> (Informant 4)

Because the New York march attracted such a huge number of participants, local activists hoped that this would fuel local engagement, which could be enforced by the fact that a local winery business near Rochester is also being threatened by plans for fracking, i.e. extraction of fossil gas:

> Change has to start locally. Political and technological change is paramount, but national leaders will look foolish [if nothing is done]. Due to the shell [a geological formation of fossil gas located near Rochester], there is a

resistance among wineries along the Finger Lakes and they are putting together a firm stand [against the exploration of fossil gas] because they are also of economic importance to the state.

(Informant 4)

Several of the informants reported that the fact that many people are actively against climate change mitigation efforts has been a severe obstacle to their local work. The informants noted that large swathes of the US public do not even accept the phenomena of climate change as such; many people still do not believe that it is anthropogenic. One of the informants, who organises climate change training programmes, reported that:

Say ten years ago, we couldn't even mention climate change. But now we say: Whether it's man-made or not, we have to address it. There will be floodings, some species will thrive, some will not, we just have to face it.

(Informant 1)

The debate seems to have slowly shifted from *if* there is global warming going on to *whether* the global warming is caused by human activity or not. One of the informants, a very engaged activist, has become accustomed to confronting this doubt (more about that below) immediately when addressing the public in meetings and gatherings: 'The word I use is *anthropogenic warming*' (Informant 3). This informant also consciously changed her rhetoric, focusing not so much on the environmental consequences of climate change as on the financial consequences of *not* adopting mitigation efforts. In a way that would be considered rather unorthodox to an environmentalist, she reported that she argues now that big financial investors had changed their minds about the future of energy:

It's all about economics, the City Bank, Deutsche Bank: They all invest in solar energy now. ... There are economic benefits. There are technological solutions, energy conservation efforts.

(Informant 3)

Shortly before this interview, in September 2014, the Rockefeller Foundation, which built its fortune on fossil fuels, was reported to have changed its future investments in energy industry to renewable energy (BBC News 2014). This was seen by the informants as a very positive sign that soon big money is going to admit that fossil fuels are obsolete. This is a good example of what Hajer (1995) and Spaargaren (1996) call *ecological modernisation*: modernity's incessant drive for economic growth and technological development combined with sustainability values. One informant commented that the more 'old-school', i.e. orthodox environmentalists, did not like the talk about solar energy 'because they thought environmentalism should be about saving energy' (Informant 4).

One informant was openly sceptical about green business. His understanding of the climate issue was more explicitly global and political than the others. He cited American military actions abroad during the last centuries: 'The empire needs a grip on the resources in the future. A lot of the warfare is about that' (Informant 5). Not surprisingly, climate change and climate mitigation are issues that lead to a broader spectrum of civilisational critique, as well as to issues of nationality and social change. What is a country like the US built upon, how will sustainability be achieved? What is the foundation for the country's persistence about climate change? Another informant commented that new shopping centres that can be reached only by car keep popping up in the towns around Rochester, despite the fact that population is decreasing in the region:

> There are not enough people to do all this shopping, it's a zero-sum-game [meaning there are only so many shoppers]. When there was a housing bubble, house prices went down and development slowed. It's about all these places and disparities, and then there is xenophobia. But we could use a lot more people to come and do the shopping.
>
> (Informant 1)

Confusing communities, inert individuals

All of the informants referred to climate work being done in the *community*. This work is being done by parent groups, religious congregations and local political organisations. It is my impression that for Americans, participation in community works as an activator: the individual connects to and takes part in society. It can be a discussion club, a soup kitchen, an organisation for helping the disabled or, as in this case, groups of people fighting to elevate climate issues and raise consciousness.

The importance of *community* in American society is obvious, but it is also curious to an outsider. De Tocqueville applied the concept of *associations* (which today could be defined as *community groups*) to describe the intense and individually based citizen participation in American local politics that was obvious in the young country even in the early nineteenth century. He lauded this coming together of groups of people to discuss an issue or solve a problem outside the official purview of 'townships, cities and countries':

> In no country in the world has the principle of association been more successfully used, and more unsparingly applied to a multitude of different objects, than in America. Besides the permanent associations which are established by law under the names of townships, cities and counties, a vast number of others are formed and maintained by the agency of private individuals.
>
> (de Tocqueville 1835/2002, 213–214)

De Tocqueville acknowledged the political role of associations in a democracy that in his day was finding its feet. He saw associations as practical manifestations of the right to promote any political agenda or 'doctrine' under the rubric of freedom of speech:

An association consists simply in the public assent which a number of individuals give certain doctrines, and in the engagement which they contract to promote to the spread of those doctrines by their exertions. The right of association with these views is very analogous to the liberty of unlicensed writing; but societies thus formed possess more authority than the press.

(de Tocqueville 1835/2002, 214)

But communities – and their role in climate change mitigation – are still intriguing to a European. The distinction between *Gemeinschaft* and *Gesellschaft* in European sociology, as stated by Ferdinand Tönnies in 1887, is central to understanding the structure of modern European society. Gemeinschaft is based on family-like structures, where personally known, collective, social interaction and family ties form the models for how society works. Gesellschaft, on the other hand, is a more formalised, non-personal society, where status is formed by individual achievement, but where individual agency is restrained and organised through legislation and legal control rather than by interpersonal pressure. Gemeinschaft and Gesellschaft do not rule out each other, even if the concepts have often been utilised to describe a shift from pre-modern to modern conditions. In many societies, Gesellschaft works as a formal, official scheme whilst many segments of people's lives are conducted within a social realm that is more reminiscent of Gemeinschaft.

Communities in the US model are voluntary gatherings that take on some of the functions that Gesellschaft does in a European setting. To an outsider, it looks as if climate consciousness raising in American society, for example, takes place in a social space somewhere between Gemeinschaft and Gesellschaft, in a layer called community. Brint (2001) attempts to sort out the ideas of community and Gemeinschaft within sociological theory. Conceptually, his text as applied to this context is confusing, as he uses community as a synonym for Gemeinschaft. He states that Gemeinschaft-like relations have six central properties:

(1) dense and demanding social ties, (2) social attachments to and involvement in institutions, (3) ritual occasions, (4) small group size, (5) perceptions of similarity with the physical characteristics, expressive style, way of life, or historical experience of others and (6) common beliefs in an idea system, a moral order, an institution or a group.

(Brint 2001, 3–4)

The group as such, rather than the individual, can negotiate with and relate to Gesellschaft, and the individual can depend on his or her community rather than on formal society. The weakness of this analysis, when it comes to climate work, is the fragmentation of a collective understanding of the field or problem.

A *community* is based on the freely chosen engagement of individuals. The geographically defined *neighbourhood* suggests a solidarity and communal relationship with those living nearby. The relationship between politics, climate activists and local society is exemplified in this announcement from the City of Rochester People's Climate Coalition, an umbrella organisation of 35 local organisations, about a local climate change public event:

> With all of the climate change wake-up calls globally and closer to home – like Hurricane Irene and Superstorm Sandy – we should be demanding bold action from our leaders. Participating in this march is something concrete and effective that we can each do. And we need EVERYONE there at the march. Please don't wait for your neighbors to do it for you. This is too important.
>
> (Baltus 2014)

In a country like Sweden, climate work and engagement might as well be done by local organisations, but the difference is that they often are formal organisations, such as NGOs, with a declared focus on, for example, environmental issues. In the American example, however, congregations and parental groups may choose to engage in climate mitigation in a way that seems more spontaneous, i.e. an outburst of engagement in one community. For example, a Rochester newspaper described a local 'climate night' organised by a local Unitarian church:

> Rochesterians interested in learning how they can lessen their own carbon footprints are invited to Climate Action Night, a free event on Tuesday.
> The event, to be held at First Unitarian Church in Rochester, features several local experts who will offer suggestions on how people can help mitigate climate change.
>
> (*Democrat & Chronicle* 2014)

This quote underscores an interesting trait that was cited in all interviews: *individual responsibility*. All informants emphasised the role of individual responsibility in halting of climate change. Informants also emphasised the massive challenge of marshalling individuals to express their responsibility for climate change mitigation. 'It's a little like herding cats', said one informant about her workplace, where she works to initiate climate engagement (Informant 2). The inertia around, and structural obstacles to, changing individual behaviour were evident: 'The greatest challenge is organisational and individual behaviour. Everyone has to change. People prefer not to change' (Informant 2). This informant reflected on America's 'culture', with its strong focus on individual freedom as it collides with a global call for solidarity:

> The worst challenge is our culture. This country has an individual focus, a strong narrative that you do it yourself. ... The government can't tell me what to do. It's very hard to launch global issues if they can't be made personal. It's hard to change that.
>
> (Informant 2)

Another informant argued that there have to be economic gains from changing, contrasting it to a need for personal freedom: 'The only thing that can change people's behaviour is if they can save some money from it individually. People don't want to sacrifice their freedom' (Informant 1). 'Freedom' in this case means physical freedom as expressed by driving a car, which will be discussed in more detail below.

As contradictory as it may seem, the problem with changing *individual behaviour* is often referred to as a result of the *structures of society*. Informants, themselves actively engaged in climate mitigation work, hint to a lack of agency among the public. One informant, however, found it 'unfortunate that climate change has become a public issue. It shouldn't have been politicised' (Informant 6). This informant also suggested that an assortment of other climate change mitigation initiatives in the same community might scatter the initiatives and decrease their political influence:

> There is no resistance against climate mitigation work in the municipality, but there are competing interests. Crime, poverty and education are priorities. ... The work tends to be fractured: one group is doing this, another that. Even if every group met with each other, the work is fractured. There are so many private initiatives.
>
> (Informant 6)

There are, thus, political obstacles as well as possibilities on the regional and local levels. Planning and policy can be enabling, but with the lack of central planning, they are more often challenging. Communities form a strong, creative contingent between Gesellschaft and Gemeinschaft, and between politics and individuals. But the basis of all behavioural change is still on the most local level: how people lead their daily lives. And that, in turn, is made more or less possible by physical structures and circumstances that are defined by forces that exist outside of and beyond individuals' choices.

The big issue: The car

I asked the informants what they considered to be the biggest challenge to climate mitigation in the US. The answer was unequivocal: the transportation system. Or, to be more exact, the car. Can this deeply rooted way of organising daily transportation, this combination of mobility and sedentary life-style, physical freedom and enclosure, be understood by an outsider? Baudrillard's take on the issue is simply to drive: 'All you need to need to know about American society can be gleaned from an anthropology of its driving behaviour. That behaviour tells you much more than you could ever learn from its political ideas' (Baudrillard 1986, 54). This statement is, of course, a gross simplification. But the fact remains that the car is central to the American way of life, and is responsible for one-third of US greenhouse gas emissions (Morrow *et al.* 2010). How did this come to be?

Rochester is one of the many cities in the US where the car has been crucial to urban development. In the first half of the twentieth century, the city was structured like most European cities, with a number of vibrant high streets. There were trams, later exchanged for a subway system. Just outside this and akin to the traditional European urban structure, was a circle of more villa-like neighbourhoods divided by more urban *avenues*, larger streets radiating from the centre. Many lived in the city centre, or, depending on economic circumstances, in one of the many surrounding neighbourhoods of villas. The subway system, which was always crowded with customers during World War II, supported local transportation (Rochester Subway 2014). But as car driving became more common after the war, wealthier people could afford to commute by car, and were soon joined by the middle- and working class. This was the beginning of the America's so-called *urban sprawl* – a semi-urban landscape started to spread out around the city. Land was plentiful and cheap:

> The county has been of agrarian areas – and cities. After WWII, this changed into big suburban areas. There has been no proper land-use planning, space was affordable. We had too much money there for a while, building [oil] pipes, and now it's so expensive to maintain our infrastructure. Gas was so cheap. It's still very cheap, it doesn't really change.
>
> (Informant 1)

Eventually, only the poorest people lived in the city. The subway was closed in 1956 (rochestersubway.com 2014) and companies began to move their offices to the suburbs. When urban sprawl increased, the city was depopulated and eventually considered a socio-economic backwater, where people avoided moving around, especially on foot. Companies that remained in the inner city arranged for parking spaces in the basements of their buildings, making it possible for employees to drive to work, taking the elevator to their office and never using the streets at all. A circle of motorways was built around the city, more or less consciously 'cutting off' the poorer, problematic parts of town from the wealthier surroundings. Today, downtown Rochester is still an urban landscape, but without many of the features that a European finds typical of a city. Very few people walk the streets, there are few cars and large department stores have long since closed. There are no cafés and hardly any shoppers. Whilst only a few hundred metres outside the city centre there are streets with restaurants, bars and people moving in the streets, the impression of depopulation is still evident (see Figure 10.2).

Around Rochester, ring roads with shopping centres and suburban housing areas stretch out, intersected by smaller roads. Car traffic has formed an 'arterial network' around which the urban structure is built (cf. Baudrillard, 1986, 55).

The causality, or the course of events that brought Rochester and countless other American cities to this juncture is complex. The availability of cheap land inverted the urban structure, forming a multi-centred landscape where car-mobility replaced the social gravity of one city centre. But even more so, cheap

Figure 10.2 Rochester's Main Street

Note: Rochester's Main Street at 10 a.m., 9 December 2014. At a time of day when a city centre should be full of people, this photograph of very few cars and almost no pedestrians indicates the current state of America's 'Main Streets'. Stores that once thrived here and drew many customers closed long ago and moved to car-dependent shopping malls.

Source: Ebba Lisberg Jensen.

oil made it possible. Between the years 1973, the year of the global energy crisis, and 2007, petrol consumption in the US went from 110.5 to 176 billion gallons annually, an increase of 59 per cent (Morrow *et al.* 2010). Meeting, eating out, shopping – all the normal tasks of daily living – take place mainly where citizens can use a car, and circle around the city rather than go into it. Still, the poorest are left in the city. The public transportation system is also considered unsafe, and mainly serves those who do not own cars, a fact that undermines the political urge to support and develop it:

> We work with something called active transportation: Environmental issues and public health. But the bus company thinks that most of their riders are poor, they don't see the point of treating them. RIT (Rochester Institute of Technology) has made tremendous drives [to make people ride the bus], RIT is now a partner in this project.
>
> (Informant 1)

But to have a car and drive has become central to American psychology, according to several of the informants. The car is the machine of freedom in a society where time is also money.

The worst challenge to American sustainability and climate work is giving up the car. We love the freedom that we have. Leaving for work ten minutes earlier is impossible for many people, if they need to go to the bus stop and change, etc. 'There are only poor people on the bus' [quoting politicians].

(Informant 1)

As all the informants pointed to 'the car' or 'the transportation system', it became clear that the US fossil-fuelled transportation system has taken the form of blood circulating in the country's body politic. The complexity of car dependency, the 'freedom' mind-set, the sprawl and inadequate public transportation systems seems to have taken on a life of its own in the challenge to mitigate climate change. The car is central to physical planning, architecture, daily lives, people's ways of thinking and acting, social activities and politicians' way of handling – or not handling – obvious problems:

One of the worst challenges is public transport. We don't walk here, we don't have that mind-set. There's so much sprawl – so there's not much incentive for public transport. [But] I try to be optimistic; we are trying to do good.

(Informant 5)

One root cause is the horrible transportation system. We simply don't have sufficient public transportation. This affects the layout of the cities. It's very difficult to make good life-style choices.

(Informant 4)

Whilst all the informants offered various 'root causes' of climate change, all of the causes they stated centred on the same complex. Is it the sprawl, the poor transportation systems, the mind-set, American culture – what is it, really, that causes this immense inertia when it comes to moving US society toward a more climate-friendly direction? Car traffic and fossil fuel dependency is growing everywhere in the world, and severely influences the physical as well as socio-economic structures of societies. Many well-formulated and well-informed people do their best to find a way to change this. However, they have powerful enemies.

Denialists: The best defence is a good offense

Naturally, for the climate activists interviewed there is no doubt about the big political issue in the coming years. 'The number one political agenda now is climate change', said one informant (5), who was determined to fight it. He formulated how climate change could be a threat to social and ecological balance as well as to food security of his country:

Global warming will probably move the [normal cause of the] wind belt: Dry zones will spread out to the Great Plains and influence food production. We will experience more severe storms, have more extreme ice storms, and freakish things like extreme frosts in early season, which will destroy crops, and droughts and high temperature in summers.

(Informant 5)

Another stated that 'The great challenge is how to talk about this [climate change]: I hold up my little can of worms, but one worm is a poisonous snake. Climate change is the World War II of our generation. We have to face it now' (Informant 3).

The central problem with climate change in the US is that from the very beginning of the understanding of climate change as a genuine global threat, the issue has been positioned as a conflict of diverging systems of value. Oreskes and Conway, in their ambitious analysis of how denial of global warning has been formulated and politicised in the American public discourse, demonstrate how one of the first reports on climate change, the 1979 'Changing Climate: Report of the Carbon Dioxide Assessment Committee' came to be divided in two (Oreskes and Conway 2010). One part of the report presented the opinion of natural scientists, who make it clear that global warming due to the burning of fossil fuel will occur in the near future. The second part presented the point of view of economists: Warming *would* occur, but could be handled within the existing [political and economic] system (Oreskes and Conway 2010:177ff).

However, the synthesis of the report was written from the economists' point of view, stating that the problems likely to occur due to carbon dioxide (CO_2) emissions would 'take their place among the other stresses to which nations and individuals adapt' (Oreskes and Conway 2010, 180). Despite the attempts to diminish the problem and blame natural fluctuations or the sun, an increasing number of climate researchers came to the consensus that the greenhouse effect was indeed occurring. What remained in the early 1990s was to prove that it was man-made, or anthropogenic (Oreskes and Conway 2010, 198).

But the denialists kept highlighting the fact that results about the causes of climate change were being changed as experiments and measuring were repeated. The core of modern science – critical thinking, retrial, and scepticism – was attacked by the denialists as the researchers' 'weak spot'. Eventually, denialism became a discourse of its own, an industry of doubt. This, of course, has made climate mitigation, and raising consciousness, problematic. 'Media avoids the topic because one might think that there are two equal sides to it', said Informant 4.

This is precisely the *doubt* that Oreskes and Conway analyse in their book: if the slightest doubt about climate change can be found, denialists sell it as being just as influential as the actual evidence. One informant expressed exhaustion, or desolation, when talking about the denialists, who made her mission so much harder: 'It's hard to read about the deniers. They think the whole climate issue is just made up, it's a hoax, they don't really accept it at all' (Informant 6). Another informant noted how denialists had managed to give the issue 'an aura of controversy'. Oreskes and Conway comment on this issue, noting that 'a wide spectrum of the media – not just obviously right-wing newspapers like the *Washington*

Times, but mainstream outlets, too – felt obligated to treat these issues as scientific controversies' (Oreskes and Conway 2010, 214). Eventually, according to Oreskes and Conway, the media in the US were pushed into conflating 'scientific diffidence with scientific uncertainty' (Oreskes and Conway 2010, 214).

When asked why the denialists are so influential in the American public debate, one informant said that sometimes the climate issue is seen as *anti-American* or *anti-patriotic*. Climate mitigation is considered a denouncement of the whole American project, where 'technology is closely connected to the free market' (Informant 4). Technology is symbolised by the car, the emblematic American machine. And the car dependency is crucial to the oil companies: 'The divide [between climate 'believers' and 'denialists'] is encouraged and propagated by the fossil fuel industry. It's heavily lobbied: money and politics. Politicians become lobbyists' (Informant 4).

Among the informants, with their strong engagement in climate issues, there were obvious differences in political radicalism. But they all seemed to be aware that climate engagement, rightfully or not, put them in a certain political 'field'. 'Conservatives generally associate environmentalists with the far left and think that they are practically socialists. All environmentalists, though, do not want to be associated with certain groups' (Informant 1).

The denialists form a peculiar ideological discourse coalition. They are often radically conservative, both politically and religiously. They do not believe in the results of modern natural science, they can be creationists and often deny evolutionism. But they are at the same time often explicitly pro-technology and pro-industrialism. Some of the informants, however, who had been challenged personally by denialists, thought that they were not '*that* many [denialists], it's more that they are a loud minority. They respond to our activism and argue with their "script" to promote their cause' (Informants 3 and 4). According to the activists, the script consists of a number of arguments that appear (in print and public comment) in the same general order and formulation. According to the informants, the central denialist arguments include:

- Climate change is a conspiracy that was financed by former US Vice-president Al Gore in his 2000 campaign for the presidency;
- The IPCC consists of fake experts;
- The 'smaller people' are being manipulated;
- Government is hated and science is distrusted; and
- It is one's patriotic duty to confront climate activists.

(Informants 3 and 4)

The denialists, the informants say, are generally 'white men in between 40 and 60' years old. They are generally very well-behaved and nice, as one informant said: 'I haven't met one climate denialist I haven't liked' (Informant 3). But some denialists are not that nice, and engage in writing letters to, and otherwise putting direct and intense pressure on climate activists. In this email written to a climate activist in 2014, the sender argues that the activist had attacked freedom of speech:

If you actually said, as a quite reliable source reported, that people who did not believe in AGW [anthropogenic global warming] should be in jail, you should be fired. ... You 'warmists' have an execrable record of prediction, and are almost certainly dead wrong, which is your privilege – unlike apparently those who disagree with you. The Earth hasn't warmed in 18 years. Scientists invested in this religious nonsense have been caught hiding data. ... you are an absolute disgrace. You remind of Mao who murdered people because of 'wrongheadedness'. You are beyond a disgrace.

I noted above that de Tocqueville had observed that the American right – and drive – to 'associate' is the social equivalent of free speech. Thus, the right of the climate activists to speak their mind is actually acknowledged by the denialist, even though he or she thinks the opposing idea is dictatorial.

The informants, however, have learnt to develop strategies to handle the outspoken denialists: 'If there are 100 people in the room, I try to focus on those 99 that are not denialists (Informants 3). Another formed a strategy that was more about adapting the message to the audience, without avoiding mention of the need for action:

One always has to size up the auditorium to know how to address them. ... Instead of talking about climate change, we have to talk about 'energy security' and independence. Homeland security, not to be dependent on petroleum from other countries. Wind, solar, etc. are all part of the independence.

(Informant 2)

The argument that dependency on fossil fuels puts America in a weak political position might be efficient. The trouble is that fracking – the extraction of fossil gas – is one of the fastest growing energy industries in the US at the moment. According to Howard and Ingraffea (2011), the greenhouse gas effect of fossil gas exceeds that of both oil and coal. Thus, whilst fracking could be the solution for energy supplies, it will exacerbate climate change. The more acute trouble with fracking, though, is the severe environmental effects it has on the local environment. But that's another story.

Concluding remarks

I have attempted in this chapter to give a picture of the central challenges to climate mitigation in the US from a human ecological perspective. To climate activists, many challenges remain. Since the beginning of the twentieth century, cheap energy and cheap land have made car dependency, and thus oil dependency, physically and economically viable in the US. The country's diverse political structure, with its traditionally strong focus on local self-control, is simultaneously an obstacle to and a possibility for climate mitigation. Cooperation is needed to make physical planning efficient and daily transportation more environmentally friendly, not to mention the critical need for an enhanced public transportation system.

The strong American tradition of creative, politically engaging community work, however, seems to be a central venue in which climate mitigation efforts can occur. Communities *do* actually work to raise climate consciousness and to influence local policy making. The question is to what extent community activities across the US have enough influence to challenge the current entrenched energy use system. The denialists appear to be much more politically influential than their grasp of scientific knowledge warrants. Moreover, on the national level at least, the climate change debate gives the impression of two sides that have an equally justifiable foundation for their opinions. It appears that the denialist position consists of a very influential minority lobbying against an overwhelming majority of researchers and an increasingly knowledgeable public who *know* that climate change is already happening.

Finally, I would like to return to the question of the role of science. Hajer (1995) wrote that the role of science regarding environmental issues changed in Europe in the 1990s. From having been focused in large part on proving that the environment was not threatened by climate change and that everything was going fine, scientists began to calibrate their methods to understand how industrial society affected the ecosystem. A strong discourse-coalition formed, in which scientists and activists were able to truly influence politics to mitigate, in a specific case from the 1990s, acid rain.

To do that, scientists and a growing climate change activist community had to gain the trust of established society in order to actually shift the burden of proof to the polluter, to those who once claimed that there was *no* environmental threat connected to industrial society (Hajer 1995, 28). This is a good example of the 'U-turn of modernity', i.e. modern society looking back at its own flaws with the help of its own rationality. The difference between acid rain, an issue that dominated environmental debate in the 1990s, and climate change is that climate change is so much more diffuse. It is caused everywhere, and by everyone, and in the end will make everyone vulnerable. To mitigate it, local groups as well as individuals will be responsible for changing not only their own lifestyles, but also invoking their responsibility to think critically.

Today, scientific evidence is available to most of us. Torcello (2011) argues that whilst our society has the expertise, it is not possible for all of us to draw our own conclusions on every topic. But if we know how science works, we can at least believe that science is efficient enough, and its climate conclusions are valid enough to override any kind of evidence as equally relevant. He also argues that seriously decreasing greenhouse gas emissions will require nothing less than 'a paradigm shift in the collective thinking of the industrialised world' (Torcello 2011, 202). But is there such a thing as a collective thinking? There are undeniably very strong forces working against the mitigation of climate change, particularly in the US. Whilst it is my impression that local initiatives are not completely without influence, the fact is, that with 'a change of just a few degrees' (Baudrillard 1986, 47), not only America, but the whole world will be faced with the overwhelming challenge to preserve its ecosystems and support its population.

References

Baudrillard J (1986) *America*, Verso, London.

Balthus, C (2014) *Press Conference: Rochester People's Climate Coalition, Rochester, NY,* [Rochester People's Climate Coalition] 8 September, 2014 (http://peoplesclimate.org/event/press-conference-rochester-peoples-climate-coalition-rochester-ny/) Accessed 28 January 2014.

BBC News (2014) *Rockefellers to Switch Investments to 'Clean Energy'*, 23 September 2014 (www.bbc.com/news/world-us-canada-29310475) Accessed 28 January 2014.

Betsill M M (2010) Mitigating Climate Change in US Cities: Opportunities and Obstacles, *Local Environment The International Journal of Justice and Sustainability* 6(4) 393–406.

Brint S (2001) Gemeinschaft Revisited: A Critique and Reconstruction of the Community Concept, *Sociological Theory* 19(1) 1–23.

Cool Rochester (2014) (www.coolrochester.org/downloads/MunicipalReductions.pdf) Accessed 28 January 2014.

Democrat & Chronicle (2014) *Event Discusses How to Reduce Carbon Footprints* 1 December, 2014 (www.democratandchronicle.com/story/news/2014/12/01/first-unitarian-church-carbon-footprint/19757639/) Accessed 28 January 2014.

de Tocqueville A (1835/2002) *Democracy in America* [Pennsylvania State University translation] (http://ir.nmu.org.ua/bitstream/handle/123456789/132813/6d828844ad7e8b7a313076ac443ae95b.pdf?sequence=1&isAllowed=y) Accessed 28 January 2014.

Foderaro L W (2014) Taking a Call for Climate Change to the Streets, *New York Times*, September 21, 2014 (www.nytimes.com/2014/09/22/nyregion/new-york-city-climate-change-march.html) Accessed 28 January 2014.

Granberg M and Elander E (2007) Local Governance and Climate Change: Reflections on the Swedish Experience, *Local Environment The International Journal of Justice and Sustainability* 12(5) 537–548.

Hajer M (1995) *The Politics of Environmental Discourse. Ecological Modernization and the Policy Process*, Oxford University Press, Oxford, UK.

Hornborg A (1994) Encompassing Encompassment: Anthropology and the U-Turn of Modernity, *Ethnos* 59(3–4) 232–247.

Hornborg A (2001) *The Power of the Machine: Global Inequalities of Economy, Technology and Environment*, Alta Mira Press, Walnut Creek, CA.

Howard R W and Ingraffea A (2011) Should Fracking Stop? *Nature* 477 271–273.

IPCC Press Release (2014) *Greenhouse Gas Emissions Accelerate Despite Reduction Efforts* [2014/19/PR 13 April] Intergovernmental Panel of Climate Change.

Knuth S, Nagle B, Steuer C and Yarnal B (2007) Universities and Climate Change Mitigation: Advancing Grassroots Climate Policy in the US, *Local Environment: The International Journal of Justice and Sustainability* 12(5) 485–504.

Lutsey N and Sperling D (2008) America's Bottom-Up Climate Change Mitigation Policy, *Energy Policy* 36 673–685.

Meadows D H, Meadows D L, Randers J and Behrens W W (1972) *The Limits to Growth*, Universe Books, New York.

Morrow R W, Gallagher K S, Collantes G and Lee H (2010) Analyses of Policies to

Reduce Oil Consumption and greenhouse-Gas Emissions from the US Transportation Sector, *Energy Policy* 38 1305–1320.

Oreskes N and Conway E M (2010) *Merchants of Doubt*, Bloomsbury Press, New York.

Pitt D R (2010) Harnessing Community Energy: The Keys to Climate Mitigation Policy Adoption in US Municipalities, *Local Environment: The International Journal of Justice and Sustainability* 15(8) 717–729.

Rabe B (2006) Second Generation Climate Policies in the American States: Proliferation, Diffusion and Regionalization Executive Summary, *Issues in Governance Studies* 6 1–9.

Rochester Subway (2014) *Rochester Subway 'About This Site'* (www.rochestersubway.com/rochester_subway_history.php) Accessed 28 January 2014.

Spaargaren G (1996) *The Ecological Modernization of Production and Consumption*, Ph.D. Thesis Wageningen University, Wageningen, the Netherlands.

Steiner D (1993) Human Ecology as Transdisciplinary Science, and Science as Part of Human Ecology, in Steiner D and Nauser M (eds) *Human Ecology: Fragments of Anti-Fragmentary Views of the World*, Routledge, London, 47–76.

Torcello L (2011) The Ethics of Inquiry, Scientific Belief, and Public Discourse, *Public Affairs Quarterly* 2(3) 197–215.

Wilson E (2006) Adapting to Climate Change at the Local Level: The Spatial Planning Response, *Local Environment: The International Journal of Justice and Sustainability* 11(6) 609–625.

11 How many thick television sets can there be in the world?

Recycling workers and customers reflect on changing roles, recycling routines and resource flows

Ebba Lisberg Jensen

Introduction

Until the 1990s, families in most parts of Sweden drove with their trolleys of debris to the nearest landfill (*soptipp*). It was a smelly, dystopian landscape of chaos. Eventually a caterpillar would pile up the garbage and prevent it from spreading into the forest. The garbage just lay there: cows' ears, broken television sets, rotting food, furniture, soiled baby nappies. Screaming seagulls circled the area. Rats fled when cars arrived. In the bigger landfills, mountains and ramps were built by roaring bulldozers, resulting in steep ridges where the public could 'tippa', i.e. dump their waste, and watch it getting mixed with stinking garbage bags delivered by trucks full of garbage from homes, hospitals, food stores and restaurants. To work at the dump was a low-prestige, low-paid job. For the public – the dump's customers – it was mainly about getting rid of their waste and leaving as quickly as possible.

Today, there are very few dumps of this kind left in Sweden. In Skåne, a county in southernmost Sweden, the regional waste management company SYSAV, which is owned by 14 municipalities, is responsible for administering the movement of waste (SYSAV 2012). Household garbage is collected and brought to a great incinerator in Malmö, which produces 1,429,000 Megawatt hours (MWh) per year for heat and electricity (SYSAV 2012). In an increasing number of places, waste food is collected separately and brought to biogas plants, where it is used to produce climate-neutral gas for cars and buses. The former dumps, or landfills, are now being closed and covered. When it comes to larger waste from households, such as construction debris and used furniture, the public is directed to recycling stations (*återvinningscentraler*). At these stations, a new professional group has emerged that serves close to 1,900,000 customers that deliver 160,600 tons of waste annually (SYSAV 2012) to recycle stations. Waste workers have become recycling workers (*återvinningspersonal*). A complex economic and infrastructural system is developing to handle the detritus of mass consumption and production.

Hetherington (2004) has argued that whilst consumption has been a thoroughly discussed area of sociological research, waste has not. This chapter is a response to Hetherington's call for research in which 'disposal [should] be seen as a necessary issue integral to the whole process of viewing consumption as a social activity' (Hetherington 2004, 158). This is where recycling stations and recycling workers come into the picture. These workers are professionals charged with producing resources out of waste and creating orderly material out of chaos.

How is recycling physically organised? What is the professional role of recycling workers? What are the obstacles to an efficient recycling process? How do the recycling workers manage the challenges of their everyday work, especially when it comes to meeting and serving the public? What are their reflections on the resource flows that are so manifest in their work? And how does the public – the customers – react to the workers' attempts to educate and instruct them?

This chapter describes how waste handling is organised at recycling stations. Its main focus is to analyse the new professional role of recycling workers, a role that is not only technical, but highly social. It also provides a glimpse into how citizens perceive the act of visiting recycling stations.

Background: Organising material metabolism

In industrial society, materials come into the system in large part as virgin raw materials. Through the industrial process, knowledge and techniques are added step-by-step. Raw materials are changed into 'artefacts' – things or products – in a process that is simultaneously material and social. Over a century ago, in 1899, the phenomenon of consumption to express prestige ('honourable consumption') was thoroughly analysed by Thorstein Veblen (1899/2005). In his day, consumption for purely conspicuous reasons was only possible in the wealthy class of society. Veblen did not predict the volume of the consumption we see today, when tons of merchandise are produced and shipped all over the world to be used hardly at all. Today, mass consumption of goods in the industrial world is often more of a prestigious or social act than consumption for utility.

When things arrive at the other end of the societal metabolism, they become *waste*. In terms of material and energy, not much has changed in them. The central change is that products are eventually *thought of* as waste, i.e. something that the owner wants or needs to throw away. The change, therefore, seems to be of a primarily symbolic transition – we re-categorise things as waste even if they are still in a useful state.

In her classic (1966) work *Purity and Danger*, anthropologist Mary Douglas demonstrates how societies culturally embrace or ostracise matter (Douglas 1966/2002). *Clean* is opposed to *unclean*, *safe* is opposed to *dangerous*; *mundane* is opposed to the *holy*. Categories have to be held separate for cultures to keep their symbolic and psychological order intact. People in most societies want some kind of orderliness, and want to be able to recognise shapes and borders (Douglas 1966/2002, 45). Messy, dis-organised masses of things are often perceived as ambiguous and therefore evoke fear or disgust.

Exactly *what* is unclean and messy differs between cultures as well as between individuals. Cultural categories by which we cognitively organise things are marked by our 'schema' (Douglas 1966/2002), a cultural pattern for how to perceive and interpret phenomena. Douglas says that our capacity to 'label' things that we perceive increases with the familiarity we have with the kind of things in question (Douglas 1966/2002, 45–46). There is also a class dimension to the possibility of distancing ourselves from uncleanness and disorder, i.e. waste. Contact with, and handling of waste is often left to the poorest class of society.

Farmers in the pre-industrial Swedish countryside used to have special, unattractive sites in their vicinity where things were left once there was nothing more to gain from them. Or as one customer informant said: 'We used to drop everything over the edge' (Interview, 21 October 2013). When asked about where 'the edge' was, he said that it was place near the farm where he grew up.

In the Swedish modern welfare state, municipalities began to establish dumps on the cheapest land available to them. Hultman and Corvellec (2012) note that it became the mark and responsibility of a functioning society that waste be kept orderly and out of sight of (most) citizens, often in 'extra-urban areas' (Hultman and Corvellec 2012). They describe this former handling of waste by a term borrowed from psychology – *dissociation* (Hultman and Corvellec 2012, 2413), i.e. the process that occurs when an individual 'cuts out' a part of reality and more or less consciously chooses not to be aware of it.

This dissociation of waste by most of society probably worked well because there was little economic value in it. Still, there seems to have been some mental and economic attraction to the scraps even before the age of recycling. 'It was really exciting going to the dump', said one informant who grew up in northern Sweden in the 1970s and 1980s. 'It smelled really bad, but we would climb around in the debris. There were no opening hours and nobody worked there'. But, said another informant who grew up in southern Sweden in the late 1950s, 'There were people going to the dumps every day, people who collected things and sold the scrap'.

Larger dumps did employ dump workers, whose job was, apart from forming mountains of trash and covering them with soil, to direct garbage trucks and cars that arrived throughout the day. If something very voluminous or poisonous was to be dumped, visitors had to get a special permit or had to pay for the deposition of, for example, asbestos tiles. Even if the workers didn't have to touch the waste with their hands, the dirty working environment rubbed off on them. They were often thought of as hostile and unfortunate: their professional prestige was very low.

Until the 1970s, landfills were accepted as long as there was room for them, and as long as nothing aggressively poisonous leaked out. Nature, like water, was often thought of as a trash recipient that was unlimited in size and scope (Hajer 1992; McNeill 2002). But in the 1980s, the main narrative of waste began to change (Corvellec and Hultman 2012). Landfills formed places of responsibilities being handled by no one. As environmental issues became part of the narrative, waste began to develop a new reputation. This change has been called *ecological modernisation* (Hajer 1992; Spargaaren 1996), paired with *industrial ecology*. The 'dissociative sociomateriality of waste' (Hultman and Corvellec 2012) was no longer an option. The perception of the role of waste changed from waste as 'chaotic leftovers' to a new double identity, as *risk* (to be handled by society) and as *resource* (to be sold):

> This is a result both of how hazardous materials hidden in products resurface with problematic consequences when the products reach the end of their commercial life … and of how waste has become economically desirable on complex markets. Enabled by the evolution of applied industrial ecology, it is increasingly possible to use waste as input in production processes. … In such circular material management, recycling is a complement to and even replacement for the extraction of 'virgin' materials.
>
> (Hultman and Corvellec 2012)

It bears noting that in order to handle risk and collect resources, people with skills and knowledge are needed.

Method

This study is built upon interviews with employees of recycling stations in Skåne (Scania) in southern Sweden that were conducted in 2011 and 2012. The informants are all employed by the waste management company SYSAV. Eleven recycling workers (*återvinningsarbetare*) – from here on called 'workers' – were interviewed. The interviews were semi-structured, and centred around the following questions:

- How do workers perceive their job? What is positive, what is negative or problematic?
- How do workers think of their role in relation to 'customers', i.e. the public that comes to sort and recycle waste? Sub-questions may deal with encounters that are smooth and functional, but also those that are conflicting and problematic.
- How do workers experience change in their profession over time? Because the waste business is in a period of marked change, the experience of recycling workers is a good indicator of what is changing in the relationships between and among the waste management company, the organisation of waste management and the public.
- Do workers see any patterns in who is throwing out or recycling what, when it is recycled, what groups of the public come often or seldom or other reflections about the patterns of customers' behaviour?
- Any other spontaneous reflections about the profession and their everyday work.

During the interviews, I took careful notes, and rewrote them on the computer immediately afterwards. The use of a recorder might have provided more verbatim citations, but it is my experience that recorders tend to dull the expressivity of informants. Also many interviews were conducted outdoors in a noisy environment, which might have complicated recording. Even though the relationship between the waste company SYSAV and its employees generally appears to be friendly and trustful, informants were all informed that answers and results would be presented anonymously. (Without the shelter of anonymity, the informant might have censored information.) In the following, citations are marked by the date when the interviews were conducted. Since several interviews were sometimes conducted on the same day, one date may index from one to three interviews.

Interviews took place at the recycling stations during the hours of the day when there was not much customer traffic. Often, we had time to sit down in cabins and offices on the site. Some interviews were conducted standing outside where arriving cars and customers could be seen by the workers and by me. The workload on a recycling station is unpredictable – a normally 'slow' day may suddenly turn very busy. Interviews were often interrupted, when informants' colleagues, or the public, popped in to ask questions or to make comments. These interruptions of work are part of participatory observation. At other times, I remained at the recycling stations after finishing interviews to observe the flow of visitors, encounters of the employees, and how employees handled different kinds of situations. Even though visitors' behaviour was not the focus of my investigation, these observations often provided useful insights into the routines around recycling habits. I also had meetings and conversations with managers of the recycling stations to discuss the overall operation. In June 2012, I attended a meeting in Scania, where approximately 30 SYSAV employees and their manager discussed urgent matters and socialised before going back to work. I was asked to present this research project briefly. During the social time after the meeting ended, I had the chance to collect comments from the workers, and then spent some hours listening to and observing their social interaction.

Since the customers' points of view are also important for the purpose of this chapter, I conducted three interviews with citizens living in the SYSAV region. One informant was a single man in his early forties, an academic who lives in a small city apartment and does not own a car. This informant held strong environmental values. Since he had been in the process of moving recently, he had experience with recycling stations. I also interviewed a man living in the countryside who used his car a lot in his profession as a construction worker. This man, single and in his late forties, owns a big house. And finally, I interviewed a female organic farmer with a big family and a very busy household. During this last interview, the husband also contributed, as did one guest, another male middle-aged farmer, who popped in for coffee. The interview thus developed into an informal focus group. However, whilst the widely differing life-styles and choices of these informants demonstrate how diverse the customers' experiences of the recycling process can be, the focus of my investigation is primarily the workers' points of view.

Recycling stations: Deconstruction and transformation

During the last 15 or 20 years, a revolution has taken place in the handling of waste. Some of the recent changes in waste handling originated in the European Union (EU); its 'European Waste Hierarchy' provides an order of priorities for handling of waste in all member states (Hultman and Corvellec 2012). The steps of this hierarchy are reduce, reuse, recycle, recovery, landfill. 'Recovery' in contemporary Swedish waste policy means 'energy recovery', i.e. incineration (Hultman and Corvellec 2012). Landfill, the previously preferred method, is today the least common: only 2 per cent of the waste is reported to end up as landfill (SYSAV 2012). Municipality waste management has turned into a combination of public service and a large-scale business in the resource and energy sector (Corvellec *et al.* 2012).

The 15 recycling stations in SYSAV's domain are well-organised sorting land-scapes. They are often organised as drive-around plateaus, with full-size open containers ordered in a circle with lower ground around it that makes it conven-ient for customers to throw their waste over the edge. Containers are organised and numbered in order of most common waste (carton, paper, metals, wood) to less common (garden debris, upholstered furniture) to least common (plaster, for example) and, finally to combustible waste and non-recyclable – waste that has to be deposited. Tractors eventually come to compress the container contents. Trucks collect the containers from outside the platform, where there is a separate drive-way not accessible for customers (see Figure 11.1).

There are also smaller containers for light bulbs, batteries and glass bottles, among others, and metal tables where paint and chemicals can be placed. Electronic waste has its own container, but television sets go in large 'cages'. Household devices such as refrigerators and washing machines are put in a special corner. Often, there is some kind of walk-in charity container, where customers can put things that can be sold again. Each station follows the same pattern, but there are local variations in how things are organised.

There are also cabins for employees. As a rule these cabins are very comfort-able, with a corner for a desk and a computer, a toilet and a little kitchen with a table close to a window overlooking the station. Normally, there are two or more recycling workers at each station, but very remote and local stations may have only one worker. Beyond helping customers, recycling workers keep statistics on the number of visiting cars, direct the trucks that come to collect the containers and collect fees from non-private customers (more about this below).

A recycling station is in all its aspects the opposite of a factory – it is an anti-factory, a *dis-assembly line*. Once the waste is sorted, companies buy the recycled material and reuse, recycle or refine the products in a number of ways. For their purposes, it is important that materials are not mixed. The main product of the recycling station is sorted material. The goal is to deliver containers with mate-rial that is as non-polluted as possible, what the workers call *clean bins*. If there is more than 10 per cent pollution, i.e. non-wanted material, in a bin, the buyer might not pay for it (Interview, 24 February 2012).

Figure 11.1 'Ditt avfall förvandlas till nya material' – *Your waste is transformed into new materials*

Note: A buyer of material picks up a container at a recycling station in Scania, Sweden.

Source: Ebba Lisberg Jensen.

During the development process of the recycling stations, new sub-categories or new kinds of material have emerged (like hard plastic, which used to be unre-cyclable) and keep on doing so. This depends on the increasing market price of raw materials. If a material can be sold, it will be recycled. Somewhere down the dis-assembly line, a new technique may make it possible to process glass fibre and plaster or hard plastics into useful materials again. This influences waste-handling companies to respond and provide stations with new containers and new sorting areas. The ephemeral character of the business keeps the workers on their toes when it comes to expertise: what they know about sorting can, and must, change quite quickly.

Recycling workers are at the stations primarily to guide, educate and control customers, not to assist them in their performing the tasks of recycling. The concept of 'customer' is of interest here. The majority of the customers do not buy or pay anything (except for compost produced by garden debris delivered by the public). They are receivers of a service being performed for them as citizens, which has been paid for through waste collecting fees and taxes. Nonetheless, they have to perform the work themselves.

Some consumers are enthusiastic about and loyal towards the system, whilst others are sceptical about and hostile towards it. It is a new way of relating to materiality, both for customers and for workers. For the customers, the recycling process is at the far end *of the spectrum* of their consumption, but for the workers, the process is about producing reusable material.

From trashman to service professional

SYSAV is very ambitious about its recycling stations. Even if a station is only a small part of the enterprise, it is the arena where the public encounters the organisation and where its structure and goals become evident. It is the ambition of the company that when the public come to sort its waste, the visit will be smooth, clean and well-organised (Interview with managers, 27 February 2011). The infrastructure must also be as efficient as possible with clear directions on how to drive through the system. Management says that the personnel, as well as the skills they develop and implement in their daily work, are also focal points of achievement from the company's point of view (Interview with managers, 27 February 2011).

In the well-organised dis-assembly lines, employees are increasingly de-proletarised: they are leaving the markers of their former blue-collar roles behind them and facing new situations with new strategies. The employer regularly provides short courses and education on, for example, hazardous waste. This is of central importance both for the working environment and security of the employees, but also because of the need to handle paints, thinners, lacquers and biocides, among others, in the most environmentally friendly way possible. At the stations, the public can put their paint on a special sorting table; it is then organised by the workers. Except for hazardous fumes and threats to the ecosystem in case of a spill, the risk of explosion must be minimised.

It is possible that the recurring education and courses are central to the fact that so many of the informants report a high degree of fulfilment and happiness with their job. One worker in his sixties is one of several who have been working for the company for many years and had experienced the radical changes in the workplace and employees' work. 'It is really nice driving to work, it is almost like a hobby', he said (Interview, 24 February 2012). Generally, informants describe their work in positive terms. It is 'changing', someone else stated, and found that it is particularly positive that workers move about between the different stations (Interview, 24 February 2012).

The work on a recycling station is felt to require many more specific skills than the work on a landfill. Despite the well-organised system of reducing waste and recycling materials, there still exist a few depository sites in Scania, i.e. places for materials that for technical, economic and legal reasons are unrecyclable. Food remains and hazardous chemicals, metals and glass are no longer put on these sites, so they are not as smelly and dangerous as they once were. But no customers visit them, because the trucks servicing the sites are those of the company. Moreover, the work at the depository sites is not perceived by the workers as meaningful compared to the work at the stations – nothing, except for compost, is produced there. But whilst the professionally fulfilling experience of flexing one's expertise is not present at these sites, by circulating among the various workplaces, employees get to know all the different stations. 'Of course, it matters [where you work]. We who work on the recycling station [as opposed to depository sites] have some more peak competence. But I have worked all over the field and have a wide competence' (Interview, 27 January 2012).

Note the worker's use of the word *competence*, a word that in Swedish is used more often to denote skills performed in more academic or corporate contexts. This same informant did not look upon himself as a trash man: he had elevated his own function to that of a service provider. His job, he said, is about 'supervision and guiding, see to it that the station really works and to give service and help'. On the other hand, one of the customers expressed a little doubt: 'They [the recycling workers] are very helpful, but sometimes they don't seem to be that sure [about the sorting]' (Interview, 21 October 2013).

Several worker informants mentioned the quality of working outdoors, in the 'fresh air' (*friska luften*). To an observer, the term 'fresh air' is somewhat dubious – some of the stations are placed close to roads with heavy traffic. The activity at the stations also doesn't promise much in the way of air quality. Many cars come and go, and many drivers leave their motors running. Visitors empty bags of sawdust, plaster, ashes, earth and old, dry foam in the bins, and place their electronic and hazardous chemical waste in the receptacles. The air is often full of dust, fumes and particles. The fact that the air is considered 'fresh' is more of a 'schema', a category of perception, than a statement about the quality of the air. '*Friska luften*' is also considered less controlled and freer in a social way than the stricter structure of indoor work.

Several workers say that their work has changed from low-qualified labour to one that demands higher competencies. It is now close to a white-collar job with a focus on service: '[I see my role] more as a helper, not a controller. It is not obvious to everybody where to throw things. We have been educated, you know' (Interview, 16 March 2012).

The shift from labour to service parallels a shift in the way workers express responsibility when it comes to solving problems. To provide service, employees may open the gates even before the station formally has opened. This also helps prevent a flood of queueing cars that may take hours to ebb:

> Sometimes, we see that there is a queue all the way down to the road, already before opening. Then we normally open up half an hour in advance. Maybe the queue is gone when the formal time for opening comes. We let out the steam and make them pass by. No customers are going to drive home [once they've arrived], and then come back half an hour later, anyway, so they might as well be let in to leave their stuff.
>
> (Interview, 27 February 2012)

Workers can also keep the station open after official closing hours so that everyone who arrived even close to closing time can sort their waste and do not have to go home with loaded trailers. (If the recycling station had been a factory or a workshop, the service ideal would have been not to let any customer leave empty-handed.) The recycling station is a place where the empty trolley is the successful result of the customer's visit.

The work is also described as 'mobile' (*rörligt*) in a positive way. Workers walk or run up and down along the ramps. They are not supposed to help the public unload their waste. 'If someone managed to get a big TV set into their car, they must be able to get it out again', said one informant. Another told me – a little 'off the record' – that sometimes 'an old lady comes and asks if one might, maybe, be so very kind and grab the corner of a waste bag. Then it's all right [and you help her]. But if someone just calls: "Hey, come and help here!" – then you don't do it' (Interview, 16 March 2012). Even if informants are willing to help when visitors really need it, they are cautious about being subject to a patronising tone from customers. The authority in their professional role may be strong, but it is also new, and has to be protected by strict boundaries. No one wants to be reduced to a trash man again, or to be ordered about.

The social worker

Recycling workers spontaneously describe their work as 'social'. They meet people who do their sorting in a variety of moods and situations. Several of the worker informants commented on the fact that sorting waste is often done during a period of shifting life situations. It is performed when children leave home, when there is a divorce, when someone moves, renovates their house or when elderly parents die. For many, according to some workers, the arrival at the recycling station is the end of a psychologically challenging process of emptying cellars and garages, or emptying an apartment. Workers express consciousness about this delicate dimension of their work.

Sorting one's waste may be almost a moral ritual, which helps to cleanse previous situations in life (Åkesson 2012). On one occasion, I observed a grey-haired couple coming into the recycling station. They might have been siblings, or man and wife. Their car was full of unopened packages of nappies for old people. They threw package after package in the container for combustible waste. They also threw an assortment of odd china and battered pots and pans, as well as some waste bags full of what appeared to be textiles into the containers. They worked in silence. When the car finally was empty, they jumped in and left. They gave a strong impression of 'that was that' – someone who had been old and ill didn't need all these things any more (Personal Observation, August 2012).

To the consumer informants, who are generally in the productive phase of their lives, the most common visit to the recycling station is called upon 'because it's time' (Interviews, 15 and 20 October 2013). 'I accumulate a pile and go there when it's time', one costumer informant said. 'Maybe once every spring and every autumn' said another, but then the family brings a whole horse trailer full of waste (Interview, 21 October 2013). One had recently emptied his apartment to move, which naturally called for recycling (Interview, 15 October 2013).

Others seem to go there just to talk a little. There are many stories to be told at a recycling station, and some workers see it as part of their job to listen to customers:

> I care about people. Often, one gets to know everything [about the customers]. This has happened so many times. Some come [to the station] for the social contact, some elderly people. Sometimes, they have almost nothing to sort; they just come to get a chat. Yep, right, I think, there is the one [customer] who likes to talk football. One tries to remember.
> (Interview, 21 October 11 April 2012)

'It is almost moving', said another informant, 'to hear customers who come and confide in what happened lately'. In many other businesses, there have been reductions in personnel, another informant noted. You can no longer chat with the post office clerk or the person at the counter at the supermarket – either they have been exchanged for machines or they are too busy. In this social sense, recycling workers have a role to play. Some of them think it is a part of their trade to know when to talk to customers or not. 'Sometimes, people from 50 to 65 [years of age] come. Then it is often homes after their parents [who have died or moved into a nursery home that are to be emptied]. One sees the old furniture and carpets that weren't exactly bought the other day. Sometimes, one shouldn't talk to them' (Interview, 11 April 2012). (This last sentence was added in a rather defensive voice, as though this informant was saying that perhaps he shouldn't put as much time into talking to customers as he really wanted to.)

Recycling workers are trained to answer questions about all materials and about where the sorted containers are going once they are collected. This inform-ative, even pedagogical part of the work is seen as an important aspect of their professional life. Together, SYSAV and the workers have produced a pamphlet with details about why materials should be recycled, and what happens to metals, cardboard, electronics and all the other sub-categories. Because the workers know where the material is going once it is sorted, they also take pride in delivering 'clean bins' (Interview, 24 February 2011).

In this systemic urge for orderliness and 'clean bins', there is a latent conflict with some of the customers, who may have an interest in getting rid of their waste as quickly as possible. This conflict is handled with a certain amount of authority and pedagogy by the workers. On one occasion, I observed a man who arrived at the recycling station with a trailer filled to the brim. The man started to shuffle out cups, toys, clothes and small electronics into the last container on the station marked 'not recyclable'. This container is normally used for the last remnants in a customer's car or trailer when everything else has been properly sorted. But a recycling worker, a young woman in her high visibility jacket, came up to the man and started to explain. She looked friendly and smiled all through the conversation, while the man looked increasingly gloomy, his shoulders sloping. He began to sort, item-by-item. I discreetly watched him do this for half an hour, reflecting on the fact that his task seemed overwhelming. He didn't protest or try to cut corners in his sorting, but seemed to accept a drill that must have been unprecedented to him. I then had an interview booked in the station office and had to leave. Perhaps when this man had filled his trailer that day, he had no idea that magazines, shoes, radios and a number of other items could not be discarded at once at the recycling station.

Reluctant customers

The work at the recycling stations is not always idyllic. Sometimes, customers demand help that workers are not allowed to provide. Here, as we saw in the example above, personal judgement seems to go before the rules. If there are very few customers and almost nothing to do, one worker said, one would rather help a little rather than stand still getting colder (Interview, 24 February 2012).

The function as 'controller' is more complex. Some informants say that they have developed the instinct to judge whether a customer somewhere at the station is ruthless about the sorting or is going to object to advice and instructions. 'Rather often, it happens that people oppose. One learns to read their body language from far away. It says, "something is not right here"'. (While saying this, the informant mimicked the flicking of a garbage bag over the edge of a container with a nonchalant gesture.) (Interview, 11 April 2012). By contrast, one of the customer informants said that some of his friends had a technique where one distracted the recycling worker with questions so that the other could throw away bags of unsorted waste (Interview, 21 October 2013).

The more the public becomes accustomed to the routines of the recycling stations, the less often these kinds of problems occur. Workers say there is an increasing awareness among the public that everyone should sort properly. 'One is so used to the system now', said one of the customers (Interview, 21 October 2013). But some customers may still continue to oppose the procedures for a long time. A worker told about a wealthy customer who owns a hotel in a nearby village. Time after time, the customer tried to get through the gate to the old landfill, which was formally closed, to drop empty bottles and cardboard from the hotel. As a non-private customer, he would have to pay to sort his waste, but he wasn't opposed to the fee as such. According to the recycling worker, this customer argued that he shouldn't have to do the sorting at all, because he had to pay for it. He would rather pay the fee and just dump everything. The customer was very persistent and had to be talked into doing the sorting for a long time before he accepted it (Interview, 27 January 2012).

Sometimes it is not the effort as such that customers oppose, but the authority of the recycling workers. According to one informant, this attitude is more common with wealthy people. 'Those who have some money [i.e. who are rich] are not that good at sorting. Some people who come in really nice cars can be patronising. Then, I am [perceived as] a small trash man who should shut up and not tell him what to do' (Interview, 24 February 2012).

Stories like this illustrate a recurring problem for the recycling workers. On the one hand, they are white-collar workers in a municipally-owned company. They are officials: it is part of their job to direct peoples' sorting. On the other hand, they don't have that much power to put behind their authoritative performance. Customers can and do disobey or oppose them. But whilst these situations may become pointed, they don't happen every day. 'One gets yelled at. But it isn't that often. We haven't been scared. It is more common in Malmö' (Interview, 24 February 2012). (This interview was conducted at a smaller recycling station in a small town. Malmö is a city commonly thought of as a 'crime city' in Sweden.) When asked whether workers had experienced violence or threats at the workplace, one informant answered: 'No. It might happen, but it is very rare. Many (workers) are reluctant to interfere with the customers; some of them may be unpleasant. But it is not that often that they [the customers] say bad things' [Interview, 24 February 2012].

A little later, though, this informant told me that he was once punched by a customer (Interview, 24 February 2012). It didn't scare him, though. 'As long as one has a colleague there, one shouldn't back off if there is a conflict', he said. Because there are fewer employees at the smaller recycling stations, workers sometimes have to work alone, even if the trade union is opposed to it (Interview, 27 January 2012). But workers feel that small stations are also more peaceful, whilst all informants associate aggressive situations with the larger stations in Malmö. More male than female workers seem to experience threatening or aggressive encounters. No one has offered an explanation for this, but my interpretation is that the cultural threshold for displaying aggression towards a female recycling worker is higher.

Irregular entrepreneurs sorting their waste

There is one structural problem that all recycling worker informants brought up in the interviews. Whilst private customers pay for their use of the recycle station through their waste fee, entrepreneurs such as carpenters, mechanics, hotel owners and NGOs have to go to recycling centres that are especially customised for them. When sorting lesser amounts, an occasional trailer, say, entrepreneurs can go to the usual recycling station, but they (until recently) had to pay in cash on site. This system was criticised by the recycling workers, who didn't feel secure carrying money. Entrepreneurs now have to pay either 400 Swedish kronor (Skr), or €43 with a credit card, or they can buy coupons in advance for 250 Skr, or € 26 each. As a consequence of this system, recycling workers have the tough task of keeping an eye on cars arriving, so that all professionals either leave for another centre or pay the fee. The fee is high enough to cause customers try to cover up the business nature of their trash and do their sorting for free.

The recycling workers cannot do very much about these customers. 'The only thing we can do is *ask them* if they are private citizens or companies. It's not normal for a private person to bring four trailers with concrete, bricks and debris here every week' (Interview, 27 January 2012). Sometimes, it's not the entrepreneur himself or herself who arrives and opposes the payment. 'I was actually once chased by a person who didn't want to pay. He had Poles [Polish labourers]. When they sorted waste without paying, I told them [that they had to pay], and they got their boss, and he came after me. But since then, he has paid every time' (Interview, 24 April 2012).

This informant and his colleague pointed out that the problems with the entrepreneurs shouldn't be exaggerated. Sometimes, they said, company cars 'just drive through'. It wasn't really clear if they just come to see if there might be a chance to do the sorting unseen. Another informant told me that at his workplace workers had let go of the control – it just isn't worth the trouble. The stress and encounters with such illegal firms and illegal labourers makes the situation even more stressful:

> The attitude [here] has become a little more relaxed. It was like a stress thing [the trouble with the companies]. Those who are not really legal, if you know. … The same trailer can come with people who are working … but if Mr. Andersson sits in the car, one cannot really prove that it's about work this particular time [and not Mr. Andersson's free time when he is allowed to come sorting for free].
>
> (Interview, 11 April 2012)

At a recycling station in Malmö, I observed how a couple of cars arrived, and to judge by the clothes and gear of the men in the cars they were obviously construction workers unloading debris and construction waste. On this particular occasion, nobody stopped them. The recycling workers had asked them about their provenance without my noticing, and had received the answer that they were privates. 'Asking is all you can do', said the informant, and he shrugged (Interview, 16 March 2012).

A moment before that, two men in overalls had begun to unload old windows from a trailer. But as soon as a recycling worker approached them, they tied up their load and left. 'They were from a company', the worker explained: they had been sent off to the recycling centre for companies. Some of the customer informants who rightly should have paid for their sorting said that they 'don't exactly put out signs that they are at work' (Interview, 21 October 2013) and the interviewed construction worker had solved the problem by letting his clients do the sorting. 'It saves time and money, both for me and them', was his explanation (Interview, 20 October 2013). 'Otherwise, they would have to pay me for doing it and pay the fee on my bill'.

How many thick TV sets can there be?

The fact that garden debris increases during the warmer season is seen as 'natural. These are things that keep on growing', as one worker said (Interview, 11 April 2012). But many recycling workers express a fascination for the never-ending stream of things that pass through. They observe and comment upon the pace with which new items are passed on for recycling (see Figure 11.2). The number of older, thicker television sets doesn't ever seem to ebb. 'We empty [exchange for empty ones] the cages [housing the discarded television sets] several times a day' said one worker.

Figure 11.2 Recycling workers reflect on the flow of electronic waste from electronic devices

Note: Electronic waste from electronic devices is often not made to last or cannot be repaired. The flow of such goods to recycling stations seems to increase every year.

Source: Ebba Lisberg Jensen.

The 'cages' are metal frames of one cubic metre each. 'And it [the circulation of television sets] has been going on for several years. How many thick TV sets can there possibly be?' he added (Interview, 24 February 2012). 'There are enormous amounts of electronics', a colleague at the same station added. At another station, a worker summed up the TV situation:

> Every day in the weekends, a bin [full-size truck container] and a half are filled up with electronic waste, and ten cages with thick TV sets. It is so sick, this consumer society [that] we are in. At least 70 per cent of it [the stuff in total] still works.
>
> (Interview, 16 March 2012)

A worker at another station made it clear why the flow of electronics has increased. 'It doesn't pay to repair the TVs. It's on purpose, all that. It shan't last too long' (Interview, 24 February 2012). His comment was an elegant summary of the phenomenon of *planned obsolescence*. Products that last decrease the need to buy something new. Therefore, many products, especially electronics, are now built not to last on purpose (see Figure 11.3).

Figure 11.3 Cages with 'thick' television sets

Note: According to one of the recycling workers, cages like this can sometimes be filled and emptied ten times a day.

Source: Ebba Lisberg Jensen.

Another worker stated that sometimes overconsumption goes directly to the recycling station, not even passing through a 'use phase'. The constant consumer wish for new things, as well as low prices, increases the flow:

> Sometimes, people go to buy three bookshelves from IKEA, and then they happen to buy five and two of them are left in their original wrapping. We often see that down in the flee-market container. Electronics also increase; it has been cheaper to buy things new [than to mend broken things]. TV sets arrive in incredible numbers. And now, the first flat screens start to arrive. Those who bought a 32-inch now want a 42 or a 55-inch – bigger than a normal house gable.
>
> (Interview, 27 January 2012)

When asked about patterns of waste they see among customers, a majority of the informants agree that younger people discard things faster. 'Older people throw mostly garden debris, and they save more things. The younger throw IKEA furniture and things that look completely whole and new' (Interview, 24 Oct 2011). One of the customer informants thought that people throw away almost new furniture (Interview, 21 October 2013). But another worker also commented that elderly people overuse their cars and the recycle stations. 'They come with a few light bulbs in a bag and some newspapers every week. Makes you wonder how environmentally friendly that is' (Interview, 24 October 2011).

Some, but not all workers reflected on their task from an environmental perspective. Another worker related the mass of waste to a:

> … fast consumption society, especially when it comes to electronics. The things break immediately once the guarantee has expired. We use natural resources to produce something new. Companies make more and more money – and we buy more and more.
>
> (Interview, 11 April 2012)

This informant reported that sometimes he 'gets all nauseous' about the amount of things being discarded. He also said that consumption trends and alarmist reports from the media have a short-term influence on the flow of waste:

> If the Christmas present of the year is a special thing that substitutes [for] something else, this other thing is thrown out. We notice that. Then there is a lot of fuzz about what can be dangerous. 'Soy can be really poisonous!' [mimicking a news reporter] – suddenly we had many litres of soy put on the shelf for hazardous waste! Media get things started. But sometimes, there are chemicals, when people have died. [There can be] 3–4 cardboard boxes with herbicides that have been banned since the fifties.
>
> (Interview, 11 April 2012)

Some things are never meant to be used. A worker told me that he wondered why there was such a flow of completely new refrigerators, freezers and cookers. He came to the conclusion that people who are about to sell their house or apartment buy these new appliances in order to make the kitchen or laundry room look fresh. Then the buyer starts to refurnish and redecorate the new home. Away go the fridge and cooker, which have never been used, or only used for a few weeks while the house was for sale. These expensive items may therefore come to the recycling station in mint condition – their only purpose had been to decorate a house for sale.

Congestion at recycling stations

In general, recycling workers describe their job as something positive. They like it, they think it is meaningful: it makes them feel like important actors in society. But sometimes the going gets tough. Except for the problem of warding off private companies or making them pay for their recycling, several informants express concern about the frequency of recycling. During weekends, there are ever more cars arriving. In springtime, when people clear their gardens and garages, the situation is often problematic; the circulation of vehicles at the station is so dense that customers can only move their cars in one direction, metre by metre. People dispose of their waste and scream at each other over the noise of running motors.

Sometimes, small accidents occur – cars scratch each other or the dense traffic threatens to injure people. 'If one comes along carrying, for example, a sofa, it doesn't feel safe at all', one customer said (Interview, 15 October 2013). 'It is a catastrophe', one worker said. (He was not being interviewed, but interrupted the interview to make this message clear.) 'We need at least two extra stations in Malmö' (Interview, 11 April 2012).

When the pressure is at its peak, the job gets really stressful. The workers all 'run and run. There is no time to sit down through the whole day, or to go to the toilet'. Drivers honk and customers are also irritated, due to the pressure, the noise and the other cars waiting with their motors running. As soon as a worker stops to inform one customer about how to sort, a flock of other customers forms and waits impatiently for advice. Several stations decided to put up a gate at the entrance to keep the flow down to a number that workers feel they can handle. But seeing and hearing all the cars lining up outside the gate may also be a pressure. The queue of cars is not allowed to exceed the distance out to the common road, where it might block traffic, so the station sometimes has to open the gate even if it is crowded. At the smaller stations, this is not as much of a problem as in urban areas.

The workers are aware that recycled material is valuable. Once it is deposited at the station, it belongs to SYSAV to be sold or incinerated. But because things that are sorted are not always waste except in the formal sense, there are people who want them. Sometimes customers pick up something from a container. From a legal perspective, it is theft, but workers do not always intrude. Often, one informant told me, it is enough to approach the 'thief', and things are returned without discussion.

But as it happens, the amount of valuable machines standing out in the open is too much of a lure to criminals. Sometimes, small lorries come in and thieves begin to load valuable things like refrigerators. Some informants expressed that this was very stressful and sometimes overtly threatening. One worker reported that thieves threatened him when he tried to stop them from stealing cookers. 'We are waiting for you outside the gates tonight', they said. He called the police and the incident ended peacefully, but it scared him (Interview, 16 March 2012).

Concluding remarks

Waste in earlier times was an object of dissociation on both the personal and societal levels. Now, increasing production and consumption have made recycling crucial, for both economic and environmental reasons. Waste has turned into *a governance issue* (Zapata Campos and Zapata 2011); in the case described here, governance has been implemented through a business model (Corvellec *et al.* 2012). Waste is materials and energy, both are valuable in economic terms. To 'extract' *the value in* products for societal gain is the obvious function of the recycling stations.

But there is also an aesthetic aspect to the sorting of waste. As the amount of waste has increased, society has decided that waste should be kept in an organised space so as not to defile the landscape or the environment (cf. Douglas 1966/2002, 9). Recycling stations function like counter-factories, as dis-assembly lines, and can be seen as emblematic of late modernity. They can also be seen as physical manifestations of ecological modernisation, where the negative outcomes of industrial society (disorderly waste) are turned into materials, and economic value is handled through the social processes of ordering.

The recycling workers produce value, but they also produce order. The order is of two kinds, the first being material order – the *clean bins*. The second is the social order – the citizen's responsibility and the level of education of the customers on the stations. Citizens are mildly disciplined into creating order even if they have little to gain from it, at least in economic terms. In some cases, as with the entrepreneurs, recycling may even cost them. Whilst some are reluctant and unwilling and others are willing to fulfil their responsibility, the recycling workers have taken it upon themselves to motivate citizens.

Recycling workers also help citizens create a private order. Domestic cluttering is known to most of us. When we buy things, we include them in our personal lives. Once they are used, we need to get rid of them. We don't want them haunting us and reminding us of situations that are no longer present (Hetherington 2004). Therefore, the act of going to the recycling station is an act of cleansing, often as satisfying as the original purchase of the products once was.

In a way, recycling is also an act of repentance. What has been consumed – sometimes with a bad conscience – is now 'returned', and dis-assembled back to what one may think of as resources. Crises or voluntary changes in life may be marked by the trip to the recycling station. To many customers, it is as unimportant where things are going once they are sorted as where they originally came from. But a recycler (somewhat righteously) may have the feeling that all the things that once were raw materials now go back to an original state – or at least can be used again by others, or by society. How this is done and what the costs are, are not always clear (Interview, 21 October 2013), not even to the recycling workers, who strive to keep production up in their dis-assembly factories, where the full life-cycle of raw-material–product–waste–material is always clear. Their job is to see to it that waste is dis-assembled into material in a smooth and orderly way.

Recycling personnel are 'the face of the company'. In the rather short time span of about 10 years, their professional role has changed completely. Their work used to be low-qualified – not to say *non*-qualified labour – as trashmen at a dump. Today, the work is about providing service in a knowledge-intensive organisation that works well, as the managers put it. The status of the recycling workers has increased tremendously, a fact that is obvious in all the interviews; all informants report a high degree of professional pride. Not only do they take pride in delivering clean bins, they also take pride in mediating knowledge and providing service to customers. At the same time, they continuously reflect on the material flows in which they take part every day.

References

Åkesson L (2012) Waste in Overflow, in Czarniawska B and Löfgren O (eds) *Managing Overflow in Affluent Societies*, Routledge, Oxford, UK, 141–154.

Corvellec H and Hultman J (2012) From 'Less Landfilling' to 'Wasting Less': Societal Narratives, Socio-Materiality, and Organizations, *Journal of Organizational Change Management* 25(2) 297–314.

Corvellec H, Bramryd T and Hultman J (2012) The Business Model of Solid Waste Management in Sweden: A Case Study of Two Municipally-Owned Companies, *Waste Management and Research* 30(5) 512–518.

Douglas M (1966/2002) *Purity and Danger: An Analysis of Concept of Pollution and Taboo*, Routledge, London.

Hajer M (1992) *The Politics of Environmental Discourse. Ecological Modernization and the Policy Process*, Oxford University Press, Oxford, UK.

Hetherington K (2004) Secondhandedness: Consumption, Disposal and Absent Presence, *Environment and Planning D: Society and Space* 22 157–173.

Hultman J and Corvellec H (2012) The European Waste Hierarchy: From the Sociomateriality of Waste to a Politics of Consumption, *Environment and Planning A* 44 2413–2427.

McNeill J R (2000) *Something New Under the Sun: An Environmental History of the Twentieth-Century World*, W W Norton, New York.

Spaargaren G (1996) *The Ecological Modernization of Production and Consumption*, PhD Thesis Wageningen University, Wageningen, the Netherlands.

SYSAV (2012) *Årsredovisning* [Yearly Economic Report] (Online) (www.sysav.se) Accessed 2 December 2013.

Veblen T (1899/2005) *Conspicuous Consumption: Unproductive Consumption of Goods Is Honourable*, Penguin Books, London.

Zapata Campos M J and Zapata P (2011) Narratives of Sustainable Waste Management in International Aid Agencies, *The 7th International Critical Management Studies (CMS)* Gothenburg Research Institute, Gothenburg.

12 Klimafesten

A case study of a municipality's intervention to engage citizens in environmentally sustainable actions

Emilie Møllenbach and Kasper Hornbæk

Introduction

Human–Computer Interaction (HCI) is a multi-disciplinary field based in computer science that focuses on the interaction between man and machine. In its simplest form, it involves a user interacting with a computerised system through some kind of mediated bodily input (e.g. typing with hands, motion activation, voice input and gaze control) and receiving feedback from the system as to the effects of the interaction. The implications of HCI in our individual and collective lives become ever more complex as the number of digital platforms, contexts and daily practices shaped by technology increases. Applying HCI to environmental sustainability is part of an emerging discourse that situates the design of technology in societal problems.

To date, the field of sustainable HCI has focused primarily on the consumption habits of the individual, for instance by providing ambient feedback on electricity use (Midden *et al.* 2008; Petersen *et al.* 2009; Crowley *et al.* 2011), persuasive information on water consumption (Kappel and Grechenig 2009; Kuznetsov and Paulos 2010; Erickson *et al.* 2012) or improving garbage disposal (Gartland and Piasek 2009; Reif *et al.* 2010). DiSalvo and his colleagues (DiSalvo *et al.* 2010) reviewed 157 papers on sustainable HCI and found that 70 per cent focused on the individual. Many researchers have pointed to the limitations of this scope and the need for interventions that target groups (Mankoff *et al.* 2007; Paulos *et al.* 2008; Dourish 2009). For instance, Dourish argues: 'Rather than using technology to provoke reflection on environmental impact of individual actions, we might use it instead to show how particular actions or concerns link one into a broader coalition of concerned citizens, social groups and organisations' (Dourish 2009, 7).

Focusing on groups holds at least two promises for sustainable HCI. First, the fact that we are inclined to align ourselves with the norms and actions of others may be used to motivate behavioural change (Lewin 1947; Snow *et al.* 1986; DiSalvo *et al.* 2010). Social networks, online communities and online logging support information exchange and are powerful platforms for developing norms. In one study 80,000 households received letters informing them about general energy conservation strategies and comparing their specific household energy use to that of their neighbours. The letters reduced the energy consumption of its recipients by 2 per cent. The study concluded that 'some combination of infor-mation, attention and social norms can cause substantive changes in consumer behaviour at population scale' (Allcott 2009, 17).

Second, environmental sustainability is a complex global, societal and politi-cal problem. It is shaped by both societal macro-structures (large-scale social organisations such as municipalities or public transport companies) and micro-structures (bodies of agency within the macro-structure, typically individuals) (Giddens 1986; Alexander 1987). We argue that HCI might benefit from the study of how agency can be facilitated by a macro-structure that would allow us to identify approaches that inherently possess scale. The challenge of environ-mental sustainability must be addressed through macro-structures, as well as at the individual level. However, the complexity of macro-structures (and their interaction with micro-structures) is rarely studied in sustainable HCI.

This chapter reports on a case study of a five-month, cross-media, multi-method intervention created by a Danish municipality focused on environmental sustainability. The intervention is called *Klimafesten* (in English, the 'climate celebration'). The foci of the case study were the intentions of the municipality, the actions and motivations of citizens and the effect of the inter-vention. We describe what happens when motivations of different actors converge, analyse types of sustainable actions and show how the secondary effects of the intervention were crucial to its success. Finally, we discuss some lessons and reflections on large-scale interventions that are intended to inspire ways to target HCI solutions at sustainable, group-based citizen involvement.

Sustainable HCI

The following presents existing research on sustainable HCI, first as an active field with panels (Khan *et al.* 2011), reviews (Froehlich *et al.* 2010) and numer-ous papers (DiSalvo *et al.* 2010; Froehlich *et al.* 2010; Erickson *et al.* 2012). Second, we discuss adjacent fields such as environmental psychology and how they qualify motivation and action. Finally, research related to the dynamics of group-targeted interventions is presented.

Environmental sustainability within HCI

One research target on pro-environmental behaviour in HCI has been the search for pervasive solutions that decrease energy consumption through remote moni-toring and control using mobile phones (Burke *et al.* 2009; Kjeldskov *et al.* 2012) or sensor-based energy management systems (Sutaria and Deshmukh 2008) to gather and deploy information about behaviour and carbon footprints (Dada *et al.* 2008). Another approach focuses on providing feedback about consumption patterns as a way to increase awareness and thereby create behaviour change. Froehlich and colleagues reviewed eco-feedback research in HCI (Froehlich *et al.* 2010) and drew attention to the relevance of integrating knowledge from fields such as environmental and behavioural psychology (Hines *et al.* 1987; Kollmuss and Agyeman 2002; Bamberg and Möser 2007).

Few large-scale studies of eco-feedback systems have been conducted (Aoki *et al.* 2009; Erickson *et al.* 2012). The reasons for the lack of large-scale studies include the complexity involved and the difficulty in establishing baselines for benchmark testing of consumption, behaviour and awareness levels. One example is from Erickson and his colleagues (Erickson *et al.* 2012), who studied feedback on water consumption in 303 households in Dubuque, Iowa, in the United States (US) over a 15-week period. The result of the change in feedback was a 6.6 per cent decrease in water consumption. They propose that showing people their consumption levels could become even more efficient if the feedback was tied to individual appliances.

Environmental sustainability in adjacent fields

Kollmuss and her colleague (Kollmuss and Agyeman 2002) reviewed environmental psychology frameworks developed to bridge the gap between environmental awareness and pro-environmental behaviour. They addressed the move from models that assume a linear progression from knowledge to behaviour (i.e. information campaigns) towards more detailed and complex models of internal (motivation, awareness and values) and external (institutional, economic, social and cultural) factors.

Motivation is a central issue in environmental psychology and is modelled in many ways that often show how to enhance the desire for altruism and pro-sociality based on incentives and disincentives. However, De Young (2002) expressed the need to expand the concept of motivation in pro-environmental behaviour. He argued that pro-environmental action should be fuelled by self-interest and provides the example of humanitarian aid workers being more inclined to continue working if they are motivated by personal growth and rewards, in contrast to being motivated by altruistic motives. Powerful motives such as self-satisfaction could be engaged to create sustained pro-environmental action.

Interventions targeted at groups

Research in environmental psychology (as well as much research in sustainable HCI) departs from a focus on the individual. The fields of social marketing and behavioural economics (Thaler 1985; Tversky and Kahneman 1986; Kahneman 2003) provide ample examples of strategies that influence group dynamics through cultivating norms. Often these strategies combine information campaigns, legislative initiatives, social events and individual incentive schemes. The cultivation of the norm that preceded the ban on smoking in many countries is such an example. Anti-smoking campaigns gradually influenced popular opinion over a number of years; it can be argued that by the time anti-smoking legislation was passed, large swathes of populations had already become accustomed to the idea of smoking as culturally unacceptable.

Humans adapt to their peers through either assimilation or differentiation (Pickett and Brewer 2001). If our friends gain weight, there is a tendency for us to gain weight (i.e. assimilation) and collectively differentiate us as a group from thinner people (Christakis and Fowler 2007). The beneficial powers of social networks to increase a sense of happiness (Fowler and Christakis 2008) as well as the detrimental effects of feeling ostracised in social contexts have been well-documented (Williams et al. 2000; Zadro et al. 2004).

Summary

This brief review suggests that large-scale interventions for environmentally sustainable HCI are difficult. When they also involve heterogeneous groups of actors with different motivations, the ambiguity of designing for specific bench-marks and describing their effects is daunting. The goal of this chapter is to address the ambiguity inherent in socio-economic content through our involve-ment in such an intervention, which targeted cultivating norms and initiating action through the distribution and generation of information. We argue that the systematic study of such an intervention adds to our understanding of the areas discussed above.

The *Klimafesten* intervention

The *Klimafesten* intervention ran in the municipality of Skanderborg from November 2011–April 2012 and focused on citizen action. The core of the inter-vention was a citizen competition on sustainable action. The intervention was designed to support the point of *self-satisfaction* as a motivational factor. The goal was to celebrate, reward and thereby motivate those already behaving or want-ing to behave in more environmentally sustainable ways.

The *context of* Klimafesten

Denmark has had a national climate strategy since 1987 and signed the Kyoto protocol in 2002. The country has set the goal of being solely dependent on renewable energy sources by 2050 ('Denmark's Climate Strategy 1' n.d.; 'Denmark's Climate Strategy 2' n.d.). In 2012, 33 per cent of the national elec-tricity supply was provided by wind power (see www.windpower.org/da/energipolitik, 2012). For decades it has been a political, economic and social focus to establish Denmark as a frontrunner in environmental sustainability. On the municipal level, environmental sustainability efforts are directed at city plan-ning, energy supply structures and citizen involvement.

The municipality of Skanderborg, Denmark, which is approximately 440 square kilometres in area and has 55,328 inhabitants, has set the goal of becom-ing CO_2-neutral with regard to heating and electricity by 2020. It is gradually relying more on renewable sources such as wind power, biogas, biofuel and solar panels for its energy supply. However, 5 per cent of the proposed reduction in

CO_2 is slated to come from cutbacks in personal energy consumption. To this end, the municipality is trying to engage both industry and citizens.

Skanderborg conducted the intervention by spearheading a series of public social events, a media campaign and an online competition where citizens were asked to post stories about environmental actions they had made. The ethos of the intervention was to highlight individuals who are already taking action and encourage others to do the same.

Methods of inquiry

The intervention comprised a network of political and societal stakeholders (the municipality, participants in events and participants in the competition) and properties of the intervention (media coverage, the website and the events), each with various intentions and motivations. We used a case study approach (Yin 2009) and observed three events, conducted 27 interviews, performed content analyses of the uploaded material and ran an online survey.

Methods for exploring the municipality

Two municipal workers supported by a design firm led the intervention. Seven interviews were held with the two municipal workers during and after the intervention period. The interviews were qualitative research interviews as described in Kvale (2006a, 2006b). The main themes of the initial interview were the goals and success criteria of the intervention, the practical details of the intervention and the challenges and technologies involved. Subsequent interviews were more informal and explored progressions, iterations and changes that occurred in the intervention. A final interview concerned the overall evaluation of the intervention. The municipality workers were also involved in the analyses of the content entries. All entries were converted to narratives and coded according to activity.

Methods for investigating the intervention

Klimafesten was mediated through three channels: traditional media (television, radio and newspapers), public events (town meetings and climate fairs) and digital media (a web competition and a mobile application).

The project also included intense and ongoing scrutiny of how the media were covering the intervention. In fact, one of the goals set by the municipality was the requirement of a certain number of mentions in the different media. An overview of the media coverage generated by the intervention was also produced.

In order to create awareness around *Klimafesten*, the municipality organized nine events; observations were conducted at three of these. Two events were town meetings held with the local supply company. The goal of the meetings was to provide citizens with knowledge about structural and behavioural changes that could reduce energy, heating and water consumption. The third event was a climate fair at which both energy supply companies and local tradesmen dealing in sustainable technology and solutions had booths.

There were a total of 17 interviews of citizens conducted at the climate fair. The topics concerned how citizens had heard of the event, their interest in participating and whether or not they had been provided the information they wanted.

Names and email addresses submitted by event and climate fair attendees constituted a survey of the broader response to *Klimafesten*. The survey was distributed to 475 respondents; 39 completed it. Other than basic demographic questions, the survey sought to clarify three issues: (1) general attitudes towards environmental sustainability issues, (2) the effect of participating in the event and (3) changes in awareness and behaviour as a consequence of participation. Survey participants were asked to list what actions they had taken after participating in an event.

Online content of the intervention was assessed by an analysis of entries in the competition on the intervention's website. Competition participants uploaded 36 entries, including posts with video and text entries (9), image and text entries (12) and pure text entries (9). Some entries consisted of several posts because people uploaded image and text in separate entries. In order to complete the content analysis, these entries were aggregated into 30 unique contributions and converted into a 10-line or less description similar to Kvale's technique of 'meaning condensation' (Kvale 2006b), i.e. summarising entries into comparable narratives. This allowed the second author of this chapter, other project researchers and representatives of the municipality to quickly understand the content.

Methods for studying citizen actions and motivations

These methods were used to investigate the public events and digital content as they relate to the actions of citizens. However, a series of interviews was also conducted to explore the motivations of citizens. Three interviews were conducted with content-providing citizens. The first was an interview conducted with the winner of the competition, a man who had upgraded his home to be environmentally sustainable. The second was with representatives from a project called 'Transition Town Ry', a village that decided to take collective action towards more sustainable ways of living. The third interview was also with a prizewinner, a woman who had made many changes in her lifestyle in order to function efficiently and freely without a car.

Analysis approach

Audio recordings were made at event observations. Also, memos were written during the events and subsequently structured according to discussion subjects and areas of interest from participants. Interviews were audio-recorded and partially transcribed. For the initial and final municipality interviews, the transcriptions were turned into reports on intention and evaluation respectively. Transcription of the interviews conducted with participants were analysed to understand motivations.

Content analysis of the uploaded content was performed in three ways. The first was with municipal workers and was coded by initiative, uploads, content types, activities generated by *Klimafesten* and activities that would have occurred anyway. The second coding was conducted with the second author in order to identify patterns of actions. The third was also conducted with the second author analysing the open questions of the survey and coded based on the actions taken by participants after events.

Results

We report on the evaluation from five angles; Figure 12.1 is intended as an overview.

The first angle of the Figure (A) is the municipality's intention to inform and motivate its citizens to take various environmentally sustainable actions. The second angle (B) considers the means through which the municipality communicated this intention. The third angle (C) considers the actions of citizens as reported in the intervention. The motivations of participants (D) are explored to understand both why they take environmental action and why they participated in the intervention. Finally, the angle of ripple effect (E) is explored, by which we mean secondary events that occurred as a consequence of the intervention, not as part of the intervention itself.

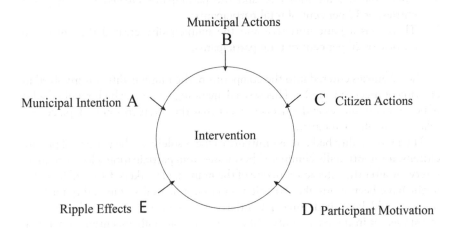

Figure 12.1 The five perspectives from which the municipality has been observed and investigated

A) Municipal intention: Intervention plan

Information in this section comes from the initial interviews, content analysis of the website and the subsequent coding of that information with the municipal workers.

A range of information was provided regarding different opportunities for sustainable living. A 'tips and tricks' section on the website covered topics such as energy conservation in the home, sustainable shopping, water usage reduction tips and recycling tips. Similar information was presented at the various events. These properties represented what the municipality considered to be sustainable improvements. The challenge was to make the intervention visible in the community and engage participants.

The municipality had anticipated that it would be difficult to attract entries to the online competition, as people had no prior knowledge of the competition's existence. This is a classic marketing and communications problem. As a consequence, the municipality initiated the first four entries by asking citizens who were known to engage in environmental action to contribute to the competition.

The strategy of municipal workers encouraging and creating entries continued throughout the intervention. Five combinations of initiative and creation factors for participation can be observed:

1   Both the initiative and the creation of the competition entry came from the participant – 11 entries, or 37 per cent of total participants.
2   The initiative came from the participant and the municipality created the entry – 9 entries, or 30 per cent of total participants.
3   The municipality took the initiative and created the entry – 1 entry, or 3 per cent of total participants.
4   There was a joint initiative and the participants created the entry – 3 entries, or 10 per cent of total participants.
5   There was a joint initiative and the municipality created the entry – 6 entries, or 20 per cent of total participants.

Of the 30 entries entered into the competition, the municipality was involved in creating or incentivising 19. This was a demanding strategy, which required a lot of personnel resources and reflects the fact that the intervention took place in a relatively small community.

The municipality had chosen initially to focus solely on the actions of private citizens: it intentionally eliminated businesses from participating. However, in an interview after the intervention, one of the municipal workers discussed how this might have been a mistake. Focusing on environmental sustainability for businesses would have had three potential consequences: (a) strengthening the private sector in the community, (b) creating a financially incentivised network for spreading both awareness and tools for environmentally sustainable living and (c) businesses often consist of groups and existing networks. Tradesmen and companies had requested to join the online competition, but had been declined.

However, in the upcoming climate campaign for the winter of 2013, the focus is on supporting business communities, both those making a living on environmental sustainability and those wanting to increase the environmental sustainability of their businesses.

B) Municipal action: Communicating through multiple channels, framing activities and events

An overview of the intervention elements is provided in this step. This outline was compiled from media clippings, an event calendar, interviews and observations. Because the municipality had originally not made plans for such an overview, the elements were created in relation to this research.

The intervention ended with a total of 85 mentions in 9 different print media and 6 mentions on local television stations. Nine public events were held in Skanderborg and the surrounding villages to create awareness regarding the environment and the intervention. These ranged from themed citizen meetings to Christmas events in the town square (see Table 12.1).

Except for the kick-off meeting and the Christmas town square event, all of the events were organised in collaboration with other public and private institutions. The recycling fair was hosted by the local Red Cross. At each of the town meetings, a representative from the local power supply company gave a presentation whilst the municipal worker only gave a brief introduction. It may sound strange that information on energy savings comes from the very source that provides energy in the first place. However, a national political initiative ensures that energy supply companies are financially rewarded by public funds for energy savings that they help generate. Energy saved is money made.

Table 12.1 An overview of social events arranged by the municipality during the intervention period

Month 2012–2013	Events		
November	Kick-off Conference	Christmas Event in Ry	
December	Christmas Event in Skanderborg		
January	Town Meeting on Energy Saving in Skanderborg	Recycling Market in Ry	
February	Town Meeting on Energy Saving in Hørning	Town Meeting on Energy Saving in Veng	Solar Power Meeting in Skanderborg
March	Energy Fair in Skanderborg		

C) Citizen actions: Awareness, behaviour and tools for change

This angle covers information from the content analyses of the online competition entries. The rules of the *Klimafesten* competition were simple: take action and post the activity online. Because what constituted an environmentally sustainable action was not pre-defined, a wide variety of contributions were made. In the online survey, participants were asked whether or not they had made any behavioural changes relative to their energy consumption after participating in the events. Forty statements about changes made were posted and subsequently categorised. Through a content analysis of both the competition entries and the survey answers, three classes of actions were identified: increasing awareness, behaviour change and introducing physical components (see Table 12.2).

Awareness actions are those that impart knowledge of environmental sustainability and involve exchange of information about the environment, climate policies, energy-conserving behaviour and practical structural solutions. Behavioural actions are activities completed during the course of everyday life, including turning off lights, choosing to use a bicycle instead of a car and recycling and sorting waste. Physical components are practical alterations regarding the acquisition, distribution and use of resources such as installing solar power, rainwater collection and distribution systems, geothermal heating and insulation.

Increasing awareness

Awareness entries in *Klimafesten* either related to global or local awareness of climate issues. Seven awareness entries came from schools. An example of a school awareness action was a mock climate summit with 50 participants from the 9th grade classes of two local schools. The idea was to emulate international climate proceedings. Whilst the goal was to reach an agreement by the end of the day, this was not achieved; the students couldn't reconcile the economic and climate agendas of the various countries. In another awareness entry, two

Table 12.2 2012 Skanderborg Climate Intervention Online competition entries categorised by increasing awareness, behaviour change and introducing physical components

	Entries	Topics of entries
Increasing awareness	11 (37%)	Energy conservation, waste disposal, climate policy, climate awareness, alternative energy, insulation, thermography imaging, transportation
Behaviour change	12 (40%)	Transportation, recycling, waste disposal, food consumption, energy conservation
Introducing physical components	8 (23%)	Rainwater collection, solar power, insulation lighting

students at a local school surveyed their school and identified areas where energy could be saved. Finally, an entry described a group awareness action in which 69 homeowners and an energy supply company collaborated to complete thermography screenings of the homes. (Thermography screenings reveal where a house is emitting unnecessary or unwanted heat.)

Behaviour change

In the behavioural change action, student participants performed sustainable activities, created venues for sustainable activities or maintained sustainable lifestyles. One activity was titled 'Sell Before You Buy'. Some young girls sold their old clothes and items at a recycling fair, saying that the acquisition of new things made more sense if old items were recycled. In another entry, a woman described how she had arranged her life so that she could get around easily without a car. She had four bicycles and a bicycle trailer, two at home and two permanently parked at train stations. (Incidentally, there was only one entry in the competition on transportation, even though transportation holds much potential for improving sustainability.) And a final example: in an effort to teach pupils in the 3rd grade about nature preservation, the students were asked to collect litter on the school grounds.

Introducing physical components

All the stories about physical components submitted to the competition dealt with home improvements in some way. Of the 18 statements made about introducing physical components in the online survey, 10 were about solar power, as were four of the eight introductions of physical components.

The stories entered into the competition included a homeowner who installed 40 solar panels to provide energy for a heat pump. A family placed 84 solar panels on the roof of their house, which covered 135 m^2 and were intended to supply 80 per cent of their energy consumption. Another type of home improvement dealt with insulation: one household used 'paper wool' to insulate their roof and installed low emission windows and a ventilation system. The winner of the competition was a homeowner who had completely renovated his house in order to make it as energy- and resource-neutral as possible using insulation, new windows, solar panels and a rainwater collection and distribution system for toilets and the clothes washer. He then allowed people to visit his house, where he explained the solutions that he had chosen. Approximately 80 people participated.

D) Participant motivation

The entries in the competition came mainly from people already engaged in environmentally sustainable activities; certainly, understanding their motives for taking environmental action might motivate others. Three entries represented three types of motivation: technology, community and lifestyle choices.

Technology motivation

The overall winner of the competition was the man who had climate-renovated his house, focusing of technology:

> I am a bit of a climate tech geek. … I had the money to do some things, we changed the mortgage on our house … now the money has run out. I guess what means the most to my wife is comfort … I am probably the one who cares more about the environment. … She still thinks we are going on holiday this winter, I have tried to tell her that this is not going to happen.

What motivated this man was the process of finding the right solution to his problems, either through the internet, being inspired by others or talking with tradesmen. Large financial investments in environmental sustainability such as this are characteristic of those who introduce physical elements changes such as a solar energy system that can easily cost €10,000.

Community motivation

Another competition entry came from the aforementioned Transition Town Ry. A couple that had helped organise a climate fair in Ry was interviewed. Their main motivation for joining the Transition Towns project had been the focus on action, not just awareness. However, it was also very important to them to have a sense of belonging to their local community. They emphasised the fact that the group organising the climate fair came from very diverse backgrounds, but all felt ownership toward the project: they created it and the potential effects of the fair would be felt in their immediate community. They were slightly sceptical about the fact that the municipality was heading the intervention: '… people will never really feel ownership of such a project (*Klimafesten*), because they don't have any relation to the people involved, when we meet, it is as much a social thing as anything else'.

Lifestyle motivation

The woman with the four bicycles exemplifies the lifestyle motivation. When asked when and why she started living this way her first answer was:

> Well, I started riding a bike when I was about six and I just never stopped, I guess … when I was young we didn't have a car. So I just got used to the fact that we rode our bikes everywhere – it has always been a natural part of the way I live.

This woman had also joined another association specifically targeted at preventing the construction of highways: sustainable transportation was her main concern. 'The rest – I mean eating organically and that sort of thing, that I can do at home'.

E) Implications of the intervention: Ripple effects

We have been discussing examples of events that were part of the intervention and the motivations of those participating. However, the impact of such an intervention goes beyond the discrete actions and events; indeed, the impact of the intervention was one of the project's main goals. We call this secondary impact *ripple effects*.

For all the participants interviewed, the internet was a place that they wanted to spend as little time as possible and they all looked rather puzzled when asked about the potential role of the internet as an instrument to further their causes. However, contributing to the event meant that they received attention for their work from people they met in the course of their daily lives. This attention from strangers on the bus or the clerk in the local supermarket reaffirmed their personal convictions about environmental sustainability.

In the online survey conducted after the intervention, over 18 statements that introduced physical elements were made. One of the events arranged by the municipality was dedicated solely to solar power; over 500 people attended this function and it was also covered by the local television news. At another later event, the climate fair, several representatives from local power supply companies were present. When asked what they considered was the most important environmentally sustainable product at the moment, they answered solar power, and said that solar power sales had gone up substantially over the past few months (the fair was held in March 2012). There were several reasons for this, they said. First of all, there is a huge financial incentive to install solar power, because there is a monetary reward – energy generated and not used makes the energy meter start running backwards. Second, supermarket chains had begun selling solar power panels so people would be exposed to them in their local store. Finally, media coverage of solar power had increased. This trend was observed in both the structural entries in the competition and statements of change from the event participants. The point here is that an intervention in a complex societal context not only creates ripple effects but also reflect ripples from external events.

Discussion

We have described the multi-method study of an intervention aimed at promoting sustainable behaviour among a municipality's citizens. The following section discusses some methodological implications and lessons learned about group synergism, implications of political and structural tensions and activity classification.

Methodological implications: Causing and observing ripple effects

The reason why such interventions are difficult to design and evaluate, especially in a full-scale real-world context, is that ripple effects cannot be pre-determined. Understanding that the effects of the intervention lay partly in the ripple effects changes the design and evaluation perspective. Design and evaluation should not only focus on the actions and interactions within the intervention, but also look for opportunities for creating ripples. Involving groups of people is a way to create ripples; for instance, we observed that school children tell their parents about the climate negotiations they had been taking part in or the collection of litter on the school grounds. Using alternate media is another way to create ripples, as shown by an article in the local newspaper about a local environmental hero or a television news story that inspires viewers to make investments in environmentally sustainable products.

Using social network outlets could perhaps help spread the message and create more ripple effects. However, it became clear through the interviews on motivation that those citizens who contribute the most in terms of sustainability were not involved in social online networks. A digital platform might not be the source of motivation for those already active or even for those wanting to take action. However, it can be a source of inspiration that can affirm and solidify social norms.

Group synergism

The group focus of the intervention worked. Among other results, it led to citizens teaching citizens about solar power and school kids informing each other and their parents about sustainability and local communities by taking collective action such as thermography readings. This differs from the typical individual-oriented campaign (Erickson *et al.* 2012) or the use of typical individual behaviour-change technology (Petersen *et al.* 2009; DiSalvo *et al.* 2010; Froehlich *et al.* 2010; Kirman *et al.* 2010). It also meant that even citizens sceptical about the intervention changed their opinion after experiencing recognition and publicity. These changes would not have been seen in an individual-oriented intervention. Thus, many key effects of *Klimafesten* were the result of the intervention's focus on groups and macro-structure.

There was no individual awareness action entry in the competition. Information exchange is a fundamental part of generating awareness: it must either come from a system, as known from eco-feedback, or from other people generating collective norms, as seen in this intervention. Both can be supported by HCI. Behaviour, on the other hand, is largely an individual activity. Whilst it may be something performed with others and can have a social motivation, as seen in the Transition Towns project, the choice to act is an individual one. Ultimately groups consist of individuals, so the goal of HCI is to provide tools that support both individual action and collective interaction. The same synergism that is causing technological innovation problems and designs to be crowd-sourced and crowd-funded through channels such as Kickstarter (www.kickstarter.com/) is represented in the group activities in this intervention. Global sustainability is a global issue and one that requires group synergised activity to be addressed. The technological infrastructure of the intervention is capable of managing, creating and inspiring group synergism.

Implications of political and structural tensions

All the people interviewed were motivated to take environmental action. In spite of having participated in *Klimafesten* and being very oriented to environmental sustainability, none of them were particularly thrilled with the intervention. This tension was perhaps due to the fact that it was created and imposed by the municipality: when an authority seeks to impose a norm, it will create tension for some and not for others (Kollmuss and Agyeman 2002).

As such, the macro/socio-structure aspect of the intervention had fundamental consequences. The municipality catalysed the activity on the website by collecting and uploading material. This was a successful strategy because of the short distance between municipality and citizens, and is most likely a result of Skanderborg being a small rural community. And while citizens accepted the bootstrapping, uploads did not happen on their initiative. In terms of future implementations, this is interesting in several ways: the size and political climate of a community play an important role in capturing the attention of active citizens.

Future interventions need to take seriously the role between the messenger and the receiver. Erickson and his colleagues (Erickson *et al.* 2012) argue that:

> Feelings of this kind [negative towards authority] may override traditional cues of authority, so that someone who has developed a dislike of government interventions may be less likely to listen to messages that they perceived to come from 'the government'. In such cases, the most effective strategy for changing behaviour may be to use third parties or downplay government involvement in a campaign or intervention.

Having the municipality as the messenger had two observable consequences: (1) some people were hesitant about participating because they do not want to become involved with authority, or (2) the opposite – they were willing to participate because the authority lends participation societal importance and legitimacy. Crowd-sourcing, which should, in this context, be understood as using the distribution power of information technology to engage and involve crowds of people in addressing and taking action regarding political issues seems to be the natural technological progression of the democratic tradition. Technology-based interventions hold the key to managing the information flow of crowds. The question is what activities are suitable to be crowd-sourced.

Action classes

The actions taken by competition and event participants reflect three focus areas for environmental sustainability research and design: environmental awareness, behaviour and structure. Each constitutes a potential design space for HCI.

Awareness as a design space is amply represented in the literature, as most eco-feedback systems target this by providing visualisations and information about consumption habits with the intention of lowering consumption.

We suggest that designing for behaviour change requires situated artifacts, that is, artifacts that are part of the behaviour. One example of this is designing for garbage disposal. Knowing that garbage should be sorted and how it should be sorted does not always translate in the situation of actual disposal. The technologies involved in structural actions might belong in large part in the engineering of sustainable technological artifacts, but the enabling and integration of such technology in everyday life lies firmly within the field of HCI.

Investments in physical elements (e.g. solar cells) were frequent in the entries of the competition. We have argued that investing in infrastructure is a type of sustainable behaviour, but it is rarely discussed in the literature. It is typically a one-time action, requires little maintenance (in the sense of the trans-theoretical model; Prochaska 1997; Prochaska 2008), but the costs are steep. Perhaps these characteristics mean that networks and discussions with other citizens about such large investment decisions are particularly important. It is easier to justify investing a substantial amount of money when there is a consensus in the community that this is a sensible investment.

The willingness to change the physical frame of one's actions is a reflection of how important comfort is. These changes require very little maintenance and are unlike behaviour change, where conscious vigilance is required in order to break habits. Installing solar panels or insulating one's home is expensive, but once completed, the change is more or less permanently implemented. This is why structural implementations on the level of groups are often the first line of attack, and rightly so. Changing a country's power supply from fossil fuel to sustainable sources has great impact; while it is expensive and not maintenance-free, the initial transformation is by far the most far-reaching. This is where eco-feedback on a large collective scale becomes an opportunity for HCI.

As smart grids and sustainable energy networks become more prevalent, the tools to visualise exactly how much energy a system has and where it is going becomes vital for effective distribution management. Perhaps some of the insights gained from understanding eco-feedback on an individual level can be translated to the collective.

Future work and limitations

Future work on *Klimafesten* could focus on the insights we have described here in order to have even more impact. When given no guidelines, people chose to engage in various types of actions regarding awareness, engaging in sustainable behaviour and making structural changes to their homes. This structure of actions might be a useful tool in designing future interventions and designing HCI. Future interventions should be designed to identify different types of ripple effects. However, measuring the exact impact of such an intervention is problematic, because both the context and the intervention are so complex. But we might be able to see the contours of impact by exploring intention, actions, actors, motives and impact.

Conclusion

This case study looked at a municipality-driven intervention that was conducted to highlight and increase environmentally sustainable actions of citizens. The intervention consisted of an online competition, a series of social events and media coverage. Our analysis found that by directing the intervention at groups, groups took action. However, the tensions among motivation, intention and actions of participants and the municipality underscore the fact that environmental sustainability is – or can be – a point of political contention.

The actions taken by the participants in the intervention fell into three classes: actions of awareness, behaviour and structure. Evaluating the intervention was a complex task of accessing impact in a rich socio-political context. We argue that interventions cause ripple effects on multiple levels. By specifically targeting future interventions toward awareness, behaviour or structural implementations, the intention, outcome and means of assessment become clearer.

Acknowledgements

We would like to thank the municipality of Skanderborg for contributing to and supporting this research.

References

Alexander J C (1987) *The Micro-Macro Link*, University of California Press.

Allcott H (2009) Social Norms and Energy Conservation, *Journal of Public Economics* 1082–1095.

Aoki P M, Honicky R J, Mainwaring A, Myers C, Paulos E, Subramanian S and Woodruff A (2009) A Vehicle for Research: Using Street Sweepers to Explore the Landscape of Environmental Community Action, *Proceedings of the 27th International Conference on Human Factors in Computing Systems* 375–384.

Bamberg S and Möser G (2007) Twenty Years after Hines, Hungerford, and Tomera: A New Meta-Analysis of Psycho-Social Determinants of Pro-Environmental Behaviour, *Journal of Environmental Psychology* 14–25.

Burke S, Snyder S and Rager R C (2009) An Assessment of Faculty Usage of YouTube as a Teaching Resource, *The Internet Journal of Allied Health Sciences and Practice* 1–8.

Christakis N A and Fowler J H (2007) The Spread of Obesity in a Large Social Network over 32 Years, *New England Journal of Medicine* 370–379.

Crowley M, Heitz A, Matta A, Mori K and Banerjee B (2011) Behavioral Science-Informed Technology Interventions for Change in Residential Energy Consumption, *Proceedings of the 2011 annual conference extended abstracts on Human factors in computing systems* 2209–2214.

Dada A, Staake T and Fleisch E (2008) The Potential of UbiComp Technologies to Determine the Carbon Footprints of Products, *Workshop on Pervasive Persuasive Technology and Environmental Sustainability* 50–53.

De Young R (2002) New Ways to Promote Proenvironmental Behavior: Expanding and Evaluating Motives for Environmentally Responsible Behavior, *Journal of Social Issues* 509–526.

Denmark's Climate Strategy 1 (n.d.) (www.ens.dk/sites/ens.dk/files/politik/dansk-klima-energipolitik/Klimapolitisk%20Redeg%C3%B8relse%202011.pdf) Accessed February 4 2015.

Denmark's Climate Strategy 2 (n.d.) (www.ens.dk/da-DK/Politik/Dansk-klima-og-energi-politik/Sider/dansk-klima-og-energipolitik.aspx) Accessed 4 February 2015.

DiSalvo C Sengers P and Brynjarsdóttir H (2010) Mapping the Landscape of Sustainable, HCI *Proceedings of the 28th international conference on Human factors in computing systems* 1975–1984.

Dourish P (2009) *Print This Paper, Kill a Tree: Environmental Sustainability Research* [Technical Report LUCI-2009-004] Laboratory for Ubiquitous Computing and Interaction, University of California at Irvine.

Erickson T, Podlaseck M, Sahu S, Dai J D, Chao T and Naphade M (2012) The Dubuque Water Portal: Evaluation of the Uptake, Use and Impact of Residential Water Consumption Feedback, *Proceedings of the 2012 ACM annual conference on Human Factors in Computing Systems* 675–684.

Fowler J H and Christakis N A (2008) The Dynamic Spread of Happiness in a Large Social Network, *British Medical Journal* 2338.

Froehlich J, Findlater L and Landay J (2010) The Design of Eco-Feedback Technology, *Proceedings of the 28th International Conference on Human Factors in Computing Systems* 1999–2008.

Gartland A A and Piasek P (2009) Weigh Your Waste: A Sustainable Way to Reduce Waste, *Proceedings of the 27th International Conference Extended Abstracts on Human Factors in Computing Systems* 2853–2858.

Giddens A (1986) *The Constitution of Society: Outline of the Theory of Structuration,* University of California Press.

Hines J M, Hungerford H R and Tomera A N (1987) Analysis and Synthesis of Research on Responsible Environmental Behavior: A Meta-Analysis, *The Journal of Environmental Education* 1–8.

Kahneman D (2003) Maps of Bounded Rationality: Psychology for Behavioral Economics, *The American Economic Review* 1449–1475.

Kappel K and Grechenig T (2009) Show-Me: Water Consumption at a Glance to Promote Water Conservation in the Shower, *Proceedings of the 4th International Conference on Persuasive Technology* 26.

Khan A, Bartram L, Blevis E, DiSalvo C, Froehlich J and Kurtenbach G (2011) CHI 2011 Sustainability Community Invited Panel: Challenges Ahead, *Proceedings of the 2011 Annual Conference Extended Abstracts On Human Factors in Computing Systems* 73–76.

Kirman B, Linehan C, Lawson S, Foster D and Doughty M (2010) There's a Monster in My Kitchen: Using Aversive Feedback to Motivate Behaviour Change, *Proceedings of the 28th of the International Conference Extended Abstracts on Human Factors in Computing Systems* 2685–2694.

Kjeldskov J, Skov M B, Paay J and Pathmanathan R (2012) Using Mobile Phones to Support Sustainability: A Field Study of Residential Electricity Consumption, *Proceedings of the 2012 ACM Annual Conference on Human Factors in Computing Systems* Austin, TX, May 5–10, 2347–2356.

Kollmuss A and Agyeman J (2002) Mind the Gap: Why Do People Act Environmentally and What Are the Barriers to Pro-Environmental Behavior? *Environmental Education Research* 8(3) 239–260.

Kuznetsov S and Paulos E (2010) UpStream: Motivating Water Conservation with Low-Cost Water Flow Sensing and Persuasive Displays, *Proceedings of the 28th International*

Conference on Human Factors in Computing Systems Atlanta, GA, April 10–15, 1851–1860.

Kvale S (2006a) Dominance Through Interviews and Dialogues, *Qualitative Inquiry* 12 480–500.

Kvale S (2006b) *Interview: en introduktion til det kvalitative forskningsinterview*, København Hans Reitzels Forlag.

Lewin K (1947) Frontiers in Group Dynamics II, *Human Relations* 1 143–153.

Mankoff J, Matthews D, Fussell S R and Johnson M (2007) Leveraging Social Networks to Motivate Individuals to Reduce Their Ecological Footprints, *System Sciences* HICSS.

Midden C, McCalley T, Ham J and Zaalberg R (2008) *Using Persuasive Technology to Encourage Sustainable Behavior*, Paper presented at the 6th International Conference on Pervasive Computing, Sydney.

Paulos E, Foth M, Satchell C, Kim Y, Dourish P and Choi J H (2008) *Ubiquitous Sustainability: Citizen Science & Activism*, Workshop Organisers at the 10th International Conference on Ubiquitous Computing (UbiComp), Seoul, South Korea.

Petersen D, Steele J and Wilkerson J (2009) WattBot: A Residential Electricity Monitoring and Feedback System, *Proceedings of the 27th International Conference Extended Abstracts on Human Factors in Computing Systems*, April 4–9, Boston, MA, 2847–2852.

Pickett C L and Brewer M B (2001) Assimilation and Differentiation Needs as Motivational Determinants of Perceived In-group and Out-Group Homogeneity, *Journal of Experimental Social Psychology* 37 341–348.

Prochaska J O (2008) Decision Making in the Transtheoretical Model of Behavior Change, *Medical Decision Making* 28 845–849.

Prochaska J O and Velicer W F (1997) The Transtheoretical Model of Health Behavior Change, *American Journal of Health Promotion* 12(1) 38–48.

Reif I, Alt F, Hincapié Ramos J D, Poteriaykina K and Wagner J (2010) Cleanly: Trashducation Urban System, *Proceedings of the 28th of the International Conference Extended Abstracts on Human Factors in Computing Systems* Atlanta, GA, 3511–3516.

Snow D A, Rochford Jr E B, Worden S K and Benford R D (1986) Frame Alignment Processes, Micromobilization, and Movement Participation, *American Sociological Review* 51 464–481.

Sutaria R and Deshmukh A (2008) Taking the Guesswork out of Environmentally Sustainable Lifestyles, *Proceedings of Pervasive 2008 Workshop on Pervasive Persuasive Technology and Environmental Sustainability* 109–112.

Thaler R (1985) Mental Accounting and Consumer Choice, *Marketing Science* 4(3) 199–214.

Tversky A and Kahneman D (1986) Rational Choice and the Framing of Decisions, *Journal of Business* 59(4 pt.2), 251–278.

Williams K D, Cheung C K T and Choi W (2000) Cyberostracism: Effects of Being Ignored over the Internet, *Journal of Personality and Social Psychology* 79(5) 748–762. (www.windpower.org/da/energipolitik_og_planlaegning/energiforliget_og_2020.html) Accessed on 23 January 2015.

Yin R K (2009) *Case Study Research: Design and Methods* (Vol 5), Sage, Thousand Oaks, CA.

Zadro L, Williams K D and Richardson R (2004) How Low Can You Go? Ostracism by a Computer Is Sufficient to Lower Self-Reported Levels of Belonging, Control, Self-Esteem, and Meaningful Existence, *Journal of Experimental Social Psychology* 40 560–567.

13 Computer games and social innovation

Participation through micro-contributions

Mette Wichmand

Introduction

> It [the computer game] was important in the sense that it made me think more proactively about what's happening around me. It made me realise that I can't just be a spectator and I have a role to play in whatever way I can … it made me realise my role in the different problem areas in the world. It definitely did change me because now, rather than just being aware of what is happening around me, I've actually seen that I also have a responsibility to do something … no matter how small it might start out.
>
> (Player of 'Urgent Evoke', World Bank's online social innovation game)

This comment tells us that a game experience can transform a player from a passive spectator to an active post-game citizen ready to take responsibility and act in order to create positive social change. It represents a dream scenario for many socio-political actors, who, in the midst of the financial crises when public money is scarce, have begun to look for technologies that can generate civic engagement.

Research has already shown us that the use of social media – with political as well as non-political content – can help generate offline civic and political engagement (Feezell *et al.* 2009; Zhang *et al.* 2010; Kahne *et al.* 2013) such as voting, helping a neighbour, making donations to charity or engaging in political discussions with friends and family (Adler and Goggin 2005). However, this engagement in civic and political life doesn't seem to be enough. What we need to continue to seek are technologies that can turn passive citizens into creative and innovative social change agents who are willing to create and implement social innovations that can help solve complex public problems such as poverty, hunger and climate change.

Over the last ten years, a small but growing niche in the computer game industry has developed that produces serious games designed to empower players to create innovative solutions to complex social problems. These games, called 'Games for Change' (G4C)[1] are framed by a participatory optimism based on two factors.

First, the average gamer today is 30 years old and has about 13 years, or 10,000 hours of game experience; 45 per cent of them are women and 25 per cent are over 50 years old.² The international community of gamers spends 3 billion hours a week playing games,³ which makes it possible for G4C developers to argue that games should be seen as a possible democratic and political tool as they have the potential to reach and engage all demographic groups.

Second, after years of research that has focused in large part on the negative outcomes of playing computer games – anti-social behaviour, aggression and violence (Sherry 2001; Grüsser *et al.* 2007) – a growing body of research is beginning to show the positive impact that games might have in relation to health and education. This relatively new attitude about the potential of computer games creates a more nuanced picture of the medium's weaknesses and strengths.

Researchers have also begun to pay attention to the impact that video games might have on civic engagement (Bers 2010). They are now suggesting that playing video games can cause players to engage in offline activities that previous research has found to promote civic outcomes (Adler and Goggin 2005). These activities include helping and guiding others, learning about problems in society, exploring social, moral or ethical issues, organising interest groups, discussing social and political issues with family and friends, raising money for charity and writing letters to political representatives in the offline world (Lenhart *et al.* 2008; Bers 2010; Neys and Jansz 2010).

Research has also shown that pro-social game play increases post-game pro-social behaviour (Gentile *et al.* 2009), promotes online and offline social support among players (Trepte *et al.* 2012) and that games have the capacity to function as a new form of a 'third place' for political deliberations (Steinkuehler and Williams 2006). These findings substantiate the G4C developers' participatory optimism, even though very little research has yet been done on the specific functioning and effects of G4C (Connolly *et al.* 2012).

So far, then, we can perhaps agree that there is a basis for a possible partnership between the political need for citizens willing to create and implement innovative solutions to complex public problems and the G4C developers claim that their games come with a built-in capacity to engage players and turn them into an army of ever-ready citizens eager to create and share knowledge and ideas online in order to contribute to the common good. And so far this partnership seems like a match made in heaven. However, the actors' shared focus on using technology to generate post-game social innovators might prove to be an obstacle for bringing into play all the human resources present in and around the G4C games.

This chapter presents data from an emerging case study of a G4C called 'Urgent Evoke' (UE). The data indicate that even though games offer new possibilities for creating player-driven social innovation, the underlying social mechanisms are perhaps more complex than just generating creators with socially innovative ideas. Drawing on the data from the study of Urgent Evoke, this chapter argues that if socio-political actors and game developers want to facilitate citizen-driven social innovation, they should decrease the single focus on the creators and develop a more network-oriented approach to game design, one that will enable the facilitation of multiple forms of participation.

The following narrative describes the game Urgent Evoke and presents this study's research methodology. The data from the case study is then presented and compared to previous studies of user participation in other forms of online social media. Because the chapter builds on an emerging case study, it ends with a discussion of the data and some possible ideas for further research.

Urgent Evoke: A social network game

The following description of Urgent Evoke's game design and play is not a comprehensive analysis of the game, but a sketch that should enable the reader to better understand the case study and its context.

Urgent Evoke is a G4C developed by the World Bank Institute, together with game developer Jane McGonigal. It is an online game that is free to play via a computer, tablet or smartphone. The game is open to players of all ages (although the recommended minimum age is 13), and can be played from anywhere in the world. (Because the World Bank has established sub-Saharan Africa as one of its key focus areas, young people in South Africa and to some extent other sub-Saharan countries were targeted specifically by the game developers.)

UE is also a social network game, which means that it concentrates the players' engagement simultaneously on one platform and is structured to foster collaboration and co-creation between and among game players. The World Bank wants to use UE to engage ordinary citizens in some of the problems the Bank deals with, including poverty, hunger and climate change. The goal of the game is to empower players to 'investigate the most pressing challenges around the world, collaborate to generate innovative and creative solutions and act to turn ideas into reality within their own communities and beyond' (Gaible and Dabla 2010, 9).

In other words, the aim of UE is not just to deliver an engaging experience or teach players about global challenges, but also to transform the initial game motivation of the players into post-game social participation, a form of participation that should materialise in the development and implementation of social innovations in the physical world.

The narrative: A story of heterogenic network of agents

Urgent Evoke is built around a narrative told in the form of a graphic novel. Every week a new chapter is released. The narrative of the game is the story of a secret social network of international agents with innovative superpowers capable of solving some of the most complex problems facing the international community. The agents can be reached by sending out an 'Evoke'. The Evoke is answered by Alchemy, the leader of the network. He puts together a team of agents that immediately goes into action. The team travels to all corners of the world to face problems like famine, epidemics and natural catastrophes. The team consists of three members – Eureka, Ember and Quinn. Each member of the group has a defining background story and characteristics, skills and knowledge that both set them apart and make them a very resourceful team capable of developing and implementing new social solutions.

The narrative introduces the 'mission of the week', but also communicates the idea that the kind of problems dealt with in the game can not be solved by one person alone. A team is needed – a heterogenic team of agents with very different strengths and capacities.

A UE player is a member of Alchemy's secret Evoke network, and is expected to help find solutions to the missions connected to the ten chapters in the graphic novel. Parallel to the work on the missions, players are presented with a weekly quest formulated to help them reflect upon and strengthen their personal capacity as social innovators.

Missions and quests: Offering structure as well as freedom

A mission and quest are also released with the weekly release of a new chapter. The missions are large and complex – such as how to solve a hunger crisis in Japan. The topics addressed in the missions are social innovation, food security, power, water crisis, money, empowering women, urban resilience, indigenous knowledge and crisis networking. Because the size and the complexity of the missions make it difficult for players to tackle them alone, they are compelled to cooperate and share their knowledge, experiences and ideas with other players. The last mission that players are asked to complete is to write a detailed and innovative plan of how the player will tackle a self-chosen socio-political challenge in the physical world after the game has ended. This plan is called an 'Evokation'.

The 10 quests are meant to help players discover their own abilities and strengths as social innovators. They urge players to think about their own capacities, potential and dreams and to express how they would like to develop personally. For example, players are asked to think about their motivation for playing UE or to describe the skills and capacities of a person they admire.

Together with the narrative, the missions and quests create a clear path for the players to follow that leads to the creation of an Evokation. But even though UE is very structured and the goal is clear, it is possible for the players to create their own game play. Players do not need to follow the progression of the game. They can take on the missions and quests they feel like doing, and spend as much time as they like (within the limits of the ten-week game period). It is possible to move back and forth between the missions, quests and chapters of the graphic novel, which means that players can catch up any time during the ten-week run time. It is also possible to investigate the resources (the links, blogs, sound files and the graphic novel) offered by the game without doing the missions and the quests. This mix of a clear structure and freedom to create one's own game play makes it possible to create a large community of players sharing an experience, even though the players might participate in the game in many different ways, ranging from light use to intense game play.

Interface: Facilitating the formation of a social network

The interface of Urgent Evoke is simple (see www.urgentevoke.com), but visu-
ally strong. The game is constructed on a Ning template (Ning is a company that
hosts and creates templates for online social communities, see ning.com). The
game is in 2D, a main opening page leads to a series of sub-pages, and a mix of
digital artefacts (links to external sites, blogs, jpegs, sound recordings) is incorporated into the site. The design of the interface is to a large extent based on
images and sound, which allows for a minimum use of text. The tone-of-voice is
open, but bidding ('You are ready, aren't you? Ready for a real challenge? It's not
enough for you to read our story…') and plain English is used. The colour scheme
creates a somewhat gloomy yet warm environment with the use of colours like
black, dusty grey, blue, green and purple.

During the game, players build up a personal profile page. This page resembles
in many ways the personal pages we know from Facebook. It functions as a
logbook, where players collect, showcase and develop their material from the
completed quests and missions (written reflections, videos, links and photos).
But the page is also a communication tool. It can be personalised with pictures
and personal information and used to communicate an in-game identity. Players
can visit each other's profiles and communicate with each other by leaving feedback or awarding each other points for missions and quests well done. Points
awarded can lead to a spot on the eight hero lists – Newest Heroes, Emerging
Heroes, Questing Heroes, Heroes on a Mission, Power Generators, Mega Heroes,
Heroes of the Week and Leading Powers.

In order to be rewarded points, players need to generate traffic on their page
and build up a network of friends. For example, this can be done by being active
in the game's chat-room where the community of players can 'talk' with each
other. Contributing to the community by being active in the chat-room can
generate traffic on the players profile page and lead to new in-game friends.

It is possible to play the game without connecting to the player community,
but the interface, together with the narrative and the complexity of the missions,
is designed to promote the formation of a social network among the players.

Recognising everybody, awarding some

To be considered for the awards offered by Urgent Evoke, players have to
complete the 10 missions and 10 quests and submit an Evokation. The Evokation
works as a bridge to the physical world, because it forces the player to focus on a
problem outside the game, problems that are no longer just drivers in a good story,
but are wicked challenges affecting the lives of flesh-and-blood people. Thus, the
kind of participation that the World Bank is looking for transcends the game. To
win, a player has to produce an Evokation that demonstrates an intention to turn
the motivation to play into a longer lasting commitment to create a better world.

The Evokations are evaluated by a team organised by the World Bank. The
most promising plans are rewarded with a mix of seed money, mentorships by

respected social innovators, entrepreneurs and international development professionals and an opportunity for the players to propose their project for crowd funding on the Global Giving Challenge. A sub-set of winners is also invited to the 'EVOKE summit', a discussion of the game hosted by the World Bank in Washington, DC.

In addition to the award recipients, players who complete all 10 missions and quests are recognised for their level of participation and become 'Certified EVOKE Social Innovators – Class of 2010'; they also receive a paper that certifies their names were mentioned on the UE website. Players who complete one or more missions and quests are also recognised as members of 'the EVOKE class of 2010 graduates' on the website. The word 'winners' is not used very often in Urgent Evoke; instead, there is talk about 'agents and agent teams selected for the various prize categories'. This way of continuously talking about a class and selected team agents serves to downplay the idea of winners and losers and recognises the value of every participant in the game.

Even though the above description of Urgent Evoke is limited and does not account for all details in the game, it should provide a general idea of how the game design is supposed to transform motivated players into post-game creators of socially innovative ideas.

Methodology

This chapter draws on data from an emerging in-depth single case study of Urgent Evoke. The case study has been chosen as the methodology because games like UE, which aim to facilitate a player-driven post-game social innovation, are relatively new and few. In fact, UE is an example of a phenomenon that has not yet been explored or described in great detail. The aim of the case study is not to construct theories or make generalisations, but to produce a rich, context-dependent description of the game that provides a first-hand understanding of a new real-life phenomenon, and helps depict the complexity and nuances of the relationship between the game and its players (Yin 2009). And because the research on a G4C like Urgent Evoke is scarce, it is, as Bent Flyvbjerg says,

> ... worth repeating the insight of Thomas Kuhn that a discipline without a large number of thoroughly executed case studies is a discipline without systematic production of exemplars, and that a discipline without exemplars is an ineffective one.
>
> (Flyvbjerg 2006, 242)

The data from the case study presented here derive from retrospective semi-structured qualitative interviews with World Bank senior advisor and Urgent Evoke's executive producer, Robert Hawkins, 11 players of the Urgent Evoke 2010 game and data from an archival document collection.

The archival document collection consists of written and visual materials from Urgent Evoke 2010 (including chat, sound files, picture files, 10 chapters of a graphic novel, blog-posts and social network data), a detailed evaluation report of Urgent Evoke written by the Natoma Group for the World Bank and written material from the Facebook group 'Evoke Founder, Class 2010'.

The semi-structured qualitative interviews were based on a study of the archival document collection. Brenda Dervin's sense-making methodology was used in the design and practice of the interviews (Dervin 1998).

The retrospective interview with the World Bank's Robert Hawkins was conducted during a visit to Washington, DC. Of the 11 interviews with the players, one interview was conducted via Skype, the rest via e-mail.

The interviews with the players all shared an interview guide. The Skype interview took about 60 minutes, the e-mail interviews unfolded over several weeks and each included between 2–8 exchanges.

The email interview is a method of communication that has not received much attention, even though the growth in information and communication technologies (ICT) in qualitative research has opened up new opportunities for researchers to examine how traditional research methods can be adopted for effective online research (James 2007). I elaborate below on the effects of using e-mail interviewing as a qualitative research method. For reasons of space, I focus on one particularity of working with e-mail as an interview tool, namely the issue of time.

Because UE players communicate a lot in writing (e.g. on the message board and in blog posts), continuing this writing tradition in interviews seemed compatible with the culture of the game. But I soon learned that the difference in pace between communicating in writing or orally creates a different density in the empirical material. Working with semi-structured interviews means making room for diversions and for exploring information brought up by the interviewee. This form of exploration took place in both the Skype and e-mail interviews.

However, in an interview via Skype, which resembles a face-to-face interview conducted in the physical world, choices about which questions to ask and how to ask them had to be made relatively quickly by the interviewer. Similarly, the interviewee had to decide how to answer a question within a short period of time because longer pauses feel awkward and break the cultural conventions of the rhythm in a conversation. By contrast, email interviews allow a slower reaction time, which made it possible for both me, as a researcher, and my interviewees to take our time to consider the questions and answers of the interview. A participant in another research project remarked after being silent between emails for some time:

> I didn't email you straight back, because I was thinking about my answer. So my responses were more carefully thought through and probably longer than if I'd tackled the whole thing in a face-to-face interview ... again, other ideas would probably not have come out because of the time pressure. This is what's good about the email process because ... it allows time to consider the questions and frame an appropriate response.
>
> (James 2007, 970)

This comment reflects my own experience with e-mail interviews: the form and the pace of the method prompt interviewees to think their thoughts through and elaborate on their ideas. The challenge of working with the email method is that the number of cues to information that could possibly be explored grows exponentially with every mail exchanged. It is therefore important to find a balance between elaboration and focus. But the reward for taking it slowly is dense and rich interview material.

Challenging the focus on creators

In the introduction to this chapter, I argue that the interest of many socio-political actors in finding technologies that can help them generate citizen-driven social innovation overlaps with the promise of the G4C developers that they can transform motivated players into post-game social change agents. It was also implied that data from an emerging case study of Urgent Evoke challenged the strong focus on the creators present among both the socio-political actors and the G4C developers. The following data is presented and discussed in relation to research on participation in other forms of social media.[4]

Traffic data were collected during Urgent Evoke's ten-week run-time between 3 March and 12 May 2010. The data show that:

- 171,958 different individuals made 286,219 visits to the game.
- 19,386 people (11.3 per cent of the visitors to the game) registered as players.
- 6,618 of the registered players (34 per cent of the number of registered players) were active and completed at least one of the ten missions or quests.
- 142 players (2.1 per cent of the active players) completed all ten missions and quests.
- 73 people (1.1 per cent of the active players) submitted an Evokation.
- 36 Evokations were awarded by the World Bank and 28 players accepted their award(s).

The data demonstrate a tension between the focus on creation connected to games like Urgent Evoke and the actual way that players use the participatory possibilities offered by the technology and the game design.

It could be tempting to conclude that bad game design is the cause of the huge gap between the number of visitors to the game and the number of players who chose to go all the way and create an Evokation. But the gap that appears in the data is a reproduction of a well-known phenomenon found in other forms of social media.

As early as in 1996, Kollock and Smith wrote an article about how the creative and collective potential of a newsgroup site called Usenet was threatened by the massive numbers of participants who chose to stay silent online and therefore did not contribute to the shared pool of collective intelligence. Kollock and Smith labelled the silent users 'lurkers', i.e. non-contributing, resource-taking members of computer communities, and claimed that it was a species that needed to be weeded out (Kollock and Smith 1996). What Kollock and Smith described in their article was later recognised by other researchers, who saw the huge gap between creators and lurkers reproduced in other forms of social media. In 2006, Ben McConnell and Jackie Huba coined the concept of 'the 1% rule of thumb', which relates to the observation that in most online communities only about 1 per cent of the users create original content and 9 per cent curate the original creations, whilst 90 per cent 'lurk'.[5]

Many researchers have attempted to nuance the debate initiated by Kollock and Smith's article by developing an understanding of the motivations of lurkers and framing their silence in more positive ways. But a shared focus has always been to find ways to 'de-lurk' the lurkers and increase the number of creators (Nonnecke and Preece 2000; Preece *et al.* 2004; Rafaeli *et al.* 2004; Yeow *et al.* 2006; Crawford 2009).

Taking the body of research on participation and lurkers in social media into account, the traffic data from Urgent Evoke is not surprising. But it can prove problematic for socio-political actors like the World Bank, which is paying for the development of a game in order to turn players into creators of social innovations. This goal does not seem to benefit from the large numbers of non-contributing lurkers. But surprisingly, the gap between the number of lurkers and creators in Urgent Evoke did not seem to cool the World Bank's enthusiasm for the game, which is expressed in their evaluation of the game as well as by the fact that they are working on further developments of UE and planning to play a second round in the near future.

One possible reason that the World Bank's is satisfied with the game as it stands is perhaps hidden in the UE traffic data described above, which reveals that in addition to the 19,386 people who registered as players, about 80,000 people were 'repeat visitors' who came back to the site several times to read the graphic novel, blog posts, link with web resources and view photos and videos made by players. These repeat visitors could be framed by the words of Kollock and Smith as 'non-contributing, resource-taking lurkers'.

But when an online survey was placed on the UE site at the end of game, 84 of the 516 responses (16 per cent) came from people who had not completed a single mission or quest. By responding to the survey, these 84 people, who could be defined as lurkers, showed a commitment to the game that made it difficult to think of them as non-contributing, even though they did not participate as 'agents' in the game to any measurable extent. The ambiguity of the traffic data relative to understanding the nature of participation in a G4C game like Urgent Evoke can also be found in the results of the research interviews, which produced, among other things, the following illustrative case stories.

Story 1: Paul Holze is one of the winners of Urgent Evoke. He is 34 years old and lives in the United States. He holds a master's degree in biology and has been working as a teacher for years. When asked about what motivated him to play Urgent Evoke, Paul Holze tells a very personal story about how he had been interested in global social issues for a long time and was searching for a way to play a role in creating positive change. In this personal development process, he sought the advice of an older female friend, who was acting as a sort of mentor to him. The mentor herself had heard about UE and visited the game to check it out. Her intention was not to play but to see how a computer game could function as a tool for citizen-driven social innovation. After her visit, she was convinced that the game could help her friend in his search for a way to become socially and politically involved and suggested that he play. Paul followed her advice and ended up one of the winners of Urgent Evoke.

Paul Holze's mentor could figure in the game's traffic data as one of the lurkers who came, peeked and went away without contributing to the game. But without her lurking, there would have been no Paul Holze in the game and one less Evokation would have been produced. It can therefore be argued that Paul Holze's mentor did contribute to the game, although in a micro-form that the game design did not plan for or recognise.

Story 2: Robert Hawkins is a senior advisor at the World Bank and Urgent Evoke's executive producer. In my interview with him, I asked: 'What surprised you the most about the game?' The question prompted a surprising answer. Robert Hawkins began talking about the lurkers, the people who were spending time in the game without playing themselves but who still contributed to the game.

Hawkins gave the example of a librarian who comes to the game and offers his help to active players who need to do research in order to develop their in-game quests and missions. The librarian is not going to play himself, but he is interested in the issues dealt with in the game, believes that Urgent Evoke can have a positive impact and would like to contribute. Even though his participation in the game is very different from that of the players and his actions are taking place partly outside the game, like the mentor in the previous case story, he is influencing the game by donating a micro-part of his professional life to help the creators. As Robert Hawkins noted, the game developers never thought about designing for people like the librarian, who were not interested in playing but saw the game as a chance to contribute to the greater good.

Story 3: The third story also comes from Paul Holze. As noted, he is one of the 73 people who went all the way in the game, chose to send in an Evokation to the World Bank and was selected as one of the winners. The Evokation he produced was a plan for a documentary film called 'The Story of Happiness'. Paul Holze's plan was not just to produce a film, but to do it in a way that empowered the people portrayed in the film to ask different questions about their living conditions and to begin looking for new answers that could help them improve their own lives.

Paul Holze has always had a passion for filmmaking and plays with a video camera and editing programmes in his spare time. During Urgent Evoke, he used his camera to produce evidence for his missions and quest, i.e. filming became a tool for expressing his ideas. He received a lot of positive reactions to his work from other UE players. When asked in the interview about what prompted him go all the way in the game and create an Evokation, Paul Holze pointed to the many people who liked and 'hearted' his work in the game. He said that this support spurred him on and gave him the feeling that he had a talent and that perhaps he would be able to turn his hobby into a living. After Urgent Evoke ended, Paul Holze decided to quit his job as a teacher and devote all his time to implementing the ideas he had described in his Evokation.

There is no way of knowing whether the people liking and hearting Holze's work were participating in UE in a light or intense way. But the story indicates that micro-contributions such as liking and hearting, which are performed in one second, can have a great effect. They are examples of a way that designers have managed to design solutions that make it legitimate to participate and contribute in ways that are different from those of a creator.

We now discuss whether Urgent Evoke's reproduction of the '1% rule of thumb' indicates that games do *not* turn players into post-game social innovators or whether releasing the narrow focus on the game's creators allows a more network-oriented view of it, a view that could enable the recognition of multiple forms of participation.

Conclusion

The starting point of this chapter is the notion that the gaming industry has something to offer the socio-political actors looking for technologies that can generate civil social innovators who then help develop and implement solutions to social complex problems such as poverty and climate change.

Urgent Evoke's aim to empower players is to 'investigate the most pressing challenges around the world, collaborate to generate innovative and creative solutions and act to turn ideas into reality within their own communities and beyond' (Gaible and Dabla 2010, 9). The game is a good example of how such a collaboration between a socio-political actor (The World Bank) and a G4C developer (Jane McGonigal) can crystallise.

However, we know that traffic data from Urgent Evoke indicate that the game is no better at generating creators than other forms of social media; as noted above, only about 1 per cent of the 6,618 people who took active part in the game went all the way and created an Evokation. It would appear that the suggested collaboration between game designers and socio-political actors may not be a match made in heaven.

But even though Urgent Evoke reproduced the findings of other previous studies of social media in general, the case stories also indicate that there is more to the game than generating winners with socially innovative ideas. What the emerging study of Urgent Evoke points to is the idea that:

> An individual often lacks sufficient expertise to innovate alone when the knowledge frontier is complex and expanding. Instead, collaboration in communities becomes an attractive means to tap diverse expertise to be recombined into innovations. Detailed studies of people who at first glance appear to be lone geniuses reveal that they have been embedded in a wider circle of friends and colleagues that enabled their innovations.
>
> (Dahlander and Frederiksen 2012, 1)

When dealing with social complex problems, as the players do in Urgent Evoke, 'the knowledge frontier is complex and expanding' and to an extent Urgent Evoke is designed to make players collaborate on the game missions and quests. There are possibilities for players to chat, give feedback and reward points to each other and there are helpers in the game hired to facilitate the communication among players.

The narrative of the game stresses the idea that innovations are the result of a team effort and that a good team integrates people with different personalities, experiences and resources. The game design also allows visitors to follow the game and players to play at different paces because they do not need to 'level up' (i.e. to 'earn' or acquire a new level in the game) in order to follow the game play to the end. The design of the game tells us that its developers were interested in creating a diverse community of players that could accommodate different forms of player personalities and allow for individual degrees of intensity among players. Still, whilst the developers' focus has been on active players and their potential for becoming post-game social innovators, the case stories cited here challenge that single focus.

Active players are not the only contributors to the game; there are others forms of participation that contribute to the game results, contributions that were not designed for and which are too small to even be registered in the traffic data. The contributors of these micro-contributions could be classified as lurkers, but given the data from Urgent Evoke, it becomes hard to write them off as non-contributing free riders.

We have heard how the lurking done by the Paul Holze's mentor led to his playing the game and we have heard how the liking and hearting by people looking at Holze's work in the game helped boost his confidence and change his perception of himself. These stories exemplify how micro-contributions can have a big impact on the result of the game and can also help enable the transformation of players like Paul Holze into social innovators.

Furthermore, there is the story of the librarian who registered as a player but had no intention of doing the missions and quests of the game. Instead, he created his own mission – to act as a knowledge broker and contribute information from his professional life to the game in order to enable the players to gain the knowledge needed to perform in the game and make it easier for the creators in the game to innovate. Taken together, these stories exemplify how users who are not interested in playing Urgent Evoke themselves still relate to the goal of the game and even develop their own strategies around the game design in order to find a way to participate and contribute to the overall goal of the game.

The three case stories also indicate that players who choose to go all the way in the game, turn in an Evokation and manage to win are not 'lonely riders', but socially connected actors embedded in a larger network of players and visitors. Beyond that, they received, accepted and used the contributions that other players donated to them and the game. Urgent Evoke shows that there are multiple forms of participation thriving in the game and that in order to understand their meaning, we have to let go of the strong focus on the creators. Research literature to date reveals that the number of creators remains relatively small across time and the type of social media. The empirical material presented in this chapter should prompt us to consider how to create social environments that facilitate and make it attractive to lurkers as well as to a range of players to contribute to the development of the 1 per cent who end up creating socially innovative ideas.

In other words, we need to recognise that not every individual is ready to go all the way and make the effort it takes to become a social innovator. But a large number of people are interested in social-political issues and are willing to contribute to the development of the greater good if they can do so in a light and easy way. The challenge is therefore not to create social innovative game winners, but to design games that facilitate and acknowledge even micro-contributions as a legitimate form of participation and thereby make it possible to cultivate social innovative communities.

Discussion

> What if our power to bring to life sophisticated and evolving infrastructures must be associated with the acceptance of the idea that we are bound to lose control?
>
> (Ciborra 2000, 39–40)

In the introduction to this book, a heuristic model of a field of tensions is presented. These tensions are between system/state/(structure) and everyday life/civil society/(actor) on one axis, and individual and community on the other.

This model could be used to visualise how different social technologies relate to the four poles and to discuss whether technologies that score high on structure and community generate more citizen engagement in e.g. climate change mitigation than technologies that focus on individual actors.

The study of Urgent Evoke challenges the use of such a model, and suggests that the way to facilitate citizen engagement is to include all four poles and allow a continuous dynamic movement between and among them.

With the design of Urgent Evoke, the World Bank has created a clear structure that communicates and lays out a path to a defined goal – Evokations (a detailed plan of social innovative projects that players want to implement post-game). But at the same time, the game also allows the players to engage in ways that they see fit. It does not force players to 'level up' and follow the planned path; instead, it allows them to influence the game by bringing in knowledge, ideas and resources from their everyday life that they find interesting and relevant.

In other words, Urgent Evoke is a top-down implemented structure as well as an open platform where bottom-up, citizen-driven social innovation unfolds. By including both poles (structure and actor) in the design, the World Bank has planned for a result (post-game social innovation), and has accepted that in order to engage the players and make it a *citizen-driven* social innovation, they need to let go of the control and let the players be co-creators of the game.

Urgent Evoke seems to argue that in order to design social technologies capable of engaging citizens in issues such as climate change mitigation, designers should not think in tensions, but in synergies. They should cultivate communities and care for the individuals in them, create opportunity structures and make room for the actors – and in the end design social technologies where the control of the experience is shared with the players.

Notes

1   In 2004, the Games for Change (G4C) movement was formed by a group of non-profit directors, game developers, artists and academics committed to generating and promoting computer games aimed at creating positive social change.
2   Entertainment Software Association: www.theesa.com/facts/pdfs/ESA_EF_2013.pdf
3   www.ted.com/conversations/44/we_spend_3_billion_hours_a_wee.html.
4   Whilst Facebook, Wikipedia and YouTube are three of the best-known representatives of social media, social media is an umbrella term that covers many different forms of communication tools that enable online co-creation, knowledge and file sharing.
5   http://en.wikipedia.org/wiki/1%25_rule_(Internet_culture).

References

Adler R and Goggin J (2005) What Do We Mean By 'Civic Engagement'? *Journal of Transformative Education* 3 236–253.

Bers M U (2010) Let the Games Begin: Civic Playing on High-Tech Consoles, *Review of General Psychology* 14 147–153.

Ciborra C (2000) A Critical Review of the Literature on the Management of Corporate Information Infrastructures, in Ciborra C (ed.) *From Control to Drift: The Dynamics of Corporate Information Infrastructures*, Oxford University Press, Oxford, 15–40.

Connolly T M, Boyle E, MacArthur E, Hainey T and Boyle J M (2012) A Systematic Literature Review of Empirical Evidence on Computer Games and Serious Games, *Computers & Education* 59 661–686.

Crawford K (2009) Following You: Disciplines of Listening in Social Media, *Continuum: Journal of Media & Cultural Studies* 23 525–535.

Dahlander L and Frederiksen L (2012) Core and Cosmopolitans: A Relational View of Innovation in User Communities, *Organization Science* 23 988–1007.

Dervin B (1998) Sense-Making Theory and Practice: An Overview of User Interests in Knowledge Seeking and Use, *Journal of Knowledge Management* 2 36–46.

Feezell J T, Conroy M and Guerrero M (2009) *Facebook is … Fostering Engagement: A Study of Online Social Networking Groups and Offline Participation*, Paper presented at the American Political Science Association meeting, Toronto.

Flyvbjerg B (2006) Five Misunderstandings About Case-Study Research, *Qualitative Inquiry* 12 219–245.

Gaible E and Dabla A (2010) *EVOKE Project Evaluation*, Prepared for Robert Hawkins by The Natoma Group.

Gentile D A, Anderson C A, Yukawa S, Ihori N, Saleem M, Ming L M, Shibuya A, Liau A K, Khoo A, Bushman B R, Huesmann L R and Sakamoto A (2009) The Effects of Prosocial Video Games on Prosocial Behaviors: International Evidence From

Correlational, Longitudinal, and Experimental Studies, *Personality and Social Psychology Bulletin* 35 752–763.

Grüsser S M, Thalemann R and Griffiths M D (2007) Excessive Computer Game Playing: Evidence for Addiction and Aggression? *CyberPsychology & Behavior* 10 290–292.

James N (2007) The Use of Email Interviewing as a Qualitative Method of Inquiry in Educational Research, *British Educational Research Journal* 33 963–976.

Kahne J, Lee N-J and Feezell J (2013) The Civic and Political Significance of Online Participatory Cultures among Youth Transitioning to Adulthood, *Journal of Information Technology & Politics* 10 1–20.

Kollock P and Smith M (1996) Managing the Virtual Commons: Cooperation and Conflict in Computer Communities, in Herring, S C (ed.) *Computer-Mediated Communication*, John Benjamins Publishing Company, Amsterdam, 109–128.

Lenhart A, Kahne J, Middaugh E, Macgill A R, Evans C and Vitak J (2008) Teens, Video Games, and Civics, *Pew Internet & American Life Project* (www.pewinternet.org/2008/09/16/teens-video-games-and-civics/) Accessed 7 November 2014.

Neys J L D and Jansz J (2010) Political Internet Games: Engaging an Audience, *European Journal of Communication* 25 227–241.

Nonnecke B and Preece J (2000) *Lurker Demographics: Counting the Silent*, Paper presented at the ACM CHI 2000 Conference on Human Factors, The Hague.

Preece J, Nonnecke B and Andrews D (2004) The Top Five Reasons for Lurking: Improving Community Experiences for Everyone, *Computers in Human Behavior* 20 201–223.

Rafaeli S, Gilad R and Soroka V (2004) *De-Lurking in Virtual Communities: A social Communication Network Approach to Measuring the Effects of Social and Cultural Capital*, Paper presented at the 37th Hawaii International Conference on System Sciences, IEEE, Hawaii.

Sherry J L (2001) The Effects of Violent Video Games on Aggression: A Meta-Analysis, *Human Communication Research* 27 409–431.

Steinkuehler C and Williams D (2006) Where Everybody Knows Your (Screen) Name: Online Games as Third Places, *Journal of Computer-Mediated Communication* 11 885–909.

Trepte S, Reinecke L and Juechems K (2012) The Social Side of Gaming: How Playing Online Computer Games Creates Online and Offline Social Support, *Computer in Human Behavior* 28 832–839.

Yeow A, Johnson S L and Faraj S (2006) *Lurking: Legitimate or Illegitimate Peripheral Participation?* Paper presented at the Twenty Seventh International Conference on Information Systems, Milwaukee, WI.

Yin R K (2009) *Case Study Research: Design and Methods*, Sage, Thousand Oaks, CA.

Zhang W, Johnson T J, Seltzer T and Bichard L S (2010) The Revolution Will Be Networked: The Influence of Social Networking Sites on Political Attitudes and Behavior, *Social Science Computer Review* 28 75–92.

Index

161, *162*; background 151–2; barriers
hindering 168; benefits of 164–5;
criteria used when prioritising areas in
climate change action plans 165–6, *165*;
data collected 152–4, 167; distinction
between corporate and community 152;
financial savings as main rationale
165–6, *166*; and institutional theory
154–5; introduction of 158–60; local
government involvement 159–62; and
mechanisms of change 155–6;
milestones completed 153–4, *154*, 167;
milestones to be achieved 151–2; and
networking 167–8; organisational set-up
163–4, *163*; presence of climate change
officer/energy manager 163–4, *163*, 167;
and project ownership 164, 167;
regulatory framework 161–2; sectors
targeted 162–3; shaping of new
organisational norms 164–5, 167;
theoretical framework 151, 154–8, 167
'Changing Climate: Report of the Carbon
Dioxide Assessment Committee'
(1979) 188
Children: environmental behaviour and
having 83
CIDEA (Citizen Driven Environmental
Action) project 39
citizen participation 28–49, 54; and
Agenda 21 29; and bureaucratic
thinking 46; citizens as policy agents
(2009–) 38–43; and climate
ambassador programmes in Denmark
122–3, 127; and climate change
mitigation 28–49; Climate Family
Project in Ballerup 40, 44, 55, 59–65;
defining 30–1, 47; democratic
perspective 28, 45–7, 49, 58;
development of instruments for
(1980s–1992) 33–5; energy renovation
in Danish municipalities 40–2; in a
global governance perspective
(1992–2009) 35–8; institutionalisation
of in environmental policies
(1960s–80s) 32–3; instrumental
arguments for 45–6; and local
governments 37; normative tradition
46–7; phases in 31–43, *43*; and policy
making 57; steering perspective 44–5,
49; and STS 56–9, 63–4; substantive
arguments for 45; towards a material
theory of 58–9; Urgent Evoke (UE)
computer game 42–3

City of Rochester People's Climate
Coalition 183
Clematide, B. 121
climate ambassador programmes (Danish
municipalities) 107–27; ambassadors
and coordinators as political reflective
navigators 110, 123–5, 127; definition
and features of 109–10; economic
incentives in 121–2; focus of 119;
organisational structures 119, 127;
overview of 111, *112*; political context
and organisational structures of
113–18, 119, 127; as public spheres
125–6; role of citizens 122–3, 127; roles
of programme coordinators 120;
shaping and impact of 118–23; skills
and competencies required 110–11;
theoretical and methodological
approaches 110–11; *see also*
Frederiksberg; Furesø; Hvidovre;
Lyngby-Taarboek
Climate Family Project (Ballerup) 40, 44,
55, 59–65; carbon accounting regime
61–2; greening citizen identities 61–3;
lessons learned from 64; and
mobilisation 60–1; 'shower duck'
device 63
climate knowledge 71–2, 74, 79–81, *81*, 86
Climate Smart Communities project 179
Club of Rome (1972) 174; 'Limits of
Growth' report 174–5
co-creation 2
collaborative arrangements, and climate
change mitigation 2, 3–5, *3*
collective learning 110, 111, 125
comfort issue: and energy renovation in
Danish households 102–3
Common But Differentiated
Responsibilities (CBDR) 7
communicative action 111
communities: and local American climate
mitigation 181–4, 191
Communities/Cities for Climate
Protection Programmes *see* CCP
programmes
community motivation 77, 78
computer games 234–47; impact of on
civic engagement 235; Urgent Evoke
see Urgent Evoke; used for energy-
saving purposes 42
Conference of the Parties (COP)
meetings 29 *see also* COP 15
(Copenhagen)

For Product Safety Concerns and Information please contact our
EU representative GPSR@taylorandfrancis.com Taylor & Francis
Verlag GmbH, Kaufingerstraße 24, 80331 München, Germany